THE BIG 50
NEW YORK YANKEES

THE BIG 50
NEW YORK YANKEES

The Men and Moments That Made
the New York Yankees

Peter Botte

TRIUMPH
BOOKS

Library of Congress Cataloging-in-Publication Data

Names: Botte, Peter, author.
Title: The big 50 New York Yankees : the men and moments that made the New York Yankees / Peter Botte.
Other titles: Big fifty New York Yankees
Description: Chicago, Illinois : Triumph Books, 2020. | Includes bibliographical references. | Summary: "This book is about the New York Yankees"—Provided by publisher.
Identifiers: LCCN 2019058799 | ISBN 9781629377544 (paperback) | ISBN 9781641254304 (epub)
Subjects: LCSH: New York Yankees (Baseball team)—Biography. | New York Yankees (Baseball team)—History. | Baseball players—New York (State)--New York--Biography.
Classification: LCC GV875.N4 B67 2020 | DDC 796.357/64097471—dc23
LC record available at https://lccn.loc.gov/2019058799

This book is available in quantity at special discounts for your group or organization. For further information, contact:
Triumph Books LLC
814 North Franklin Street
Chicago, Illinois 60610
(312) 337-0747
www.triumphbooks.com

Printed in U.S.A.
ISBN: 978-1-62937-754-4

Design by Andy Hansen
All photos courtesy of AP Images

*For Tyler and Hayley,
easily my greatest moments.*

[Contents]

[Foreword]

When I first came to the Yankees, I was a little bit surprised by the fact that most marketing efforts were to basically point out the tradition of excellence that the organization has had over the years. Back in the early '90s when I got there, the club was not doing as well as it had in the past and I just kept questioning why they were not really putting emphasis on us, the current players, and always reaching back and talking about the past so much.

As I kept playing, as the years kept rolling by, I really started to understand the tradition of the franchise and feeling a lot of pride in being a part of that whole fraternity. It's a fraternity of players just to have played in the major leagues, but I think it's a quite exclusive one—not only the players who have played for the Yankees franchise, but also who have been part of World Series championships. It really fills me with tremendous pride to be a part of that legacy.

When I signed I was aware of the more recent history of the late '70s and '80s. I remember watching at my uncle's house in Puerto Rico when Ed Figueroa got his 20th win in 1978. Those teams were around the time that I really started looking at baseball as a way of playing organized sports. Thurman Munson, Roy White, Willie Randolph, Bucky Dent, Chris Chambliss. Reggie Jackson, of course. Ron Guidry, etc. It was great to sign with the organization and have the opportunity to meet all these people who were my baseball heroes. Some of them were really influential in my development as a player, and all of them really embraced our generation with the Yankees. They were the last generation before us to win it all—just like Mickey and Yogi and Whitey Ford were before them. I really came to appreciate them, not only as baseball players, but also as human beings because I had the opportunity to be close to them and learn from them.

When I first got to New York in 1991, that was a different story. Some of the veterans on that team gave me a hard time. In hindsight I look at it all as part of the process of becoming a successful major league player. Some weren't what you'd call embracing, but at the same time, they were trying to toughen me up. At least that's the way I choose to look at it now. Some other people may have other opinions about it. But to me, it was a process, in which I learned a lot about myself, resilience, and being focused on my goals. I had to realize that I was there to not only make the team, but also to hopefully be there for a long time. It ended up being my whole career. Sometimes they were good experiences and sometimes they were less than desirable, but from all of it, I was able to learn.

In 1989 I went to spring training in the big leagues for the first time, and those were some of my first real interactions with Don Mattingly. I took a liking to him from the very beginning because of his demeanor and his approach to the game. His reputation preceded him as a hard worker and a leader on the club. I was very lucky to have the influence of Donnie early in my career. It really taught me about being a professional baseball player. He was very kind to the young players and definitely related to us because of the circumstances when he was a young player himself. He had to make himself into a great player. He wasn't highly touted, but through hard work, resilience, and persistence, he was able to make himself into one of the best hitters of his generation and a great defensive first baseman. He also was so well-respected through the whole league, and that was always the model that I wanted to follow as a player.

Gene Michael was the most important part of the movement that was taking place. It was not only the moves that he made, but he also allowed the young players to come up and prove themselves before making any determination on what the organization would do with them. Before the Core Four, when guys like myself or Jim Leyritz came on the scene, there finally was a movement of trying to hold on to the young guys after years of trading all the prospects away. Stick was probably the most important piece of that puzzle and why guys like me were able to stick around.

I know there were several offers for him to trade me, but he really shielded me from what he used to call the wrath of Mr. Steinbrenner, who I really admired. But let's face it: he hadn't always been the most patient when it came to young players. Stick was the one who saw in me qualities that I didn't even see in myself at that time. He trusted his instincts and allowed me to play through my growing pains and really establish myself as a Yankee. I don't think I ever would have stayed as long as I did without him.

As heartbreaking as losing the division series to the Seattle Mariners in '95 was, everything that happened immediately afterward changed the whole atmosphere. I loved Buck Showalter. He was very influential in my career and my being a switch-hitter, but bringing Joe Torre into the scene was like the final piece that we needed. The core of young players who had started to establish a sense of what it took to be in the playoffs first with me, Mo, and Andy, then Derek and Jorge, and all the veteran guys that Stick had brought in before that, it was a perfect combination of factors that allowed us to embark on the beginning of that great run.

To win it all that first year with Joe in '96, especially against the Atlanta Braves and what was maybe the best pitching staff in modern baseball history, it really carried over to the subsequent years. We had that little hiccup in '97 against the Cleveland Indians, and as hard as '95 was, '97 was even worse for me because I made the last out of that series with Paul O'Neill as the tying run on second base. I was so devastated. Heartbroken. But I know for me personally and the whole team, that adversity really set the tone for the next several years. They were the best years of my career, and I attribute it to that failing moment against Cleveland.

Joe was the perfect fit for that group. He knew how to handle the media. He knew how to handle the different personalities on the team. He was a great player in his own right and he had fallen short a few times as a manager, but he had a slightly different attitude when he came to us. It was a great working atmosphere, buying into his philosophy of playing the game. He had Don Zimmer and Mel Stottlemyre, who were the perfect guys to be sitting next to Joe, with him. That team was assembled with players who could surround the young core with a championship mentality like Wade Boggs, Charlie Hayes, Cecil Fielder, Jimmy Key, Chili Davis, and on and on. David Cone, Tim Raines, Darryl Strawberry, Doc Gooden, they all had that winning experience and were true professionals, and we all appreciated having them there.

To be on a team that was allowing the young guys to find their way and develop, that was the most important change that happened. What stood out right away was their work ethic more so than just their obvious talent. Mariano made it to the Hall of Fame unquestioned. Nobody voted against him. I believe that Derek definitely deserved to have the same.

The thing that makes it interesting for me about the Core Four was always the conversation and debate that really followed. There's the Core Four, and my name always gets mentioned with it. It probably works more in my favor to have the Core Four and then to have me mentioned separately. I laugh about it when people say, "Is he part of it? Is he not?" I always look at it that at least I'm in the conversation, right? That's just icing on the cake. Those guys are my great friends, and they deserve all the praise they get. I take such enjoyment in looking back on my time and playing with those guys and everyone on those championship teams.

I mentioned the heartbreak of '97, but if I could summarize 1998 in one word, it would be magical right down to a guy like Scott Brosius winning MVP in the World Series. I ended up winning the batting title that year, but more than anything, that was a true team that showed up from beginning to end to win. Racking up 125 wins is amazing. It started right from the start of spring training that year. There was just an amazing focus by everyone, and the failure in '97 was a big motivator that never went away. That's why it was so important to keep the core together and add pieces along the way.

In saying that, it's true that I nearly left that winter and signed with the Boston Red Sox as a free agent at least until I had that conversation with Mr. Steinbrenner and made the decision to stay. That whole process and especially that conversation were very difficult. I felt like I owed it to myself and my family to see what was available. I didn't even think the money was that important. All you want is for the team to say they appreciate what you've done for us and to want you to continue to be a part of this. Looking back, it definitely was the right decision for me. In the grand scheme of things, being a Yankee for my whole career was so important and valuable to me.

Of course, we won another championship in '99 and then again against the New York Mets in 2000, and I definitely knew I made the right call. The series against the Mets, there was a lot of talk about what Mr. Steinbrenner wanted and demanded, but I think there was this misconception that everyone was anxious and tense looking at George, trembling in fear. I felt it was more the expectation that we collectively had as a team. We wanted to win for ourselves. There was not a bigger motivator than that for us. But there definitely were some bragging rights to fight for, too. I remember Derek saying how he was interacting with people in his apartment building in New York. He always heard: the Yankees couldn't lose to the Mets. It seemed like the whole baseball world stopped for these two weeks to watch the two local teams play. If we didn't win, we knew we wouldn't hear the end of it. Obviously, winning was the icing on the cake and one of the coolest moments of that dynasty.

The next year, of course, was very different because of 9/11. Not only the Yankees, but also every sports team in New York teamed up to support the relief effort, to see how we could make a difference in any small way. It was such a heartbreaking human-interest story that transcended the game itself. I remember going to the Armory and to the Javitz Center and the hospitals and seeing people who were working from all over the country trying to help the people of New York. We really took it as our motto to do something, anything we could, to help the city recover. It felt like the whole weight of the city was on our shoulders during that World Series against the Arizona Diamondbacks. We really took that responsibility to heart to win the championship. We came up short, but those two games in New York with the home runs in the ninth inning by Tino and Brosius, walk-off wins in both games, I feel like it really lifted the spirits of the city in a way we never expected. I'm still so proud of being a part of that process, not only for New York, but also for the whole nation. We provided some normalcy and let everyone know that terrorists weren't going to change our way of living. It was one of the highlights of my career, even though we lost. When people ask me the best World Series I played in, I always say it was 2001. It was so meaningful to people—even if we all wish we could have won.

Of course, I have so many other memories that make me proud to have worn the pinstripes. I had an opportunity to meet Mickey Mantle at an Old Timers' Day early in my career. Clete Boyer, who was the Yankees' third-base coach and had been one of our coaches in the minors, said to me, "Hey kid, Mickey Mantle wants to meet you."

I said, "He wants to meet *me*?" Clete brought me to the coach's locker room, and there was Mr. Mantle. To my surprise he knew who I was and even signed a ball that said, "To Bernie, you're great. Mickey Mantle." I still have that ball and remember that occasion with so much pride. It was like he was sort of passing the torch.

There was a similar situation with Mr. DiMaggio, too. He was going to throw out the first pitch during one of those playoff series and he couldn't have been more encouraging. He really made me feel like I was part of a very exclusive fraternity of center fielders playing for the Yankees. For him to be so supportive of me playing the position he played in that same outfield, I can't put into words what that meant to me. Those men made it one of the most famous positions to play in all of sports. I am very proud to be part of that legacy.

That's why the older I get, the more I appreciate the fans in the Bronx and all over and their reactions to me. It's really hard to explain what that means to me. When I look at my time with the Yankees, which encompasses so much of my adult life, it just really feels that those were some of the best times that I had. Living the dream, playing my whole career for an organization that was so tied to tradition, and being a part of teams that won championships for that organization, you're a part of something bigger than yourself. That's the only way that I can explain it.

So when they see me or Derek, Mariano, Jorge, Andy, Paul O'Neill, Tino, any of us, it makes you proud to be one of those guys that represented our generation. I think we hold a special place in the heart of the fans, just like the championship teams and players who came before us. I guess we've become the new generation of relics, and now it's our time at Old Timers' Day. It is such a great treat to come back to Yankee Stadium and be associated with our winning teams of the '90s. Certainly, we can be in the conversation with the teams of the '70s, and the '60s, and all of the decades before that back to Babe Ruth and Lou Gehrig. In my mind we have something in common with all of them and basically did our part to add to this great tradition of Yankees baseball. For that I appreciate every time the fans demonstrate that love.

I never expected my No. 51 to be retired with all of the big numbers out in Monument Park. It's just the pinnacle of my career and a way of validating the time I was there. I really had no idea when I started out that it would happen that way. How could you? To be in the same place with my number retired, especially with this organization, it's an incredible honor that I've never taken for granted. To have my kids, my grandkids, and everyone who comes from my lineage 20, 30 years from now or more, for them to be able to see that, it's just such a source of pride. Representing my parents that worked so hard and my country of Puerto Rico, to have that success in this organization, it puts me in a very special group and a very special place.

Now I am putting everything I learned as a ballplayer and that same passion and determination into being a musician. Even when I was playing for the Yankees, music was always on my mind. It was always a very important part of my life and always will be.

There's a misconception that some people think I just picked it up when I finished playing, but I started with the guitar around the same time I started playing baseball. I was around seven or eight, and it's always been a very important part of my life. It was a reasonable turn of events for me to gravitate to music for the second half of my life.

To have the opportunity to sort of reinvent myself as a musician is something that not a lot of people get a chance to do after having a full career. It's allowed me to live my life on my terms, and I'm really happy the way things have turned out. Just to have this outlet for me right now has been really important to keep my sanity. And to have something that I can pour my spirit, adrenaline, and passion into has been a really special thing in my life.

With that said, I don't think I ever will be in a position where I will detach myself from my experience with the Yankees. That will always be there and always be such a great thing to look back on. All of the moments, all of the tradition, all of those memories, it truly was the greatest time of my life...so far.

—**Bernie Williams** *is a five-time All-Star and a four-time World Series champion who played for the New York Yankees from 1991 to 2006.*

[Foreword]

Ihave been a Yankees fan forever. My father was a big Yankees fan, a big Joe DiMaggio fan, based on the whole Italian thing. My dad came over from Sicily, and that's the way it was.

People before had Ruth, Gehrig, and DiMaggio. We had Mickey, Whitey, Yogi, and Roger. After that we had Reggie and that whole team, Mattingly, and then Jeter, Mo, and Joe Torre.

That's some list, but I'm ready for them to win again.

I remember the first time my father took me to a game. It was in the '50s. Walking through the tunnel, the green grass, the sounds, seeing Mickey Mantle in person for the first time, those are memories I'll never forget. Mick was the star of the Yankees then, and I was completely enamored by him. We all were growing up in my neighborhood in the Bronx. I remember there was a pullout section in one of the papers and I cut out the photo of Mantle and Roger Maris and had it on my wall.

I was crushed when Bill Mazeroski hit that home run in Game 7 in 1960, and we lost the World Series. I was devastated, just devastated. I still get that way when I think about it because it brings back bad memories. The thing that got me about the series was we were beating them like 16–3, 12–0, 10–0, and they were beating us like 3–2, 5–2. And then they won Game 7 10–9. I was 9, but I still remember like it was yesterday. Yogi looks back, and the ball goes over the wall.

That's why I put that story from *A Bronx Tale* in there about The Mick crying and Sonny asking C why he's upset about it. That kid was based on me. That's exactly how I felt, and that's what the Sonny in my life told me. I've thought a lot about why it really affected me. It was just in my blood. I still get so upset whenever the Yankees lose. When they lost four straight to the Boston Red Sox in 2004, I laid in bed for like a day. My daughter, who was like 8 at the time, brought me a cold compress to put on my head. Of all of the teams to lose to? And after we were up 3–0 in the series? I didn't watch the television, a news show or read a newspaper for a month. I had to let it go away.

I've been a Yankees fan forever. I was rooting for both of them, Mick and Roger, to break Ruth's record in '61. I was a Mantle fan, but it wasn't like I cared who was gonna break it. Some people didn't want Maris to break it. But it didn't bother me at all. He was a Yankee.

I root for the laundry even during those bad years we had in the late '60s or in the '80s. On the flip side, that magnificent run they had in 1998 was one of the most fun Yankees teams. It was like the most amazing thing I ever saw.

I have a screening room with a big TV, like 110″, where I watch the games. I get really nervous if the game gets really tight like when Aaron Boone hit the home run against Boston in '03. I was sitting there in my office watching it and had to shut the sound off in the extra innings. With the sound on, the pressure was just too much. Then when it gets really tight, I make the room darker. I'm a grown man here doing this crazy stuff. I get to the point where I go into the kitchen, where I have a 12″ television and go through the same thing. And then I go into the pantry and close the door before peeking through. It's like a tradition at my house. My wife thinks I'm nuts. When Boone hit the home run, it was like 1:30 in the morning. I was screaming, I woke the whole house up. I'll never forget it. Oh my god, Mo was kneeling on the mound. To beat Boston like that...

I work out every morning and will watch the encore of the game from the night before, but only if they win. I still get annoyed even when I know what's going to happen. I love the current team. I mean, Aaron Judge. Wow! I like Boone as a manager. I got to know his predecessors, Joe Torre and Joe Girardi, well, too. Derek Jeter came to my restaurant a bunch of times when I had it in Baltimore. I don't know Derek very well and wouldn't claim to, but he was always very cordial. A good guy, always a gentleman, nice, and respectful he was.

I never met Mantle, though, and that's one regret. I would go down to the Mickey Mantle restaurant sometimes by Central Park to see if maybe I'd see him there. Some people have told me it was better maybe that I never saw him or met him because he was drinking a lot then. There's that famous Mantle saying: "If I knew I was going to live this long, I would have taken better care of myself."

Could you imagine Mantle with two healthy legs? Or if he played in a smaller stadium like that bandbox in Atlanta? Tony Kubek said that he would count the flyball outs by Mantle into left-center field. Called "Death Valley," it was like 461 feet away, and those would have been home runs in any other park. He thought Mantle would do that 20 to 25 times a year, maybe more. But don't forget that until Jeter, Mantle played the most games of any Yankees player. Even with the bad knees and all the other injuries, he played 18 years and he showed up to play. The guy would have had 750 home runs if he was fully healthy.

Think about this: in the history of Pittsburgh's old stadium, no one had ever hit it entirely out of the stadium. Mantle played there four games and did it twice. What the hell? It's crazy, man. That's like insane. I loved that guy. Mickey Mantle—that's like a baseball player's name, right? He was named after Mickey Cochrane. To me, he's the ultimate baseball player. If you were a Yankees fan at that time, he was your guy. I was at the game when he hit the façade in 1963. We didn't have a lot of money back then, but my dad would always take me to the games.

We'd sit in the second or third deck to the left or right of home plate. It was like the nosebleed seats, but to me I was in my glory. It was like the scene in *A Bronx Tale* at the fights. That's what we could afford. A lot of times when I go to the games now, I sit real close, and a player will flip me a ball. But I still go up to the third deck, where I used to sit with my dad, even though it's a different stadium now. When I see a father with his son or daughter, I tell them that I used to sit here with my father when I was a kid. Sometimes they'll ask me to sign a ball for them. I was doing that for a long time and never said anything to anybody. Occasionally, someone will tweet it out, and so people started finding out. I could never afford to sit in these seats that I'm sitting in now. It was a huge thrill for me as a kid just to be there. When I had my son, he was like 13, and Torre let me bring him into the dugout before a game. That was a thrill for us to get to do that.

So yes, the Yankees have meant a lot to me my whole life. They still do. My wife says I'm crazy, but I've talked about wanting the inside of my coffin to be lined in pinstripes—like of a really nice material but with the Yankee pinstripes. She'll say, "no way" and tell me I'm nuts. But the Yankees just mean so much to me. They're just part of who I am. They always will be.

—*Chazz Palminteri is a Bronx-born actor who has appeared in multiple films and television shows, including* A Bronx Tale, Bullets over Broadway, The Usual Suspects, Analyze This, *and* Modern Family.

THE BIG 50
NEW YORK YANKEES

1

THE BAMBINO

The storied history of the New York Yankees, as we now know it, unmistakably begins with one name. The Yankees had been in existence for nearly two decades before Babe Ruth arrived (even if they weren't always called that) and in the century that followed they would cement themselves as the most popular, the most successful—and, hence, both the most beloved and hated—team in all of sports.

Baseball's first true anointed national superstar, its first can't-miss gate attraction, its first slugger of incredible renown, its first headline writer's dream, George Herman Ruth was the mold-breaking template for all of the sports legends to follow in the United States. A hard-drinking, crude-talking, woman-chasing, homer-smacking, record-setting oversized former orphan with a bunch of cool nicknames playing for the marquee team in the United States' biggest and brightest city? Yes, please.

Just imagine if he played today with TMZ, ESPN, Page Six of the *New York Post*, and the ugliness of the Internet following and detailing his every exploit, both on and off the field.

"When you think of baseball, Babe Ruth is the first name that comes to mind," Derek Jeter, the Yankees' biggest star a few generations later, said in 2016. "He was a larger-than-life figure. Even if you're not a baseball fan, even if you're not a sports fan, you know who Babe Ruth is."

In the Roaring '20s, an era that also featured boxer Jack Dempsey and golfer Bobby Jones, Ruth became the breakout star, drawing fans back to baseball after the 1919 Black Sox scandal.

The Yankees were not the Yankees until Ruth stormed into the Bronx and into the national consciousness after owner Jacob Ruppert agreed to purchase the burly and boorish pitcher-turned-outfielder from the Boston Red Sox more than one century ago in January of 1920. The franchise had been founded as the Baltimore Orioles when the

American League was formed in 1901 and relocated to New York as the Highlanders, so named because their first home ballpark, Hilltop Park, was constructed on one of upper Manhattan's highest points.

They officially were renamed the Yankees, a moniker used years earlier by some in the local press, after moving in as cotenants with the New York Giants at the Polo Grounds in 1913.

Abandoned at St. Mary's, a reformatory school for boys in Baltimore, by his parents when he was seven years old, a 19-year-old Ruth arrived in Boston in 1912 and immediately established himself among the top pitchers in the league, going 78–40 with a 2.02 ERA from 1915 to 1918. The Red Sox were pure baseball royalty, winning the World Series three times in those four seasons.

Boston manager Ed Barrow, who would take over as the Yankees' general manager by 1921, also eventually began employing Ruth, a promising hitter, in the outfield on a part-time basis. Ruth led the league with 11 home runs in 317 at-bats in 1918 and again with a record 29 in 1919, though Boston's record slipped to 66–71.

By that time Ruth and Red Sox owner Harry Frazee were clashing regularly over the dual threat's salary. Frazee was in heavy debt over a few Broadway shows he was producing, and with lagging attendance at Fenway Park, a deal was struck with Ruppert for $100,000 to purchase Ruth's contract plus a $300,000 loan. "It would have been an injustice to keep him with the Red Sox," Frazee said in the book, *Emperors and Idiots: The Hundred Years Rivalry Between the Yankees and Red Sox.* "We would have become a one-man team."

The Yankees were perfectly glad to do so. Ruth ripped a record-shattering 54 home runs—35 more than runner-up George Sisler of the St. Louis Browns—in his first season with the Yankees. He then crushed 59 the following year with what turned out to be a career-best 171 RBIs.

The Yankees even outdrew the Giants at the Polo Grounds by about 5,000 fans per game, becoming the first team in baseball history to reach one million (1,289,422) in attendance in 1920. Giants co-owner/manager John McGraw told Ruppert that the Yankees had to find another place to play by 1923. In the interim the Yankees would reach the World Series for the first time in 1921 and again the following year.

Both times they lost to their landlords, and Ruth batted just .118 with no homers in a Giants sweep in 1922.

Yankee Stadium opened the next spring across the Macombs Dam Bridge in the Bronx. It quickly would be dubbed "The House That Ruth Built" by sportswriter Fred Lieb after Ruth homered on Opening Day. "Before long they will be lost sight of," McGraw said in the book, *Remembering Yankee Stadium*. "A New York team should be based on Manhattan Island."

The Babe led the Bronx-based Yankees to their first championship in its inaugural season; he blasted three home runs in a six-game victory against McGraw's Giants, the first of an incredible 19 titles for the franchise over a 40-year period. The famed Murderers' Row team won consecutive titles in 1927–28, and Ruth became the first player ever to crush 60 home runs in one season.

The 1932 World Series against the Chicago Cubs marked the Yanks' fourth championship in 10 seasons. It always will be remembered for one of the most debated moments in sports annals: Ruth's supposed "called shot," a home run off of Cubs hurler Charlie Root in the fifth inning of Game 3. This was radio announcer Tom Manning's call: "And now Babe Ruth is pointing out toward center field, and he's yelling at the Cubs that the next pitch is going out to center field. Now he's looking toward the stands. And here's the pitch. The count is ball two and strike two. It's coming. Babe Ruth connects, and there it goes. The ball is going, going, going. High into the center-field stands, into the scoreboard, and it's a home run!"

There have been differing accounts over the years—mostly doubting ones—but Ruth later maintained that the home run, which snapped a 4–4 tie, was in retaliation for the poor treatment he and his wife, Claire, had received at Wrigley Field. Former Yankees infielder Mark Koenig was a member of the Cubs. He said years later, "I don't think he actually pointed to center field. I think he was just acknowledging he had two strikes. But Ruth did so many great things. He'd say, 'I feel real good today. I think I'll hit one.' Nine times out of 10, he did."

Either way, it would be Ruth's final World Series appearance, though he had a few more milestones ahead. Ruth belted the first home run in Major League Baseball's first All-Star Game the following year at

Babe Ruth lofts another one of the 60 home runs he hit during 1927 into the right-field upper deck at Yankee Stadium.

Comiskey Park in Chicago in July of 1933. He connected for the 700th of his 714 career home runs—a record that would stand until Hank Aaron broke it 1974—barely one year later.

Still, years of partying, ignoring his health, and insubordination had caught up with Ruth, and 1934 marked his final season with the Yankees. When Ruppert and Barrow dismissed his request to replace manager Joe McCarthy in 1935, The Babe finished out his career with a trade to the Boston Braves, serving as an assistant coach and part-time player.

Ruth also briefly coached the Brooklyn Dodgers before returning to Yankee Stadium in 1939 for the ailing Lou Gehrig's farewell speech. He made one of his own on April 27, 1947, with his body thinned and his voice raspy and low from a bout with lymphoepithelioma, an inoperable malignant tumor at the base of his skull and neck. "There's been so many lovely things said about me," Ruth told the crowd. "I'm glad I had the opportunity to thank everybody."

When the 53-year-old Ruth died in 1949, nearly 80,000 people viewed his open casket over two days at Yankee Stadium. At his funeral Mass at St. Patrick Cathedral, an estimated crowd of 75,000 queued outside. The weird thing about a figure so compelling is that the two biopic movies made about Ruth's life are pure trash. Somebody get Steven Spielberg or Spike Lee on the case already.

The 1948 film *The Babe Ruth Story*, starring William Bendix as the main character, was "low-grade fiction," according to Bosley Crowther of *The New York Times*. "It is hard to accept the presentation of a great, mawkish, noble-spirited buffoon, which William Bendix gives in this picture as a reasonable facsimile of the Babe," he wrote, adding the baseball scenes were "patently phony and absurd."

The Babe, starring John Goodman in the title role, was an even deeper disaster, especially considering the advancements in filmmaking technology since the first movie. Famed critics Gene Siskel and Roger Ebert roundly panned *The Babe*, calling it one of the worst films of 1992. Siskel said it "poisoned two hours of our lifetime."

There was at least one accurate quote in *The Babe*, however. According to Tom Meany's 1947 biography *Babe Ruth: The Big Moments of the Big Fellow*, Ruth did once explain his salary being higher than president Herbert Hoover's during the Great Depression: "I had a better year than he did."

As for the so-called "Curse of the Bambino," it wouldn't become part of the common vernacular until at least the 1990s. The Red Sox would not win a World Series for 86 years after 1918, while the Yankees would capture their first four championships with Ruth as their leading man and then 23 more through 2019. In the four major North American sports, no team had won more often than the Yankees' 27 titles.

George Vescey of *The New York Times* did refer in passing to a Ruth-related curse after Bill Buckner's error in the 10th inning enabled the New York Mets to defeat Boston in Game 6 of the 1986 World Series before winning the championship two nights later. Four years later Dan Shaughnessy, a columnist for *The Boston Globe*, wrote a book titled *The Curse of the Bambino*, widely popularizing the term across New England.

The common belief for decades was that Frazee sold Ruth to New York to finance his upcoming play, *No, No Nanette*. Although this became the accepted story over the years, Leigh Montville, in his in-depth Ruth biography *Big Bam,* reported that Frazee's play, *My Lady Friends*, which opened in 1919, actually was where the Ruth money was allocated.

Despite the presence of arguably the greatest hitter in baseball history, Ted Williams, the Red Sox would not win the World Series until 2004, when they became the first team ever to overcome a 3–0 deficit with four straight wins to beat the Yankees in the American League Championship Series. Following a loss to the Yankees in May of 2001, Red Sox ace pitcher Pedro Martinez proclaimed: "I don't believe in damn curses. Wake up the damn Bambino and have me face him. Maybe I'll drill him in the ass."

Ruth had been part of baseball's inaugural Hall of Fame class in 1936, joining Ty Cobb, Honus Wagner, Christy Mathewson, and Walter Johnson. Martinez joined Ruth among the game's immortals and was enshrined in Cooperstown in 2015. "We are teammates. I had the opportunity to go over and look at [Ruth's] statue, and I did apologize for the comments I made that day," Martinez said. "I said those things because I didn't believe in curses. But I know, especially after that moment, I got to really appreciate how good the Bambino was. He forgave me for what I said, and we've moved on now. I'm counting on him to go deep and I'm going to get the next eight shutout innings."

In 2018 another big league pitcher, free-agent reliever Adam Ottavino, also took a curiously ill-timed public shot at Ruth. "I would strike out Babe Ruth every time," he said. "I'm not trying to disrespect him, but it was a different game. I mean, the guy ate hot dogs and drank beer and did whatever he did." Ottavino, a Brooklyn product, signed with the Yankees as a free agent barely one month later and instantly claimed he regretted those remarks. "Babe Ruth is probably a name I shouldn't have used in this example. I caught a lot of flak for it," he said.

The reliever even allowed himself to be a butt of the joke thereafter, taping a promotional video for MLB's website that showed him in grainy black-and-white footage being taken deep time and time again by Ruth.

Another famous parody occurred in the 1993 baseball movie *The Sandlot*. Ruth's ghost appears and says to the Benny "The Jet" Rodriguez: "Remember kid, there's heroes and there's legends; heroes get remembered, but legends never die."

Babe Ruth was the Yankees' first hero and their first legend. The Yankees wouldn't be the Yankees without him.

2

LOU GEHRIG

Lou Gehrig did not plan to speak that day. He did not plan to say the words that still are recalled and invoked more than 80 years later as among the most heartbreaking, poignant, and courageous speeches in baseball history, if not American history. "Today," Gehrig said, "I consider myself the luckiest man on the face of the earth."

Those words only gained deeper meaning in the ensuing decades as more and more was revealed about the iconic Yankees first baseman and the rare, debilitative disease that would soon take his life and ultimately would bear his name. Mere weeks after his illness had been diagnosed yet not fully understood in its gravity, those heartfelt words came on the Fourth of July in 1939 between games of a doubleheader during a somber celebration in Gehrig's honor at Yankee Stadium. "Class and leadership: obviously those are the qualities that you hear about and read about when you're learning about Lou Gehrig," Derek Jeter said in 2016. "It's hard to imagine anyone who was more well-respected than him."

Henry Louis Gehrig was the Yankees' first homegrown star, a native New Yorker born to German immigrant parents in 1903, a former football and baseball player at Columbia University who would pair with Babe Ruth for three Yankees championships (1927–28, '32) and with Joe DiMaggio for three more (1936–38) before his sudden midseason retirement in 1939.

Known as the Iron Horse, Gehrig compiled prodigious offensive statistics: a career batting average of .340; 493 home runs; 1,995 RBIs, including the American League record of 185 in 1931; and a lifetime OPS (on-base percentage plus slugging percentage) of 1.080, which ranks behind only Ruth and Boston Red Sox legend Ted Williams in baseball history.

After replacing an ill Wally Pipp on June 2, 1925, Gehrig appeared in a remarkable 2,130 consecutive games—a major league record that stood until Baltimore Orioles ironman Cal Ripken Jr. surpassed it in 1995—until his body betrayed him and forced him to remove himself from the lineup on May 2, 1939 in Detroit. Pipp, whose name would become synonymous with players losing their jobs due to injury or illness, coincidentally happened to be in the stands as a spectator that day at Briggs Stadium (later known as Tiger Stadium).

Babe Dahlgren replaced Gehrig, as the latter once had done to Pipp, who reportedly told then-manager Miller Huggins he couldn't play due to a headache. "I took the two most expensive aspirins in history," Pipp joked years later.

Dahlgren's grandson, Matt, authored a book in 2007 titled *Rumor in Town*, which recounted memories he heard for years about Gehrig from his late grandfather. "Babe grew up in San Francisco idolizing Lou Gehrig. As a kid all throughout his teenage years and high school years, he'd actually draw pictures of Lou Gehrig on his school binder," Matt Dahlgren told me in 2019, "never in his wildest dreams thinking one day he'd replace him."

Dahlgren was acquired by the Yankees from Boston in 1937 and initially was stashed away in the minors with the Newark Bears before serving as a utility player with the big club in 1938 and '39. Unaware of his pending medical diagnosis but knowing he was not right physically, Gehrig was batting just .143 when he asked Joe McCarthy to remove him from the lineup against the Tigers. He never would play again. "It was a surreal moment, a heavy moment because everyone realized the streak was coming to an end. My grandfather said it was the one day in his life that he didn't want to play baseball," Matt Dahlgren said. "During batting practice word started to spread around. Photographers were trying to get pictures with Babe and Gehrig together. Just before the game started, my grandpa went up to Lou and said, 'You really put me in a tough spot here. Please get out there and keep your streak going.' And Lou said to him, 'You're gonna do just fine, kid.'"

Gehrig's wife, Eleanor, soon arranged for him to undergo tests at the famed Mayo Clinic in Minnesota. He was diagnosed to have amyotrophic lateral sclerosis, an incurable neuromuscular illness now commonly referred to as ALS or "Lou Gehrig's disease." Yankees

75TH ANNIVERSARY OF THE SPEECH

In 2014 the Yankees compiled a video of their players—led by Derek Jeter and also featuring manager Joe Girardi—reciting Lou Gehrig's entire speech on its 75th anniversary.

Gehrig: "For the past two weeks, you've been reading about a bad break."

Jeter: "Today, I consider myself the luckiest man on the face of the earth."

Jacoby Ellsbury: "I have been in ballparks for 17 years and have never received anything but kindness and encouragement from you fans."

Brett Gardner: "Look at these grand men. Which of you wouldn't consider it the highlight of his career just to associate with them for even one day? Sure, I'm lucky."

Mark Teixeira: "Who wouldn't consider it an honor to have known Jacob Ruppert? Also, the builder of baseball's greatest empire, Ed Barrow? To have spent six years with that wonderful little fellow, Miller Huggins?"

Girardi: "Then to have spent the next nine years with that outstanding leader, that smart student of psychology, the best manager in baseball today, Joe McCarthy. Sure, I'm lucky."

Kelly Johnson: "When the New York Giants, a team you would give your right arm to beat and vice versa, sends you a gift, that's something."

Brian Roberts: "When everybody down to the groundskeepers and those boys in white coats remember you with trophies, that's something."

Brian McCann: "When you have a wonderful mother-in-law, who takes sides with you in squabbles with her own daughter, that's something."

Carlos Beltran: "When you have a father and a mother who work all their lives so you can have an education and build your body, it's a blessing."

David Robertson: "When you have a wife who has been a tower of strength and shown more courage than you dreamed existed, that's the finest I know."

Jeter: "That I might have been given a bad break, but I've got an awful lot to live for."

pitcher Catfish Hunter also died from complications of the illness in 1999.

During a game at Fenway Park in 1935, Dahlgren was playing first base for the Red Sox when Gehrig stumbled rounding first base on a single to left field. "As my grandpa used to tell it, Lou took a fall and went down basically flat on his face in fair territory and couldn't move," Matt Dahlgren said. "Babe was yelling for the ball because Gehrig was an easy out, but the umpire screamed timeout. My grandfather thought, *Gehrig is laying in fair territory. How can we call time here?* It was unlike anything my grandpa had ever seen. The Yankees' trainer and teammates all ran out and circled around Lou. I have a picture of that. My grandfather is on his knees—even as the opposing player— right at the head of Gehrig. It looks like he's just making sure he's okay."

Gehrig was removed from that 1935 game with what was reported as a back injury, and the Yankees' next scheduled game was rained out. Many believe that break in the schedule might have preserved Gehrig's streak. "Two days later Lou was back in the lineup, and that kept the streak going," Matt Dahlgren said. "But my grandfather couldn't help but wonder looking back if that was a precursor of the early stages of ALS affecting Gehrig way back in '35. No one will ever know, but he couldn't help but wonder that."

Barely two months after the streak ended, the Yankees held Lou Gehrig Appreciation Day at Yankee Stadium. Ruth, Tony Lazzeri, and several other members of the legendary 1927 Yankees team were in attendance. Pipp was there, too. The 36-year-old Gehrig's No. 4 would become the first retired by any team in baseball—and the first of 22 men to be so honored by the Yankees through 2019.

The Bronx crowd of more than 61,000 was informed the emotional Gehrig would not address them, but McCarthy leaned in to Gehrig and nudged him to the microphone. "If you look at those photos, you see Gehrig standing there, and the Yankees are lined up on one side of him, and the Washington Senators are on the other side of him. In proximity to Lou, my grandfather was the closest teammate in that moment," Matt Dahlgren said. "Before Gehrig spoke, McCarthy also walked by my grandfather, and said, 'If you see him start to wobble, don't let him fall. If you see him start to go down, catch him.'"

Gehrig, though, did not fall, literally or figuratively, that day. Instead of lamenting the cards he'd been dealt, the stoic first baseman remarkably offered a public lesson in gratitude and about the blessings of life—not one simply about defiance or perseverance in the face of adversity. Dignitaries, former teammates, fans—even Gehrig—fought back tears. The following day, *The New York Times* called it "one of the most touching scenes ever witnessed on a ball field."

Some even have referred to it as baseball's Gettysburg Address. "My grandfather would get choked up whenever he would talk about that day," Matt Dahlgren said. "He never got choked up talking about the day he replaced Gehrig because to him that was an historic day obviously, but when it happened, no one really knew Lou's fate yet. So there wasn't that emotion tied to it yet. But whenever Babe would talk about the speech, he'd get a knot in his throat, and you could definitely sense all those years later that it was such an emotional thing for him to relive."

In retirement Gehrig would accept a job briefly from New York mayor Fiorello La Guardia as a member of the city's Parole Commission before dying less than two years later on June 2, 1941.

Following Gehrig's death, there wasn't another Yankee named captain until catcher Thurman Munson in 1976. A pilot in a private plane that crashed in 1979, Munson also died tragically. Popular stars Don Mattingly and Jeter also became synonymous with the pinstriped captaincy in ensuing decades. Willie Randolph was the first African American captain in team history, sharing duties with Ron Guidry from 1986 to 1988. "Very humbling. When you say 'Lou Gehrig,' it's one of the biggest honors of my life," Randolph said. "I'm proud to be linked with all of those guys all the way back to Gehrig, who's still to this day the person you think about when people talk about a Yankee captain... We all took that responsibility seriously and how important it was to be a captain in the history of this franchise. It all started with Lou Gehrig."

The Yankees fittingly were the opponent when Ripken's subsequent record for consecutive games eventually ended at 2,632 games on September 20, 1998. I was in Baltimore that night; my game story for the *New York Daily News* took on a biblical tone: "And in the 2,633rd game, Cal Ripken rested."

Upon breaking Gehrig's franchise record for career hits of 2,721 in 2009, Jeter described it as the finest individual accomplishment of a career that would finish with 3,465 hits—sixth all time through 2019—and five World Series titles. "I can't think of anything else that stands out more and I say that because of the person that I was able to pass," Jeter said. "Lou Gehrig, being a former captain and what he stood for, you mention his name to any baseball fan around the country, it means a lot. Passing him makes it stand out that much more."

3

THE BOSS

George Steinbrenner's opening remarks when he took over as the principal owner of the Yankees might have been the greatest example of the idiom "famous last words" in the history of spoken language. "We plan absentee ownership as far as running the Yankees is concerned," Steinbrenner declared on January 4, 1973. "We're not going to pretend to be something we aren't. I'll stick to building ships."

During more than 35 years in The Bronx, the former Cleveland-based ship magnate fully restored the Yankees back to their championship pedigree while mixing in a chaotic frenzy of free-agent spending, back-page declarations, and changes in managerial and front-office personnel that forever altered the business of baseball and how it was covered by the media. Though he never threw a pitch or swung a bat, Steinbrenner—originally dubbed "The Boss" by longtime *New York Daily News* columnist Mike Lupica—was easily the touchstone figure of the Yankees for more than three decades. He probably sold more newspapers in New York than anyone in sports history. "George changed everything," former Yankees closer Goose Gossage said in 2019. "How that man isn't in the Hall of Fame is astounding, a total joke."

As of 2019 Steinbrenner had not been enshrined in Cooperstown, but several others—both former players and opponents—have taken up the cause to get him there since his death, following a heart attack in his adopted hometown of Tampa, Florida, on July 13, 2010. Under The Boss' watch, the Yankees added seven championships to the 20 that were procured before his arrival. His signings of free agents such as Catfish Hunter, Reggie Jackson, Gossage, and Dave Winfield and his formation of the YES Network revolutionized the way baseball business was done.

He also was often too irrational and impulsive when it came to changing managers, including the firing of Billy Martin five times. And he was suspended twice by Major League Baseball for illegal campaign contributions to president Richard Nixon early in his tenure and for paying a slimy gambler named Howie Spira $40,000 to dig up dirt on Winfield and his charitable foundation in 1990 before reinstatement in 1993. (Steinbrenner also infamously had publicly branded Winfield "Mr. May" in 1985, as opposed to Jackson's "Mr. October" moniker.)

Still, Steinbrenner turned an $8.7 million sale price of the Yankees, including just a $168,000 personal outlay, into one of the most valuable professional franchises of all time. According to *Forbes*, the team was worth $4.6 billion by 2019, making it the second most valuable franchise in all of American sports and only behind the Dallas Cowboys. "You can't argue with the return on investment. There's no doubt about that," said son Hal Steinbrenner, who took over as the team's general partner in 2009. "A lot of things got lost in the shuffle with George: some of the charitable stuff that was kept quiet, the chances he gave to so many people over the years, but I think now people are starting to appreciate more and more of what he did. The media was rough on him, the fans were rough on him. They weren't exactly singing his praises all the time, and some of it was deserved. But I think now that he's passed, and retrospection is possible, I think people appreciate him more and more."

Barely a year before Steinbrenner snagged the Yankees, a potential purchase of his hometown Indians with former Cleveland star Al Rosen fell through when the team's owners, who also owned Stouffer's frozen foods, backed out of an agreement to sell. By the summer of 1972, Indians president Gabe Paul heard the Yankees were for sale and steered Steinbrenner toward a deal with CBS, the team's previous owners since 1964. (Paul served as the Yankees' general manager from 1974 to 1977.)

Steinbrenner initially controlled just an 11 percent ownership stake, the highest figure among a sizable group of investors that also included John DeLorean and Broadway entrepreneur James Nederlander. John McMullen, later the owner of the Houston Astros and the New Jersey Devils of the NHL, also had been a limited partner of Steinbrenner's during the 1970s. "Nothing is so limited as being one of George's limited partners," he joked.

Every reporter who covered Steinbrenner regularly over the years also has at least one personal tale of The Boss to share. Here's mine: each year the New York media faced the Boston media in baseball games (yes, actual baseball) at Yankee Stadium and Fenway Park. In 1999 my seven-year-old son, Tyler, was coaching first base for our side. George Rose, the interpreter for Japanese pitcher Hideki Irabu, got picked off first base in the final inning, and we lost a close game to the Red Sox media. I don't know how he found out about it, but the next time I spoke on the phone with Mr. Steinbrenner, he brought it up. "If the young man's not ready to be on the field, he can't be on the field," he told me. It truly felt like a scene out of *Seinfeld*, which lampooned The Boss for several seasons with his permission.

ESPN reporter Buster Olney, formerly the Yankees beat writer for *The New York Times*, once wrote about a time he was interviewing Steinbrenner in his office when a manager from Yankee Stadium's concession services knocked on the door. Steinbrenner halted the interview and pulled a pretzel out of his desk drawer, ranting about how there needed to be more salt on any pretzel sold during games.

Players and underlings, of course, often had different experiences. General manager Bob Watson once said The Boss' trusted baseball people were little more than "voices inside his head." As former media relations director Harvey Greene told *The Times* in 2010 about noticing the light flashing on his hotel phone: "You knew that either there had been a death in the family, or George was looking for you. After a while you started to hope that there had been a death in the family."

Said Gossage: "You'd love him one minute and fricking want to kill him the next. But it was all by design. You never got comfortable around George. You hated to see that man coming. We'd look at each other and go, 'Well, whose turn is it today?' But then he'd do something really nice for us, too. But I'll also say this: on top of hating to see that man coming, now I miss seeing that man coming. He definitely made our lives as Yankees more interesting."

Dave Righetti told me one story he'd never discussed publicly about the hand injury he suffered during his first season as the team's closer in 1984. Steinbrenner ordered everyone involved to take lie detector tests because he didn't believe their back story, costing

LEAD, FOLLOW, OR GET THE
HELL OUT OF THE WAY!

George Steinbrenner, who owned the Yankees
from 1973 to 2010, sits at his office desk in Yankee
Stadium in 1981.

bullpen coach Jerry McNertney his job. "Joe Altobelli was the Orioles manager. They'd won the World Series the previous year, and he told me I was going to make the All-Star team," Righetti said. "The next day I was in the clubhouse before the game, and for whatever reason, wrestling was on. Sergeant Slaughter was fighting the Iron Sheik. I was going to the bullpen before the game started and I got down there, and Mike Armstrong was there. I was telling him how The Sheik just put Sergeant Slaughter in a freaking camel clutch, and then the Sergeant took his helmet off and hit Sheik in the head with it. As I did that, I swung my arm, pretending I had a helmet in my hand, and I cut it on the metal water cooler behind me in the bullpen, an absolute accident. I looked down at my hand, and it was like a perfect slice, and I'm bleeding everywhere. And this is where this story gets crazy."

Steinbrenner made McNertney and bullpen catcher Dom Scala take lie detector tests, but he still wasn't satisfied with the results since Righetti landed on the disabled list for a few weeks and missed the All-Star Game. "I told him we were talking about wrestling, but all he heard was that we *were* wrestling," Righetti said. "I told him the coaches had nothing to do with it. But he reassigned Jerry. The other players probably were half-mad at me for seeing this poor guy go back down to the minor leagues. I was pissed, I was really hot, and I never forgot it. George chewed my ass out. If you want to get mad at me, fine. I'd be glad to take the blame for all that. But poor Jerry took the fall."

Wade Boggs, the five-time American League batting champion with the rival Boston Red Sox in the 1980s, was a free agent while Steinbrenner was serving his second suspension in 1992. Boggs and agent Alan Nero met with Steinbrenner's son-in-law, Joe Molloy, at the Bay Harbor Hotel, which Steinbrenner's family owned in Tampa, to hammer out a contract. "There was a gentleman at an adjacent table behind a newspaper, and he lowered it and gave me a wink and a nod of approval," Boggs said. "It was Mr. Steinbrenner. He wasn't allowed to be there, but he was at the table next to us, and I didn't even realize he'd been sitting there the whole time. That's the beginning of my five-year history with the Yankees. It was pretty funny, like something you'd see in a movie."

Steinbrenner also deserves credit for providing second chances to fallen former New York Mets Dwight Gooden and Darryl Strawberry, following their bouts with substance abuse, as well as several additional opportunities to troubled reliever Steve Howe in his attempts to come back from drug issues. Several players—Bucky Dent, Boggs, Chili Davis, Johnny Damon, among them—said Steinbrenner told them upon arrival, "I've always wanted you on my team" or something similar. "Here's a good one," Chris Chambliss said. "When I first got there, Bill Virdon was managing, and George was on suspension. He was not allowed to be at the stadium. We were not playing well, and he wanted to get a message to the team. So he taped this rant. He really must have wanted to bawl us out and probably wanted to do it in person, but he couldn't. So he sent a tape, and Virdon called a meeting and plopped down this cassette player in the middle of the room and pressed play. George was just reaming us out that we needed to start playing better or he'd make some trades and get rid of some guys. Guys were laughing hysterically."

Steinbrenner's players put up with all of it because the man who once vowed to "stick to building ships" turned out to be all about winning 'ships, as the kids say. "Even with some of the tirades, all the stuff that went on, the meddling, the stuff he'd do or say in the papers that would piss you off to no end, I understood George," Willie Randolph said. "At the end of the day, he was all about winning for the Yankees and the city of New York. That's all he cared about. If you took stuff personally, you couldn't play for the man. There were times I wanted to curse him out. Everyone did. But he was the best. I don't care what anyone says. There were times I wanted to choke him, man. A lot of guys wanted to choke him, but I look back in retrospect, and there isn't another owner I'd rather play for. All he wanted to do was win."

4

JOE D.

There were two professional athletes that prompted me to immediately call my father upon meeting them. One was Sandy Koufax, whom I shared an elevator ride with at Dodger Stadium during the 2015 National League playoffs. It was just the two of us, and we made small talk for a brief minute. Pretty cool, right? The other was the far more important one to my dad, who grew up a die-hard Dodgers fan in Brooklyn, but whose favorite player in a lifetime of loving baseball was the same as many New York kids, particularly those of Italian descent.

So with my first clunky Nokia cell phone, I breathlessly called Dad after interviewing Joe DiMaggio one-on-one briefly as he sat in a golf cart ahead of his final Old Timers' Day appearance in 1998. It was a few steps away from the sign that contained his famous quote: "I want to thank the Good Lord for making me a Yankee." Derek Jeter respectfully touched that sign before every game as he made his way down the ramp from the home clubhouse to the dugout at the original Yankee Stadium.

Known as the Yankee Clipper, DiMaggio was the owner of one of the sport's most enduring and seemingly unbreakable records, a 56-game hitting streak in 1941. He was both an American war hero and dubbed in 1969 as baseball's "greatest living ballplayer," a designation he requested be used every time he was introduced at Yankee Stadium until his death during spring training of 1999, which coincided with my second full year on the Yankees beat for the *New York Daily News*. "In a country that has idolized and even immortalized its 20th century heroes from Charles A. Lindbergh to Elvis Presley, no one more embodied the American Dream of fame and fortune or created a more enduring legend than Joe DiMaggio," Joseph Durso wrote in DiMaggio's obituary in *The New York Times*. "He became a figure of unequaled romance and integrity in the national mind because of his consistent professionalism on the baseball field, his marriage to the Hollywood star Marilyn Monroe, his devotion to her after her death, and the pride and courtliness with which he carried himself throughout his life."

Indeed, Joe D. was a transcendent superstar with an almost regal dignity about him both on and off the field, earning him mentions in pop culture throughout the remainder of his life.

The son of a San Francisco-area fisherman, he was referred to in *The Old Man and the Sea* by Ernest Hemingway, who wrote about wanting "to take the great DiMaggio fishing." The Les Brown Orchestra recorded the song "Joltin' Joe DiMaggio" in 1941. As Betty Ronney sang, and many baseball fans thereafter can attest: "He'll live in baseball's Hall of Fame, he got there blow by blow. Our kids will tell their kids his name: Joltin' Joe DiMaggio."

In their hit song "Mrs. Robinson" more than a quarter-century later during the tumultuous times of the 1960s, Simon and Garfunkel asked, "Where have you gone, Joe DiMaggio? A nation turns its lonely eyes to you." Of course, children of my generation knew him more as a pitcher than an outfielder—that is, as a celebrity endorser in commercials for Mr. Coffee and for The Bowery Saving Bank. DiMaggio also would be referenced in dozens of movies and TV shows. In *Seinfeld*, Kramer even claimed to have seen Joe D. dunking into his coffee cup at Dinky Donuts.

Soon after his baseball retirement in 1951, DiMaggio, who previously had married and divorced actress Dorothy Arnold, was wed to Monroe for nine months in 1952. Some wrote the marriage splintered because DiMaggio was uncomfortable with Monroe's public sex symbol status from movies such as *The Seven Year Itch*. Still, when the 36-year-old actress overdosed in 1962, DiMaggio took over her funeral arrangements and famously sent flowers to her grave for years after her death. In perhaps the most famous anecdote from their relationship, Monroe returned from a trip entertaining U.S. troops in Japan and Korea. She said to DiMaggio, "Joe, you've never heard such cheering."

DiMaggio's reply? "Yes, I have."

Joe D. most certainly had. Directly upon arrival in the Bronx in 1936 and two years after Babe Ruth's departure, he batted .323 with 29 home runs and 125 RBIs as a rookie. With Lou Gehrig as his teammate until The Iron Horse's abrupt retirement due to illness in 1939, the Yankees won four straight World Series titles—and nine in all—during DiMaggio's 13 seasons. Imagine how much better his personal numbers would have been had the prime of DiMaggio's playing career not been interrupted from 1943 to 1945 by military service in the U.S. Army Air Forces during World War II. He finished with a career batting average of .325 and slugged 361 home runs while unfathomably striking out only 369 times.

By comparison center-field successor Mickey Mantle whiffed 1,710 times over 18 seasons, and Reggie Jackson shattered that number with a Major League Baseball-record 2,597. To illustrate how much the game has changed in the ensuing decades, current slugger Aaron Judge struck out 402 times in his first two-plus seasons with the Yankees.

In 1941 DiMaggio most notably recorded at least one hit in 56 consecutive games from May 15 until July 17. Cleveland Indians third baseman Ken Keltner robbed him of potential hits twice with sparkling backhanded plays to halt the streak. Only one player in the ensuing 78 seasons—Pete Rose with 44 in 1978—has even reached 40 consecutive games. Interestingly, DiMaggio immediately began a new hit streak of 16 consecutive games for an incredible stretch of 72 of 73. He won the American League MVP award for the pennant-winning Yankees over Ted Williams despite his Boston rival batting .406 (the last player to hit .400 or better) with 147 walks for a whopping .553 on-base percentage. "I was terribly impressed with DiMaggio and I thought that he was the best player—all-around player—for sure," Williams told broadcaster Joel Alderman in 1975.

DiMaggio, whose brothers Vince and Dom also played in the majors, also was named MVP in 1939, when he batted a career best .381 in Lou Gehrig's final season, and in 1947, when he edged Williams by a single point in the voting.

According to Matt Dahlgren, whose grandfather replaced Gehrig at first base, Babe Dahlgren also had an interesting origin connection to DiMaggio. "This goes back to the Pacific Coast League. In 1932 my grandfather was with the San Francisco Missions," Matt Dahlgren said. "During batting practice the manager told Babe to get his first baseman's glove because he wanted him at first base to take some throws from a kid that was trying out as a shortstop. They hit some ground balls, and the kid took some swings in the cages, and the manager said, 'You know what? He's not ready. Why don't you come back and see us next year?' They let him go. That kid was Joe DiMaggio. A few weeks later, the San Francisco Seals had some injuries, and DiMaggio's brother, Vince, was on the Seals. He told the manager, 'My brother can come out.' And they tried him out, and he ended up signing with the Seals. In 1932 when Joe DiMaggio played his very first professional baseball game, it happened to be against the Missions, my grandfather's team. Babe played all throughout 1933 and 1934 against DiMaggio, and then as fate would have it, they would be teammates with the Yankees and win championships together."

The World Series ring DiMaggio won during his rookie year was the one he regularly wore throughout his life, and because of that, the only original one of the nine he earned in his 13-year career that still was in his possession at the time of his death. While on a business trip in the 1960s, DiMaggio's other eight rings were stolen from a hotel suite. On the final day of the 1998 regular season, when the Yankees managed their team-record 114th victory, he was honored before the game and presented replicas of the eight missing rings as a gift from George Steinbrenner.

Still, many Yankees of those latter generations wished they could have enjoyed better relationships with DiMaggio. "Joe D. was a little harder to talk to than some of the other old timers. He was more private, more quiet," Don Mattingly said. "But there was a sportswriters' dinner one year, and we were on the dais. It was me and Joe and Keith Hernandez sitting together. Keith was from San Francisco, too, so he was asking Joe all this stuff, but Joe wouldn't really open up. Finally, Keith asked, 'What did you like to do in this situation when you were hitting?' It was like it turned on a light for Joe. He started talking hitting with us a little bit, and I'll never forget that conversation. It was awesome. Because I knew at Old Timers' Day, he didn't really enjoy guys coming up to him and especially asking him to sign things."

Paul O'Neill, Wade Boggs, Goose Gossage, and others also recounted tales of failed attempts to get autographs from DiMaggio.

But sometimes those pursuits did work out successfully. "I asked one year at Old Timers' Day to have a bat signed, and Joe just said, 'I'm not signing today,'" O'Neill said. "A couple of years later, he came up to me and said, 'Paul, do you still want that bat signed?' So I always remember thinking how cool it was that he remembered that. But I always thought it was cool that we could have these iconic guys like Joe DiMaggio getting dressed at our lockers. That was always one of the coolest things about playing for the Yankees."

5

THE MICK

Mickey Mantle might have been the last of baseball's truly mythical figures. Perhaps it was the aw-shucks innocence, the reluctance to fall in line with the Yankee greats who preceded him, the debilitating injuries he played through year after year, the astounding feats of athleticism, the rhythmic name that sounded like what a baseball superstar's name should be, or even the knowledge years later of his carousing and drinking that gave him a tragic hero-like quality.

Two prophetic quotes have stuck out whenever I've devoured articles or books about Mantle or listened to tales and gushing remembrances of him. Relatives, celebrity fans, former teammates, even media members old enough to have seen him play recounted his saying, "If I'd known I was going to live this long, I would have taken better care of myself" and "Don't be like me. I was given so much and I blew it."

Everyone, of course, wanted to be just like Mantle, the most powerful switch-hitter in the history of baseball. The blonde-haired, muscle-bound heir to Babe Ruth, Lou Gehrig, and Joe DiMaggio, he went on to earn a deserved place besides his legendary Bronx forebears on the Mount Rushmore of Yankees history with an awe-inspiring yet flawed career that still stands up among the greatest of the greats.

Still, such endearment, blind devotion, and hero worship aren't borne simply from rote statistics on the back of a baseball card. It was more than Mantle's 536 home runs, the most all time for a switch-hitter. It was more than his Triple Crown in 1956, joining Gehrig as the only two such seasons in Yankee annals. It was more than his three American League MVP awards in 1956, 1957, and 1962. It was more than his 18 World Series home runs, another record unlikely to be matched, or his seven World Series championships.

Emblematic of an era of kids and adults who worshipped him for reasons even they could not fully explain, longtime television broadcaster Bob Costas grew up a rabid fan of Mantle and the Yankees on Long Island in the 1950s and 1960s. Costas carried around a Mantle baseball card well into adulthood. Later in Mantle's life, they sat down for a lengthy soul-searching interview together and became friendly enough that Costas was asked by the Mantle family to speak at his funeral in 1995. "For reasons that no statistics, no dry recitation of the facts can possibly capture, he was the most compelling baseball hero of our lifetime. And he was our symbol of baseball at a time when the game meant something to us that perhaps it no longer does," Costas said during his eulogy. "We knew there was something poignant about Mickey Mantle before we knew what poignant meant. We didn't just root for him, we felt for him. Long before many of us ever cracked a serious book, we knew something about mythology as we watched Mickey Mantle run out a home run through the lengthening shadows of a late Sunday afternoon at Yankee Stadium. There was a greatness about him but vulnerability, too. He was our guy."

Costas was elected to the Baseball Hall of Fame as a broadcaster in 2018, 50 years after Mantle played his final game for the Yankees. Struggling through shoddy knees, Mantle batted just .237 in 1968, dropping his career batting average below .300 to .298, a number he regretted throughout the remainder of his life. "Mick was only still playing then as a favor to the Yankees to draw in the people, to say that we still had Mickey Mantle on the team," said former teammate Roy White, a bridge between the end of the Mantle era and the Yankees' championship teams in 1977–78. "Our team was so underwhelming in those years that I think he stayed on a couple of seasons more than he really wanted to."

A few years later, Jim Bouton, a pitcher for the Yankees from 1962 to 1968, released the seminal book *Ball Four*, which in part detailed Mantle's philandering with women and his heavy drinking with teammates such as Whitey Ford and Billy Martin. Until then, disclosing such untoward stories publicly was considered taboo not only for teammates, but also for reporters covering the team. "We didn't know about Mickey's personal demons until after he was done playing. My feeling always was there's a difference between a baseball hero and role model. Mickey Mantle was my favorite baseball player. Nothing I learned about him subsequently changed my feeling on that," Costas told me in 2019. "But what I also definitely think added to the feeling that he was that tragic figure was this idea: that as great as he was, he could have been even greater. Maybe my father's generation compared him to DiMaggio, but for kids of my generation, we knew who Ruth and Gehrig and DiMaggio were, but he was our Yankee hero in the here and now. It all added to the mythology of it. I don't know if kids feel that way about anyone now."

Wade Boggs told me one of his most meaningful days with the Yankees was getting Mantle's autograph for his father. Jason Giambi's father also was a massive fan; Giambi said he took No. 25 with the Yanks because the numbers added up to Mantle's No. 7.

Named by his father, Mutt, after former Philadelphia A's and Detroit Tigers catcher Mickey Cochrane, Mantle was born in Oklahoma in 1931. Mutt Mantle, once an aspiring ballplayer, would come home each day from working in the zinc mines to teach his son how to hit from both sides of the plate. A Yankees scout named Tom Greenwade signed the switch-hitting shortstop for a $1,500 bonus upon his graduation from high school in 1949.

By 1951 the 19-year-old Mantle made it to the Yankees. They converted him to right field as DiMaggio entered the final season of his storied career in center. The rookie initially was given the uniform No. 6 in the line of succession with Ruth (No. 3), Gehrig (4), and DiMaggio (5), a designation he'd resisted. Two months into the season, manager Casey Stengel sent the struggling Mantle to the Yankees' farm team in Kansas City. He switched to No. 7 upon his return, and that number wound up in Monument Park.

Mantle assumed center-field duties the following season, sharing the position in New York as part of the renowned power trio "Willie, Mickey, and the Duke" with Willie Mays of the Giants and Duke Snider of the Dodgers for the next several years until the other two local teams departed for the West Coast in 1958. "In the World Series in 1951," Mantle said, according to *The New York Times*, "I tripped on the water-main sprinkler in the outfield while I was holding back so

DiMaggio could catch a ball that Willie Mays hit and I twisted my knee and got torn ligaments. That was the start of my knee operations."

Still, Mantle's health concerns expanded far beyond typical muscle pulls and broken bones. Mutt Mantle died at age 40 from Hodgkin's disease, which also led to the deaths of Mantle's grandfather and two uncles. "You don't have to talk to me about pensions," Mantle joked. "I won't be around long enough to collect one."

Mantle's drinking only worsened in retirement; he was diagnosed with liver cancer and cirrhosis in 1992. Two years later at the behest of his son, Danny, and former Giants kicker and football broadcaster Pat Summerall, who also was a recovering alcoholic, Mantle entered the Betty Ford Center in Palm Springs, California, to undergo treatment. He later recalled a doctor telling him: "Eventually, you'll need a new liver. I'm not going to lie to you: the next drink you take may be your last."

There would be no more drinks, and Mantle indeed would undergo a liver transplant on June 9, 1995. It sparked a public debate over whether an abusive alcoholic deserved a functional organ, and whether his celebrity had enhanced his prospect of receiving one. It also finally sparked some clarity for Mantle, however, and fostered the poignant comeback Costas later discussed in his eulogy as The Mick's "ninth inning" of life.

On July 11 the 63-year-old Hall of Famer held a press conference at Baylor Medical Center in Dallas imploring children: "Don't be like me" and urging people everywhere to register for organ donations. "All you have to do is look at me and see where [my life] was wasted," a frail Mantle said. "I want to get across to the kids not to drink or do drugs. Mom and Dad should be the role models. That's what I think. I was given so much and blew it."

Dale Berra told me that it was Mantle who often played catch with Yogi's three sons during spring training, calling the superstar "the nicest, most fun guy to be around for the kids."

In 1995 Mantle lamented his relationship with his estranged wife, Merlyn, and their four sons, saying, "I wasn't even like a father to my boys. I was like a drinking buddy. That has changed. I feel more like a father now."

Billy Mantle, who also suffered from Hodgkin's disease, died in March of 1994 at age 36 of a heart attack while at a treatment center for substance abuse. Mickey Jr. died at 47 of liver cancer in 2000. Mickey was devastated by his son Billy's death so soon after completing his own alcohol treatment. But he also genuinely was surprised at the outpouring of well wishes he received in the form of thousands of letters while in rehab and an estimated 20,000 more following his transplant surgery. "After he came out of Betty Ford, Mickey actually said to me, 'I get it better now. I understand better now,'" Costas recalled. "More or less he said, 'I never completely understood why people made such a big deal out of me until I got all those letters.' Teachers of a certain age told their kids about him, and he began to understand that he had an effect on people. He was more at peace. He understood his life better, he was better able to embrace the adoration that people had for him. And then the rug gets pulled out from under him."

On July 28, 1995, Mantle returned to Baylor for treatment of cancerous spots in his right lung. By August 9 the hospital revealed the cancer had spread to his abdomen. Ford, Yogi Berra, Moose Skowron, Tony Kubek, Bobby Richardson, and more teammates rushed to Dallas, where Mantle died on August 13.

Batting right-handed, Mantle once crushed a ball thrown by Chuck Stobbs of the Washington Senators over the 55-foot-high wall in left field at Griffith Stadium. The prodigious blast was measured at 565 feet from home plate. But as Dr. Goran Klintmalm, the medical director of transplant services at Baylor, remarked about a dying Mantle's public pleas, "This may become Mickey's ultimate home run."

6

YOGI

This chapter ain't over 'til it's over. A lot of the content might even strike you as déjà vu all over again. Yes, I went there. But Yogi Berra was so much more than the wise, if malapropping, philosopher of baseball he often was portrayed to be. He was more than the deliverer of witty and prophetic Yogi-isms that many fondly remember him for and can recite with exuberance and reverence upon request.

Berra also was a devoted family man and friend to all, an American hero and icon who stormed the beach at Normandy, as well as a three-time MVP, the heart and soul of a Yankees dynasty, a link from DiMaggio to the Mantle/Maris era, and the winner of 10 World Series rings amid 14 total appearances in the Fall Classic as a player. The latter stats rank as the most in baseball history. "We get mad as a family, my brothers and I, when people say Ruth, Gehrig, DiMaggio, Mantle, and they forget Berra," Yogi's son Dale Berra told me in 2019. "That happens too much. It often goes from those four guys straight to Jeter and Mariano, who—don't get me wrong—are all-time great Yankees and deserve all of the accolades they receive. But Berra is skipped? That's absolutely insane based on what Dad did. It's like people almost forget how good he was at baseball with all of the other stuff."

Lawrence Peter Berra grew up with Italian immigrant parents in the St. Louis, Missouri, section known as "The Hill," living the true American Dream in a generation defined by such pursuits. He was given the nickname "Yogi" by a teenaged friend who thought he resembled a character in a movie he'd seen: a Hindu man doing various yoga poses.

Future major league player Joe Garagiola also was a close childhood friend, and four other kids from their predominantly Italian neighborhood were members of the United States soccer team that upset heavily favored England in the 1950 World Cup. Berra, who dropped out of school at 14, also played soccer growing up before receiving a $500 bonus to sign with the Yankees in 1943.

Berra's baseball career was delayed by a stint in the United States Navy during World War II; he served as a gunner's mate on the USS Bayfield during the D-Day invasion of Normandy. He received several commendations for his service, including the Presidential Medal of Freedom from president Barack Obama in 2015. "Dad talked about the service all the time, the camaraderie of it. He was so proud of it," Dale said. "Volunteering for a mission that he ended up on the D-Day invasion on Day One, just amazing. He'd talk about pulling bloated bodies out of the water and taking gunfire and firing on the beach—all at 18 years old. We'd say, 'Were you afraid, Dad?' He'd say he didn't have time to be afraid. He was too young to be afraid. That was definitely a different generation."

The 5'7" catcher soon would come to mean so much to multiple generations of New York baseball fans. In his first seven seasons, the Yankees won six World Series titles and then four more through 1961. As DiMaggio's fabled career was coming to a close and Mantle's was just beginning, Berra was as integral to success as any star on the team. He won the American League MVP award in 1951, 1954, and 1955 and finished second in 1953 and 1956.

Berra eventually was enshrined in the Hall of Fame in 1972. Shared with his catching mentor, Bill Dickey, his No. 8 was co-retired to Monument Park that same year. "He isn't much to look at, he looks like he's doing everything wrong, but he sure can hit," Casey Stengel said, according to *The Guardian*.

When Berra retired in 1965, his 358 career home runs were the most for any player whose primary position had been catcher. And talk about a different generation. The lefty slugger struck out just 414 times over 19 seasons, including a *dozen* in 656 plate appearances in 1950. "Ridiculous," Dale said. "Even the top guys strike out now 12 times in a week."

By 1958 Yogi Berra was a household name, so it was natural to assume the popular cartoon character that debuted that year, Yogi Bear, was named after him. Berra briefly considered taking legal action for defamation, but he didn't follow through when creators from Hanna-Barbera Productions insisted the connection was purely coincidental. Sure it was.

The Jellystone Park-dwelling Yogi certainly loved his pic-a-nic baskets and was hailed as "smarter than your average bear."

By that point Berra also had earned the reputation for colorful one-liners, a sage collection of wit and paradoxical wisdom that further endeared him to millions. His 2010 autobiography was titles *I Really Didn't Say Everything I Said*. Everyone has a favorite—whether Yogi actually said the words or not:

- "When you come to a fork in the road, take it."
- "Baseball is 90 percent mental. The other half is physical."
- "No one goes [to that restaurant] anymore. It's too crowded."
- "You can observe a lot by watching."
- "Always go to other people's funerals, or they won't go to yours."
- "Never answer an anonymous letter."
- "He hits from both sides of the plate. He's amphibious."
- "A nickel ain't worth a dime anymore."
- "I want to thank everybody for making this day necessary."

Upon retirement Berra immediately took over as manager of the Yankees, winning 99 games and the team's fifth straight AL pennant in 1964, before falling in the World Series to his hometown St. Louis Cardinals in seven games. The team legend was fired after one season in charge and oddly replaced by St. Louis manager Johnny Keane.

Berra's two eldest sons, Larry and Tim, were called out of their classes by their school's headmaster that morning. "I have terrible, awful news about your Dad,'" he told them.

"They looked at each other and were worried if Dad was okay," Dale said. "But the headmaster then told them the Yankees had let him go. And they were like, 'That's it? He's okay?' I was too young for that. I remember the news trucks being outside our house. But for Dad he didn't skip a beat. He went to spring training the next year with the Mets. Casey was the manager. It was all baseball to him. He didn't even think twice about it."

Yogi would feel much differently the next time he was axed by the Yankees.

After replacing deceased New York Mets manager Gil Hodges in 1972, Berra guided them to a surprise appearance in the 1973 World Series, losing to future Yankee stars Reggie Jackson and Catfish Hunter and the Oakland A's in seven games.

Dale reached the major leagues with the Pittsburgh Pirates in 1977 and he was traded to the Yankees in 1985. He also had started using cocaine while with the Pirates and credits a post-career intervention staged by his father with saving his life. "Dad just called me to the house one day. He never was concerned about himself ever or the Berra name. It was always just worried about me," Dale said. "He looked at me and pointed to my brothers and said, 'Those two will not be your brothers anymore. And I will not be your father anymore. I will have two sons. The second he said that, I knew I would never take another drink or do another drug for the rest of my life. And I haven't for 28, almost 30, years of sobriety now."

Berra had been named the Yankees' manager again in 1984, taking over after the third of five managerial stints for former teammate Billy Martin. Despite assurances from The Boss, he lasted only 16 games into the next season and was fired with a 6–10 record on April 28. He was replaced once again by Martin. "Billy got fired before, but this was different. Yogi was Yogi," pitcher Dave Righetti recalled. "Guys were crushed, and guys were pissed. Dale, I can't even imagine what he was thinking."

Said Dale: "I was coming home. To be able to play for Dad in New York was tremendous. But I mean, 16 games? Come on. We didn't have a healthy Mattingly, Winfield, or Henderson to start the year. It doesn't take a smart baseball man to know that when those three got healthy, we're gonna win a lot of games. But typical Dad, he was like, 'I'll be fine. I'm going golfing tomorrow.'"

Only, he was not fine with anything. He was furious, especially that George Steinbrenner sent general manager Clyde King to hand him the pink slip without a personal phone call. Berra vowed never to return to Yankee Stadium while The Boss still owned the team.

In fact, more than 14 painful years passed before the prideful, prodigal son returned.

Suzyn Waldman brokered the truce in 1999. She'd been assigned to host a WFAN show from the newly opening Yogi Berra Museum and Learning Center on the campus of Montclair State University. (Berra raised three sons with his beloved wife, Carmen, in Montclair. His son, Tim, made it to the NFL as a wide receiver with the Baltimore Colts, and son, Larry, played minor league baseball.) Program director Mark Chernoff asked Waldman, "Wouldn't it be great if you could get George and Yogi to make up" on the air?

"A few days later, I was talking to George about something else, and I said to him, 'I need to talk to you about Yogi.' And George immediately said, 'Why, what's wrong?' When I heard that, I figured okay, maybe he'd finally be open to it," Waldman said.

After several weeks of back and forth planning—with Waldman and the Berra brothers serving as facilitators—it finally resulted in Steinbrenner flying from Tampa, Florida, to Teterboro Airport in New Jersey during a January snowstorm to issue the public apology over the New York airwaves. "I started with: 'Mr. Berra, you know Mr. Steinbrenner,'" Waldman recalled. "At one point during a break, they went into another room together, and all you could hear was yelling. I was leaning up against the wall, and Tim Berra said to me, 'What are you doing?' I said, 'I'm listening to my career going up in smoke.' But Carmen went in, and everyone calmed down, and we kept going."

Waldman called Steinbrenner later that night at his hotel and asked him how he thought the segment went. "He called it a great day for the New York Yankees in that George voice of his," she said. "And then he goes, 'It wasn't too fucking bad for you either, Waldman.'"

Dale also gave an assist to his father's ailing former teammate DiMaggio, who died during spring training of 1999. "It was Joe D. who really put it over the edge," Dale said. "He told George while he was dying: 'Whatever it takes, get Yogi back to Yankee Stadium.' And of course, Suzyn piggybacked on top of DiMaggio. She was wonderful. But as soon as DiMaggio told George that, there was nothing he wouldn't do to get him back."

In turn, Yogi's family urged him to finally relent. "We kept saying, 'Dad, you have grandkids who have no idea, who have never seen you in a Yankee uniform,'" Dale said. "They don't associate you with being there and hearing the crowd cheer for you. Nine grandkids had never seen that. Let them see you walk out to a standing ovation at Yankee Stadium. It meant everything to him to become part of that again."

Berra finally found his way back for the 1999 home opener against the Detroit Tigers on April 9. He threw out the ceremonial pitch to thunderous applause and few dry eyes throughout Yankee Stadium. Accompanied this time by 1956 World Series perfect game collaborator Don Larsen, he returned again for Yogi Berra Day on July 18. David Cone incredibly threw another perfecto that day. "I was in the dugout when Yogi came out in that convertible and I was crying," Waldman recalled. "I remember thinking, *I did that. It wouldn't have happened without me.* Because everybody had tried. From [Steinbrenner adviser] Arthur Richman to Stick Michael, a thousand people had tried. I was very proud of that."

In 2000 I received the opportunity to sit down with Yogi to ghostwrite a first-person column under his byline to lead a special pullout section for the *New York Daily News*, commemorating the franchise's first 25 titles through the end of the 20th century. Working together on a column titled "Yogi on Rings and Things" (by Yogi Berra, as told to *Daily News* sports writer Peter Botte) was a massive thrill and a ton of fun, as you'd imagine. "Getting over the problems with George really made [1999's] World Series more enjoyable for me than when they won in '96 and '98," Berra wrote. "It was great to be around the team again after so many years away. George finally said the right things, and I came back. I can say now that it always seemed a little bit strange to be apart from the Yankees for all of the time I was away."

Berra became a staple around the team for the next decade, building a particularly strong relationship with manager Joe Torre and shortstop Derek Jeter. In subsequent years, Ron Guidry drove Berra around during spring training in Tampa, Florida, while wearing a "Driving Mr. Yogi" hat, a play on the popular late-1980s movie *Driving Miss Daisy*, starring Morgan Freeman and Jessica Tandy. Mattingly, a member of the 1985 club when Berra was fired in the first month of the season, donned No. 8 as a tribute to Berra when he became manager of the Los Angeles Dodgers in 2011. As he put it, "Everything Yogi touches turns to gold."

"It was very important for all of us to have Yogi back," Hal Steinbrenner said in 2019. "Nobody wants to have a situation like that, and it was so sad and unfortunate for all of us. Yogi and Carmen were an important part of the family, and I'm glad that got worked out before it was too late."

Carmen Berra died in 2014, and her husband passed away the following year. He was 90 years old. Baseball and beyond mourned the loss of a true original and an American treasure, but Yogi Berra's legacy—and words—live on forever.

7

ENTER SANDMAN

The greatest closer in baseball history emerged from the home dugout to thunderous applause as the last former Yankee to be introduced at his first appearance in Old Timers' Day festivities at Yankee Stadium in 2019, commemorating his pending induction into the Baseball Hall of Fame as the first player in history to garner 100 percent of the vote. "What it means to me to be a Yankee, I have a lot of great moments in baseball, but my greatest moment in baseball was just wearing this uniform," Mariano Rivera said. "It was just putting this uniform on for 19 seasons. That was the greatest moment. That's what I believe, that's what I think about the pinstripes. It's legend. It's majesty. It's prestige. It's all of that, and I was blessed that I wore this uniform for 19 years. It's spectacular. It's priceless."

In my opinion, Rivera and career teammate Derek Jeter unmistakably have vaulted themselves to the cusp of the greatest of the pinstriped greats just outside the incomparable Mount Rushmore foursome of Babe Ruth, Lou Gehrig, Joe DiMaggio, and Mickey Mantle, as well as Yogi Berra, on the organizational masthead of immortal Yankees.

Fittingly, baseball's all-time saves leader (652) closed out the 2019 Hall of Fame induction speeches in Cooperstown for a six-man class that also featured Seattle Mariners nemesis Edgar Martinez and former Yankees teammate Mike Mussina. With Hal Steinbrenner, Jeter, fellow Core Four brethren Jorge Posada and Andy Pettitte and teammates Bernie Williams and Tino Martinez seated in the crowd, Rivera opened his speech by joking, "I don't understand why I always have to be last."

The son of a fisherman also spoke seriously about growing up as a shortstop while using a glove fashioned out of cardboard in the small Panamanian village of Puerto Caimito, dreaming of becoming a mechanic or maybe even the next Pele—not the revolutionary one-of-a-kind player Brian Cashman called "without a doubt the best relief pitcher ever."

Rivera also fondly recalled his tearful final appearance for the Yankees in September of 2013, when manager Joe Girardi sent Jeter and Pettitte to the mound to remove their longtime friend and teammate for the rarest of pitching changes. "My two brothers came in and took me out of the game," Rivera said. "That moment was special for me. I was grateful to the good Lord that allowed me to play in New York with the greatest fans and end my career the way I did: with my two brothers next to me and me hugging them and crying over them and being thankful for them."

Williams also played "Take Me Out to the Ballgame" on his electric guitar during the ceremony, even mixing in a couple of riffs from the tune that has become synonymous with Rivera—Metallica's "Enter Sandman." In 1999 a Yankee Stadium game operations staffer started playing the song whenever Rivera entered a game. The lyrics perfectly fit a pitcher adept at putting the opposing team to sleep: "Take my hand, we're off to Never Neverland!"

Rivera admittedly listened more to Christian music than to heavy metal, but he appreciated the Rock & Roll Hall of Fame headbangers showing up at Yankee Stadium for a surprise live rendition at his final home game in 2013. Metallica also tweeted out a video congratulating Rivera on the night of his Hall of Fame election. Lead singer James Hetfield declared: "We, Metallica, took a vote here, and it's unanimous."

As Rivera has noted, the 425 voters from the Baseball Writers' Association of America who checked the box next to his name on the ballot (including me) was a fitting number, too. He wore uniform No. 42—the last grandfathered active player to do so after Major League Baseball universally retired it for Jackie Robinson—and won five World Series championships in his 19-year career. For the numerologists Rivera also recorded an unrivaled 42 postseason saves. The previous electorate mark had belonged to Ken Griffey Jr., who fell three votes shy of unanimity in 2016 with 99.32 percent. "The first unanimous, I never would say or would never pretend to be better than anybody else. That is just a humbling recognition," Rivera said. "It's amazing. It's something that you have to embrace."

Discovered by scout Herb Raybourn and signed for a mere $2,500 in 1990, Rivera made his major league debut as the Yankees' starting pitcher on May 23, 1995 against the California Angels. He promptly was hammered for 17 runs in 15 innings over his first four outings and sent back to Triple A Columbus, Ohio.

With the Yankees debating whether to start Jeter in the majors the next spring, they nearly traded Rivera to the Mariners for stopgap shortstop Felix Fermin, a .259 hitter with four career home runs who was out of baseball by 1997. He also had been left exposed and went unclaimed by the Florida Marlins and the Colorado Rockies in the 1992 expansion draft. "My God, can you imagine?" Joe Torre said. "We would have never known."

We would have never known the pitcher, who, relying almost exclusively on a bat-shattering cut fastball, registered a career ERA of 2.21 and WHIP of 1.000, the lowest in the live-ball era among qualified pitchers. Rivera was even better in October, compiling a miniscule 0.70 ERA along with those 42 saves over 16 different years with at least one postseason appearance.

"I had the best view in the stadium, watching him for all those years," Williams said on the YES Network from Cooperstown. "The fact that everybody in the park, everybody watching, everybody everywhere, knew what he was going to throw, and he was still the most successful closer in the history of the game, it was just mind-boggling. To watch him throw that pitch over and over again and have bats being shattered, it was just fun to see. I was just glad I never had to face him or I would have been one of those guys, too."

After emerging as a breakout multi-inning shutdown set-up man for John Wetteland during the 1996 championship run, Rivera succeeded him as closer the following season. He surrendered a game-tying home run to Cleveland Indians catcher Sandy Alomar Jr. in Game 4 of the American League Division Series before the Yankees were eliminated in five. Still, from the beginning, the even-keeled Rivera was famously unaffected by his infrequent failures. Jeter called him "the most mentally tough person I've ever played with."

He endured two other notable blown saves in postseason play. In 2001, nearly two months after the September 11 terrorist attacks, the Yankees had Rivera on the mound with a one-run lead in the ninth inning of Game 7 in Arizona, looking to close out their fourth consecutive title. He committed a key throwing error and lost the game on Luis Gonzalez's bases-loaded single.

During their historic comeback from an 0–3 deficit in the 2004 American League Championship Series, the Boston Red Sox got their comeback started by getting to Rivera in the ninth inning of Game 4 on a walk to Kevin Millar, a stolen base by pinch-runner Dave Roberts, and a game-tying single by Bill Mueller before David Ortiz homered against Paul Quantrill in the 12th inning. The next season Rivera was introduced to a derisive standing ovation at Fenway Park. Typically, he smiled broadly and doffed his cap to the crowd. "I can't tell you whenever I heard that damn song that it ever made you feel good," former Red Sox manager Terry Francona said. "We had some really heavyweight go-arounds with them. It's just hard not to admire guys that do it in a way that's respectful to the game. Jeter, too, obviously. It's hard when you play them because you want to beat their brains out. But that doesn't mean you don't have a ton of respect for them."

Rivera was universally respected in the Yankees' clubhouse, even attempting to counsel Alex Rodriguez through his PED suspension in 2014. "What fans will always remember about him was how unflappable he was on the mound, how stoic in victory or in those rare moments of defeat," A-Rod wrote in a piece for ESPN.com. "But the Mo I know is fully capable of bluntly chewing out somebody who needed it. Like me. In the worst of my trouble with the commissioner's office, Mariano called me all the time. He got on a plane, flew down to Miami to see me, and was very direct: 'What the hell are you doing?' He never supported the crap that I did. He is filled with conviction and was always true north. I made a lot of mistakes, and he called me out directly, looking me in the eye and chastising me. But he never did it in a way that made me feel like he looked down on me; he made me feel that it was possible that I could find my way through, if I made better choices. Mariano never turned his back on me and he gave me hope."

After A-Rod owned his mistakes, Rivera texted him: "Why weren't you doing this your whole career?"

During Rivera's entire and incomparable career, he set the saves record, went to 13 All-Star Games, won five championships, and did goodwill and charity work through his foundation, which includes the construction of a church and learning center in his adoptive hometown of New Rochelle, New York. "Mariano, there's only been one," longtime team broadcaster Suzyn Waldman said. "Mariano has done something for longer than anyone and did it the best of all time. When people are great, they change the sport. Babe Ruth changed the sport. Bobby Orr changed the sport. Bill Russell changed the sport. Mariano Rivera has changed the sport. There's one. There are people that came after that were good. But they'll never be another Ruth. And there will never be another Mariano."

8

DEREK JETER

If you had to pick just one moment as Derek Jeter's greatest with the Yankees, what would it even be? The specific components of his list are as expansive and significant—and as diverse and impressive—as anyone's in franchise history. From the flip play to his dive into the stands. From Mr. November to Mr. 3,000. From passing Lou Gehrig to passing the torch from one Yankee Stadium to the next. From his first hit in 1995 to his walk-off hit in his final Bronx at-bat. From Mariah to Minka to his marriage to Hannah. From the "Re2pect" commercial to "Dancing with George" to "Derek Jeter's Taco Hole" on *Saturday Night Live*. From owning the New York Mets and others in the World Series to owning the Miami Marlins as far away from the World Series as a team can be.

Bob Sheppard's introduction as "Numbah 2" echoed for 20 seasons in New York, but Derek Sanderson Jeter clearly was No. 1 in the hearts of an entire generation of Yankees fans while conjuring reverential images of the multiple generations of champions who preceded him.

"I was asked recently if I could trade places with one person, who would it be? There isn't a person or player I would trade places with that's playing now or ever," Jeter said when his number was retired in 2017. "You play in New York for 20 years, I learned that time flies, memories fade, but family is forever. I'll be eternally grateful to be a part of the Yankees family."

Jeter's plaque in Monument Park fittingly refers to him as "the cornerstone of five world championship teams, a leader on the field and in the clubhouse, setting an example for his teammates with his uncompromising desire for team success."

The 13-time All-Star shortstop was all of that and so much more. He was a true superstar in the mold of guarded and private predecessor Joe DiMaggio. He was a .310 lifetime batter, and his 3,465 career hits were sixth on the all-time list as of 2020. No active player is remotely close to eclipsing that total.

Jeter famously also dated a bevy of prominent singers and actresses until marrying model Hannah Davis, nearly 16 years his junior, in 2016. I was the beat writer for the *New York Daily News* during spring training 1999, when pop star Mariah Carey started showing up at games.

One night a few beat writers were eating at an Italian chain restaurant in Tampa, Florida, when the New York tabloids' newest "it" couple arrived.

This was an actual exchange overheard in the men's room: "Whoa, did you see Mariah Carey's here?"

"Yeah, who's that she's with?"

"I don't know. Some guy."

Jeter still might not have been recognizable to everyone in Tampa that early in his career, but he'd later become one of the city's foremost residents, building a splashy mansion in the Davis Island section that would come to be known by the locals as "St. Jetersburg."

He mostly kept the details of his private life out of the New York gossip pages during his career, but perhaps the only true public clash he ever had with George Steinbrenner over two decades involved The Boss' concerns about his nightlife. In December of 2002, Steinbrenner told Wayne Coffey of the *Daily News* that Jeter needed to "focus on what's important," implying that he hadn't been the previous season. He batted .297 with 18 homers, 75 RBIs, and 14 errors in 2002, and the Yankees failed to reach the World Series for the first time since 1997. "When I read in the paper that he's out until 3:00 AM in New York City going to a birthday party, I won't lie. That doesn't sit well with me," Steinbrenner said. "I want to see Jeter truly focused. He wasn't totally focused last year. He had the highest number of errors he's had in some time. He wasn't himself."

Jeter responded by telling Roger Rubin of the *Daily News* that he didn't see any reason to change anything in his game or his private life. I can tell you, though, he hardly was thrilled when the paper's back page the next day read: "PARTY ON!"

Derek Jeter celebrates his game-winning single against the Baltimore Orioles during his final home game on September 25, 2014.

Shortly thereafter, The Boss made up for the public jab by agreeing to appear in a Visa commercial with Jeter, making light of the situation. "Derek, you're our starting shortstop. How can you possibly afford to spend two nights dancing, two nights eating out, and three nights just carousing with your friends?" The Boss asked.

When Jeter smiles and flashes his Visa card, Steinbrenner simply replies, "Oh." The spot ends with the two of them dancing in a conga line at a nightclub.

By June of the 2003 season, Steinbrenner named Jeter the 11th captain in Yankees history and the first since Don Mattingly retired in 1995. "I always cherish how respectful Derek was with my father. They don't make them like that anymore," daughter Jennifer Steinbrenner told the *Daily News*' Christian Red in 2014, the year Jeter retired. "He's like family to the Yankees. You think of Lou Gehrig; Derek is an equal kind of personality. He's the modern-day pride of the Yankees."

Jeter would go on to eclipse Gehrig's longstanding team record for hits when he inside-outed a single to right against Baltimore Orioles pitcher Chris Tillman on the eighth anniversary of the September 11 attacks. That single occurred in 2009, the year he won his fifth World Series ring after a nine-year gap. He said the achievement of having the most hits in team history was something he "never imagined, never dreamt of."

The sixth overall pick in the 1992 draft out of Kalamazoo, Michigan, Jeter grew up an admirer of Dave Winfield and a fan of the Yankees from spending summers at his grandmother's house in New Jersey. The Yankees were concerned he'd choose to attend the University of Michigan rather than sign with them, but scout Dick Groch convinced the front office "the only place Derek Jeter is going is Cooperstown."

Jeter debuted with a 15-game cameo under Buck Showalter in 1995, earning his first major league hit on May 30 with a single against Seattle Mariners pitcher Tim Belcher. His career took off the following year, winning the American League Rookie of the Year during the 1996 World Series season while recording a .314 batting average, 104 runs, 10 homers, and 78 RBIs in 157 games. He playfully rubbed the heads of venerable bench coach Don Zimmer and Yogi Berra and respectfully called his first-year manager "Mr. Torre." Everyone ate it up.

"Derek Jeter is like royalty in the Berra household. Great player, great human, great teammate, great Yankee," Dale Berra said. "My dad used to kid him about his 10 World Series rings and say, 'You got a long way to go before you catch me, kid.' But he loved everything about Derek. Dad loved winners. Derek was a winner."

Jeter also homered on Opening Day in Cleveland, caught the final out of Doc Gooden's no-hitter in May, and was credited with a game-tying home run in Game 1 of the American League Championship Series against Baltimore when 12-year-old Jeffrey Maier leaned over the fence and pulled the ball into the stands. Not a bad opening act, especially considering Joe Torre, third-base coach Willie Randolph, and former general manager Gene Michael had to convince Steinbrenner the 21-year-old Jeter was ready to make the team out of spring training, following an injury to projected starter Tony Fernandez. "Derek was something, even as a 21 year old, as far as maturity. He just had this cool confidence about him," Torre said. "He was the same guy from Day One until the day he left. He definitely gave everyone their money's worth."

By the start of the 2001 season, Jeter was a perennial All-Star and MVP candidate, and the Yankees had won championships four times in his first five seasons. He was MVP of the 2000 World Series against the Mets, hitting a leadoff home run off Bobby Jones in Game 4.

He was signed to a 10-year contract extension worth $189 million in 2001. That put any potential contractual concerns off for a decade, but his next negotiation turned ugly. Agent Casey Close publicly called the Yankees' 2011 offer "insulting" to Jeter, who was told by Brian Cashman to shop it around to see if he could top it. When Jeter asked who he'd rather have as his shortstop, Cashman replied, "Do you really want to answer that?" He then named Colorado Rockies All-Star Troy Tulowitzki as one such player. The 36-year-old Jeter ended up agreeing to a three-year deal worth $51 million. "I am sentimental and I am respectful, but I get very protective of the brand," Cashman said. "Other than being called out as being insulting to our star player, I thought we should be having bouquets thrown to us by our star player because we were taking care of him in such a great way. Being put in an antagonistic role by them first, that's why I responded the way I did. It was like if you call me out, I'll come out."

A decade earlier in the 2001 American League Division Series, the Yankees dropped the first two games in the Bronx before a ridiculously heads-up play by Jeter in the seventh inning of Game 3 dramatically shifted the momentum of the series. With the Yankees leading 1–0 behind Mike Mussina and a fifth-inning homer by Jorge Posada, Terrence Long of the Oakland A's ripped an extra-base hit into the right-field corner with Jeremy Giambi on first base. Right fielder Shane Spencer overthrew the cut-off tandem of Alfonso Soriano and Tino Martinez, but Jeter sprinted to the first-base line to back up the play. He fielded the errant throw and made a backhanded flip in one motion to Posada, whose sweep tag nipped the non-sliding Giambi on the leg before his foot touched the plate. "We actually had worked on that. I still have trouble convincing people of that," Torre said with a laugh.

A's and future Yankees outfielder Johnny Damon called it: "the most heads-up play I've ever seen, probably in the history of baseball. It swung the whole series."

"I was on both sides of it, but for me, it was always the little things that Derek does," said A's first baseman Jason Giambi, Jeremy's brother, who signed with the Yankees that winter. "That's who Derek Jeter is and that's what Derek Jeter does. He saves the day."

To reach the magical 3,000-hit plateau, Jeter dramatically rocked a home run against Tampa Bay Rays pitcher David Price as part of a magical 5-for-5 day. It was such an incredible performance that the Hall of Fame asked me for my scorecard from the game. Outside of the clubhouse, Jay-Z called Jeter's feat "Incredible" and "what a storybook."

Storybook described Jeter's career right up until the end. In his final home game on September 25, 2014, he sliced a game-winning single against Baltimore's Evan Meek in the bottom of the ninth for a 6–5 Yankees victory. It was a silver-lining conclusion to one of only three seasons in his career that the Yankees did not make the playoffs.

Jeter's patented jump throw from the shortstop hole had been a logo for his Nike brand, and the company pulled out the heavy hitters for their "Re2pect" campaign as he retired. The ad featured the likes of Michael Jordan, Phil Jackson, Jay-Z, Billy Crystal, Spike Lee, former Boston pitcher Jon Lester, and even a few Red Sox fans tipping their caps to the Yankee captain.

Like Jordan, Jeter fulfilled a stated goal to transition into team ownership when he joined the investment group that purchased the Marlins in 2017. But the criticism that followed was vastly different than anything he'd faced in New York. He fired popular front-office figures and traded $325 million slugger Giancarlo Stanton to the Yankees and future MVP Christian Yelich to the Milwaukee Brewers to heavily slash payroll and start over. Jorge Posada joined him as an advisor and Mattingly, his manager, received a two-year contract extension at the end of the 2019 season. "Right after he was approved, I called Derek right away and told him I'm always available with any questions he might have any time he wants to ask," Hal Steinbrenner said. "He's got his hands full down there. But he's just gonna have to weather the storm for a few years because it's going to take at least that. He's a very intelligent guy and he'll get it done down there, just like he always has."

9

DON LARSEN'S PERFECT GAME

Don Larsen is not a member of the Baseball Hall of Fame. He never won more than 11 games in any major league season. He owns a career record below the .500 mark. The so-called imperfect man still is an unquestioned legend.

In the most prolific single-game performance in the history of baseball, considering all of the circumstances, Larsen penned the only perfect game in the history of World Series play, a span of 672 games. Larsen's gem—a 2–0 win in Game 5 of the 1956 World Series against the Brooklyn Dodgers, which was punctuated by the leap of catcher Yogi Berra into his arms—was so unexpected, so improbable based on his track record that legendary sportswriter Shirley Povich of *The Washington Post* led his column the next day by saying: "The million to one shot came in. Hell froze over." It was the *New York Daily News'* Joe Trimble, at the suggestion of Dick Young, who opened his dispatch with: "The imperfect man pitched a perfect game."

Why all the negativity surrounding Larsen? Well, following a two-year Army hitch mostly at a base in Hawaii, Larsen went 10–33 with a 4.27 ERA in his first two seasons with the St. Louis Browns and the relocated Baltimore Orioles through 1954 before he was acquired by the Yankees in a massive 17-player trade that took weeks to complete.

He arrived with a reputation of being lazy on the field and a partier off the field who often broke team-imposed curfews. Casey Stengel quickly tired of Larsen's carousing and buried him in the minors for the first half of 1955. Larsen eventually returned and finished the season with a 9–2 record and 3.06 ERA in 19 appearances—only to be drubbed for five runs in four innings in Game 5 of the 1955 World Series. The Dodgers won in seven games for Dem Bums' long-awaited first championship after losing to the Yankees five times from 1941 through 1953.

During spring training with the Yankees in 1956, Larsen also crashed his car into a light pole in the early morning hours. According to Baseball Almanac, that prompted Stengel to say, "He was either out pretty late or up pretty early." Things got late early, as Yogi would say, for the Yankees in the World Series, dropping the first two games.

The 27-year-old Larsen had rebounded with a career-best 11–5 record and 3.26 ERA over 38 games (20 starts) in 1956, eliminating the windup in his delivery in a late-season shutout of the Boston Red Sox. He had a 6–0 lead in Game 2 against Brooklyn, but he lost the plate, walking four and allowing four runs without getting out of the second inning in an eventual 13–8 loss.

After the Yankees won the next two to even the series, Stengel didn't initially announce a starter for Game 5 until that morning. Yankees coach Frank Crosetti placed a ball in Larsen's glove in his locker, indicating he'd be on the hill. Mickey Mantle homered in the fourth inning, and the Yankees added another run on Hank Bauer's single in the sixth. Larsen's control didn't betray him this time. He needed just 97 pitches to complete the perfecto. Pee Wee Reese's at-bat in the first inning represented the lone Dodgers batter to work a three-ball count.

By the latter innings, Larsen tried to engage his superstitious teammates in the dugout, but Mantle and the others typically avoided him. "I had no tension on the mound," Larsen told the *New York Daily News*, "But the dugout was a morgue. No one would talk to me. I was more comfortable on the mound than there."

Stengel had Whitey Ford warming in the eighth and ninth innings, but Larsen was one out away when .311 career hitter Dale Mitchell was sent to pinch hit for pitcher Sal Maglie.

On a 1–2 count, a borderline fastball caught Mitchell looking for the 27th out, prompting Berra to leap into Larsen's arms in a picture for the ages and this call from Hall of Fame broadcaster Bob Wolff: "Mitchell waiting, stands deep, feet close together. Larsen is ready, gets the sign. Two strikes, ball one. Here comes the pitch. Strike three! A no-hitter! A perfect game for Don Larsen!"

Dale Berra was born December 13, 1956, meaning his mother, Carmen, was seven months pregnant during the World Series. How's this for an origin story? "You know why I'm named Dale, right?" Yogi's son said. "This is what my mom always told me: she was sitting next to Joan Ford during Game 5 and she had told Whitey's wife before Mitchell came up that she really liked the name Dale because in those days you didn't know if you were having a boy or a girl, and it could be used for either sex. As the story goes, before the last out, my mom told Joan Ford, 'If Larsen gets Dale Mitchell out to finish the perfect game, I'm going to name the baby Dale.'"

Also in the announced crowd of 64,519 was a 16-year-old catcher and Giants fan from Brooklyn who had scored a couple of tickets from his older brother, Frank, a rookie first baseman for the Milwaukee Braves. "I was going to St. Francis Prep and I had to go to the principal's office to show them I had tickets, and they let me out of school because the World Series was still all day games back then," Joe Torre recalled. "I sat in the third deck halfway between the left-field foul line and third base. Just to be there was incredible. If you grew up a Giants fan, you hated both the Yankees and the Dodgers. I guess somewhere around the seventh inning or so, you wanted to see it happen."

Torre, Don Zimmer (a member of that Dodgers team), public-address announcer Bob Sheppard, and longtime *Daily News* baseball columnist Bill Madden, who was at Larsen's gem as an 11-year-old with his father, are the four people I know of who attended all three perfect games in Yankees history. "As far as I know, we're it," Madden said. "I wrote that twice in the paper, and no one ever checked in to say they were at all three, too."

Mantle ran down a Gil Hodges drive in left-center in the fifth inning, the hardest hit ball against Larsen all day. Jackie Robinson also nearly managed a hit in the second, when his smash bounded off third baseman Andy Carey to shortstop Gil McDougald, who barely threw him out.

Clem Labine blanked the Yankees in Game 6 before they pounded Don Newcombe, including two homers by Berra and a grand slam by Moose Skowron to avenge their World Series loss the previous year.

Nicknamed Gooney Bird by his teammates, Larsen was tabbed as MVP and received a Corvette. His license plate read "NY000" to depict the line score. "Before yesterday, no one knew I was alive," Larsen said one day after his Game 5 masterpiece, according to his autobiography,

The Perfect Yankee: The Incredible Story of the Greatest Miracle in Baseball History. "Today, everyone is telling me they went to school with me."

Larsen's family had moved from Michigan to San Diego when he was 15, and he starred in baseball and basketball at Point Loma High School. One of his classmates was Marion Ross, who went on to play Marion "Mrs. C" Cunningham opposite Ron Howard's Richie and Henry Winkler's "The Fonz" in the popular '70s sitcom *Happy Days*.

The other famous Point Loma alum is David Wells, who became one of two Yankees pitchers to also hurl perfect games in the late 1990s. Also known as a partier, Wells tossed his perfecto against the Minnesota Twins in May 1998, and David Cone followed with one against the Montreal Expos the following July. Larsen and Berra incredibly were in attendance at the latter. "It really has become a special bond. Boomer and I really feel a kinship with Don," Cone said. "Of course, Don and Boomer already had that connection because they went to the same high school. Some people have asked if I went there, too, because we're so closely connected. It's something that we'll always have because those games all happened at the old stadium. They're etched in stone, etched in time. And there's a lot of similarities with us. We like to have fun. We like to go out and have a drink together. We're all a little off-kilter, definitely fun lovers. I think we all can relate in that way."

Larsen would win two more World Series games for the Yankees, one each against the Milwaukee Braves in 1957 and 1958. The next year he and Hank Bauer were included in the trade with Kansas City that imported Roger Maris.

But Larsen's name always will be synonymous with perfection. "I think about it every day," Larsen, who passed away in 2020 at age 90, said after Cone's perfect game. "Sometimes it's hard to believe it happened. But I'm glad it did because everybody thinks about that and forgets all of the mistakes I made in my life."

10

61*

"**T**wo balls, no strikes on Roger Maris. Here's the windup... Fastball, hit deep to right! This could be it! Way back there! Holy cow, he did it! Sixty-one for Maris! Look at 'em fight for that ball out there! Holy cow, what a shot! Another standing ovation for Roger Maris! Sixty-one home runs, and they're still fighting for that ball out there!" Those were Phil Rizzuto's words in the Yankees' radio booth as he detailed the culmination of perhaps the single most fascinating summer in baseball history.

Two pinstriped teammates, Roger Maris and Mickey Mantle, dueled for months to see which one would catch and surpass Yankees legend Babe Ruth's exalted home run record. The underdog Maris emerged on the final day of the regular season with No. 61 (no asterisk!) against Boston Red Sox pitcher Tracy Stallard and hit one into the right-field stands at the Stadium on October 1, 1961. "Whether I beat Ruth's record or not is for others to say," Maris said that day, referring to the dispute over validating records accomplished in the longer 162-game schedule. "But it gives me a wonderful feeling to know that I'm the only man in history to hit 61 home runs. Nobody can that away from me."

That didn't stop folks from trying. The controversy began with a midsummer edict from commissioner Ford Frick—Ruth's former ghostwriter—that anyone who hoped to eclipse The Babe's record had to do so before his team's 155th game since the old mark had been set when a season lasted 154 games. No asterisk ever was actually used in an official capacity, but until 1991—six years after Maris' death—he and Ruth were acknowledged in the record books separately. Many in the public in 1961 apparently agreed with Frick, as only 23,154 fans attended Game No. 162 at Yankee Stadium.

Thirty-seven years later, sluggers Mark McGwire of the St. Louis Cardinals and Sammy Sosa of the Chicago Cubs similarly staged an assault on Maris' mark. Both surpassed him. McGwire did so first on September 8, 1998 and finished with 70. Sosa also beat Maris' record, totaling 66. Both of them were eclipsed in 2001 by San Francisco Giants outfielder Barry Bonds, who hit 73.

All three of those players later were alleged to have used performance-enhancing drugs, though only McGwire publicly admitted his steroids usage. He even phoned Maris' wife, Pat, to apologize in 2010. The Maris family had embraced McGwire's run in '98, appearing at his record-setting game against Sosa's Cubs. Afterward, a tearful McGwire said he touched the bat Maris had used against Stallard, which was on loan from the Hall of Fame, for luck. "The family feels that it's his record," Roger Maris Jr. said of his father at Yankee Stadium in 2011 on the 50th anniversary of No. 61. "I know that's arguable with a lot of people, but that's just how we feel."

Added brother Randy Maris: "I think there needs to be a distinction. Obviously, unfortunately I think Major League Baseball turned an eye to that era. We appreciate everything Mark did with respecting my dad and stuff like that, but it's got to be noted. If you look at since they started drug testing, where are the numbers now? It just hasn't been there. So definitely there's got to be some kind of distinction."

Mantle ended up belting 54 homers before missing several games down the stretch—and appearing in only two games in the World Series—due to an abscess in his hip. Ralph Houk replaced Casey Stengel as manager in 1961 and flipped the lineup to have Maris batting third—one spot ahead of Mantle, a reversal from the previous season. "I was nine years old and I still can remember it very clearly. It's probably the first season that I truly remember—if not every game then the way most of the season played out," said Hall of Fame broadcaster Bob Costas. "I liked Roger Maris, my friends liked Roger Maris, but Roger Maris wasn't a lifetime Yankee. Absolutely nothing against him, he was an admirable man and player. I think almost all of us were rooting for Mantle."

Maris had been acquired from the Kansas City Athletics before the 1960 season for a package featuring Hank Bauer and perfect-game author Don Larsen. The reserved Fargo, North Dakota, product won the American League MVP award in his first year with the Yankees with 39 home runs and a league-best 112 RBIs in the final season of the 154-game slate.

Mantle and Maris shared an apartment together in 1961 in Queens with fellow outfielder Bob Cerv, but Mantle emerged as the clear-cut choice among the fans and much of the media to break Ruth's mark of 60 in 1927. "This story that's taken hold after the fact that everyone was antagonistic toward Maris. I don't think that was true at all," Costas argued. "We just hoped Mickey hit 61 and Roger hit 59. We liked them both, but Mantle had our affections before Maris arrived."

Another lifelong Yankees fan, actor Billy Crystal, produced and directed the movie *61** in 2001 for HBO, which detailed that season. Crystal said while promoting the film that he noticed actor Barry Pepper in Steven Spielberg's *Saving Private Ryan* and thought Pepper was a dead ringer for Maris. Thomas Jane portrayed Mantle but had to learn how to swing from both sides of the plate. Famous for such John Hughes 1980s teen classics as *Sixteen Candles* and *The Breakfast Club*, Anthony Michael Hall was terrific as ace Whitey Ford. Crystal's daughter, Jennifer Crystal Foley, played Maris' wife, Pat. "I liked it very much. I think Billy knew the story and I think it was authentic for the most part," Costas said. "There's always going to be some license taken. But Barry Pepper looked remarkably like Roger Maris. Thomas Jane had the attitude of Mickey exactly right. He wasn't as convincing a ballplayer as Barry Pepper was, but as Billy said, 'All I need; give me two or three times where you make decent contact from either side, and I'll use those shots over and over.' But I thought Jane had the body language and mannerisms and the ballplayer's attitude down pretty good."

The chase by the M & M boys overshadowed some wonderful performances elsewhere on the 109-win club, which ended in a five-game defeat of the Cincinnati Reds in the World Series. Elston Howard hit .348, backup catcher Johnny Blanchard ripped 21 homers in only 243 at-bats, and Yogi Berra and Moose Skowron combined for 50 more. Ford won a career high 25 games and earned the lone Cy Young Award of his career. Luis Arroyo won 15 more with a 2.19 ERA out of the bullpen. Ralph Terry, who'd surrendered the World Series-losing home run in Game 7 to Bill Mazeroski of the Pittsburgh Pirates the previous

Roger Maris (left) and Mickey Mantle (right) pose during their epic home run chase in 1961.

October, finished 16–3. (Terry also was named the 1962 World Series MVP in a seven-game defeat of the San Francisco Giants.)

But Maris' blast remained the enduring highlight of that year. He fittingly hit 61 in '61.

The homer was caught by Brooklyn teenager Sal Durante; Maris told him in the clubhouse afterward to collect whatever cash he could get for the historic ball.

Maris edged Mantle for a second straight MVP award, but he'd never duplicate that success. The seven-time All-Star was traded in 1967 and played his final two seasons with the St. Louis Cardinals. Maris' No. 9 was retired by the Yankees in 1984, one year before he died.

His plaque in Monument Park is subtitled "Against All Odds." It reads: "In belated recognition of one of baseball's greatest achievements ever, his 61 in '61. The Yankees salute him as a great player and as author of one of the most remarkable chapters in the history of Major League Baseball."

MR. OCTOBER

After Broadway Joe and Willis Reed—but before Captain Messier—there was bold and brash newcomer Reggie Jackson, who provided the greatest clutch performance in a New York sports generation. So much so that no fan of the Yankees can even utter the name of one particular month without conjuring Jackson's well-deserved nickname. Jackson emerged from the depths of a tumultuous first season after clashing with his manager, Billy Martin, and his teammates in New York to hammer four home runs on four consecutive swings of the bat over two games in the 1977 World Series, including three in the Game 6 clincher against the Los Angeles Dodgers.

Welcome to the Bronx, Reggie, you are forever dubbed Mr. October. "Somebody asked me if I was afraid my star would get lost somewhere else, and I told him, 'I didn't come to New York to become a star. I brought my star with me,'" Reggie wrote in his autobiography, *Becoming Mr. October.* "Somebody asked me then, 'But wouldn't your star have got lost if you'd gone to Kansas City or Montreal?' I told him, 'Fort Knox is in Kentucky. But Fort Knox isn't lost. Everybody knows where Fort Knox is.'"

Following a four-game sweep by Cincinnati's Big Red Machine in the 1976 World Series, the Yankees first opened the vaults to ink Cincinnati Reds ace Don Gullett, who had throttled them in Game 1. The lefty went 14–4 in his first season of a six-year deal, but Gullett suffered a career-ending shoulder injury the following year.

Jackson, the 1973 American League MVP and a three-time World Series champion with the Oakland A's, landed his riches with the Yankees after spending one season with the Baltimore Orioles, following a fire-sale trade from the cash-strapped A's. However, the free-agent deal he struck with George Steinbrenner—a five-year deal worth $2.96 million, plus a Rolls-Royce—actually was worth less than the Montreal Expos' offer.

In 2019 the beloved Jackson accompanied the Yankees on their trip to London for a landmark game against the Boston Red Sox. Of course, a robotic Jackson had been part of the classic baseball scene in the 1988 comedy *The Naked Gun*, in which he infamously held a gun and declared, "I. Must kill. The Queen" of England, who was in attendance at the fictitious game. Asked by WFAN's Sweeny Murti if he had any difficulty getting through customs and into Great Britain over his cinematic threat, Jackson said, "No, I'm not a wanted man. I am welcome here."

More than four decades earlier, not everyone with the Yankees had welcomed Jackson with open arms. All-Star catcher Thurman Munson actually endorsed the signing initially to Steinbrenner, who in turn promised his captain he'd always be the highest-paid player on the team—other than ace Catfish Hunter.

In his first spring training with the Yankees, however, Jackson referred to himself as "the straw that stirs the drink" in an interview with *SPORT* magazine, adding that Munson "only can stir it bad." When backup catcher Fran Healy tried to tell the furious Munson that Jackson claimed he'd been misquoted, which he has insisted publicly for years, Thurman shot back, "For six fucking pages?"

It actually was Munson's acerbic sarcasm that supplied the moniker that Jackson would answer to for the remainder of his life. Following Game 2 of the 1977 World Series, Jackson was sporting an anemic .100 batting average in his first postseason as a Yankees hitter. He'd even been benched by Martin in Game 5 of the American League Championship Series against the Kansas City Royals before delivering a key pinch-hit single late in a 5–3 comeback win. Jackson publicly criticized Martin for his use of the sore-shouldered Hunter, his former Oakland teammate who'd pitched poorly in Game 2 against the Dodgers. Munson then remarked to a reporter that Martin "probably just doesn't realize that Jackson is Mr. October."

Munson and Jackson became friendlier in the ensuing years; Reggie even previously flew with Munson in his private plane before the Yankees captain died tragically while flying in 1979.

"It hit me hard. I don't know if we ever hated each other," Jackson told *Newsday* years later. "I think that's too strong a word. I never hated Thurman. I don't even know if I disliked him. I don't know that Thurman Munson hated Reggie Jackson. Thurman Munson didn't hate anybody."

If only the New York Mets hadn't botched the 1966 draft, Reginald Martinez Jackson would have arrived in New York about a decade sooner. The Pennsylvania native attended Arizona State on a football scholarship but switched to the baseball team after his freshman year.

The Mets bypassed Jackson with the first overall pick for high school catcher Steve Chilcott, who never played a game for them due to various injuries. Chilcott later signed with the Yankees in 1972, but he was released after only 24 minor league games.

Jackson was selected next by the Kansas City A's, who moved to Oakland in 1968. One year later Jackson emerged as a superstar on the national stage with 47 home runs, 118 RBIs, and a career-best 1.018 OPS (on-base percentage plus slugging percentage). He also clubbed a mammoth home run in the 1971 All-Star Game off Dock Ellis onto the roof at Tiger Stadium in Detroit.

Even then, Jackson saved his biggest performances for October for an A's team that won five American League pennants in a row, including three consecutive titles from 1972 to 1974. Jackson was injured during Oakland's first championship run before ripping three homers and driving in nine while capturing his first of two World Series MVP trophies in 1973.

His second would come four years later but not before a trying first season in the Bronx. His brash, showy personality endeared him to Steinbrenner, but it rubbed more than just Munson the wrong way. Jackson nearly came to blows with Martin after being pulled from a nationally televised game in Boston in June. The fiery manager sent Paul Blair out to right field in the middle of an inning to replace Jackson for what he felt was loafing after a ball hit by Jim Rice.

They had to be separated in the dugout by coaches Yogi Berra and Elston Howard. Jackson called Martin an "old man" and barked "You never wanted me on this team."

All of that was forgotten—or at least better tolerated—when Jackson carried the Yankees to their first World Series title since 1962. Beginning with Game 3, Jackson batted .571 over the final four games and crushed five home runs, a World Series record. Three of those highlighted a staggering Game 6 performance, and four came on as many swings over the final two games. (Jackson had walked on four pitches in his first at-bat that night.) "That performance took away everything that was said and done," pitcher Mike Torrez said after winning twice in the series, including a complete game in the clincher.

"I only hit one World Series home run in my career. And it was in the second inning that night, so no one remembers it," Chris Chambliss joked.

With L.A. leading 3–2 in the fourth inning, Munson was on first base when Jackson ripped a laser off Dodgers starter Burt Hooton that just barely made the right-field seats to put the Yankees ahead. He also went deep on the first pitches he saw from Elias Sosa in the fifth inning and knuckleballer Charlie Hough in the eighth, driving in five runs in an 8–4 victory. The chants of "Reg-gie, Reg-gie, Reg-gie" were deafening. "That was Reggie stepping up to the plate on the biggest stage in baseball," Willie Randolph said. "By the third one, are you kidding me? But I really just remember not even being that surprised that he did it. He put us all on his back. The Billy stuff, all the stuff that went on early on with Reggie and Thurman, we always dealt with that stuff well. It was the Bronx Zoo, man. But we let it all roll off our back when we got on the field. We were like a family, maybe a little dysfunctional sometimes, had our share of fights, our issues, but like a typical family, we always stuck together. We were a team that always fought with each other, but also fought for each other. It was a pretty sweet night."

Earlier in his career with Oakland, Jackson once had proclaimed if he ever played in New York, "they would name a candy bar after me." Following Jackson's 1977 performance, Standard Brands' Curtiss Candy produced the "Reggie!" bar, a round mixture of milk chocolate, caramel, and peanuts. Thousands were distributed to fans at the home opener in 1978, and when Jackson belted a homer in the first inning, many in the crowd hurled them onto the field. "When you unwrap a Reggie! bar," Hunter quipped, "it tells you how good it is."

Reggie was pretty damn good. Just ask him.

In five World Series appearances, Mr. October belted 10 home runs with 24 RBIs while batting .357, almost 100 points better than his career mark. The 14-time All-Star totaled 563 home runs, 2,548 hits, and 1,702 RBIs in 21 seasons. He was a first-ballot Hall of Famer in 1993.

Mr. October only played for the Yankees for five seasons, appearing in three World Series, including back-to-back titles his first two years, before signing with the California Angels in 1983. But he made enough of an impact in that short time to have his No. 44 retired to Monument Park and to remain a front-office advisor well into his retirement.

12

THE 1996 YANKEES

The Yankees never have had a longer World Series drought. Theirs did not rival the decades-long stretches of futility endured by the Boston Red Sox, the Chicago Cubs, or the Chicago White Sox, but by the Yankees' lofty standard, 18 years without a championship was long enough. The storybook 1996 season marked the first year after immensely popular captain Don Mattingly had retired and the final season of four decades with Phil Rizzuto in the broadcast booth.

The emotional first year of Joe Torre's successful tenure in the manager's seat and the first full year of Derek Jeter's illustrious career was punctuated by the team's first parade down the Canyon of Heroes since 1978. "It was kind of the perfect storm, that first title," Paul O'Neill said. "You had seen the tide turning the previous couple of years, but Joe turned out to be the perfect fit, and with the Core Four showing up and making an impact, and having been there for a few years before, it was incredible and a blast to be a part of that season."

Under a newly instituted wild-card format, the Yankees finally returned to the playoffs in 1995 for the first time since a 1981 World Series loss to the Los Angeles Dodgers. Mattingly homered to thunderous applause at Yankees Stadium and batted .417 in his long-awaited first postseason appearance. Backup catcher Jim Leyritz won Game 2 with a 15th-inning blast, but the Yankees flushed a 2–0 lead in the best-of-five division series, dropping a heartbreaking Game 5 in Seattle.

Manager Buck Showalter abruptly was dumped, and after George Steinbrenner reconsidered but failed to convince him to return, Torre was brought in for the fourth managerial job of his career. New general manager Bob Watson swung a key trade with the Seattle Mariners in December, bringing in Tino Martinez to replace Mattingly at first base, along with valuable reliever Jeff Nelson, for infield prospect Russ Davis and pitcher Sterling Hitchcock.

Martinez was booed early in the season before registering a team-best 117 RBIs. New catcher Joe Girardi also heard it from the fans while struggling to replace another popular player, Mike Stanley, but he also reversed that reaction by season's end.

The Yankees had resisted the Mariners' wishes of subbing out Hitchcock with another homegrown lefty, Andy Pettitte, who had won 12 games as a rookie in 1995. Pettitte wound up fronting Torre's initial pinstriped pitching staff, winning 21 games in 1996. Cone, a former 20-game winner with the New York Mets and a World Series winner with the Toronto Blue Jays, was projected to be the ace of the staff, but he suffered an aneurysm in his right shoulder in May that sidelined him for three months.

Another former Mets pitcher, star-crossed former All-Star Dwight Gooden, was given a fresh start by George Steinbrenner after years of substance abuse issues, and he replaced Cone in the rotation. With his father awaiting heart surgery the following morning, Gooden threw a no-hitter against the Mariners on May 14, outdueling Hitchcock in a 2–0 win. "Doc's no-hitter was the first indication to me that '96 was starting to have some magic to it," Wade Boggs said.

Cone didn't return to the rotation until September 2 and he nearly threw his own no-hitter in his first start off the disabled list. He stifled the Oakland A's over seven innings before Torre lifted him over pitch-count concerns a few months after surgery. "It was incredible," Torre said. "But Coney understood there was no shot we were leaving him in."

The Yankees had resided in first place since April 28, adopting the "We play today, we win today, that's it," mantra of second baseman Mariano Duncan, who led the team with a .340 batting average.

The other Mariano to emerge that season, of course, was Rivera. The Panama native developed into an absolute weapon for Torre in the latter innings as a multiple-inning set-up man for closer and eventual World Series MVP John Wetteland. Rivera posted a 2.09 ERA and struck out 130 in 107⅔ innings over 61 relief appearances. "We didn't really know what we had in Mariano until he started pitching the seventh and the eighth inning all the time," Torre said. "That to me was the key to the whole season for us. I only had to manage six innings, and it was over."

The other impactful homegrown star that year was Jeter. He homered on Opening Day and never looked back on his own Hall of Fame track. "Jete never seemed like a rookie that whole year," O'Neill said. "You could see his leadership abilities right away."

The Yanks finished 92–70—four games ahead of the Baltimore Orioles in the American League East—before defeating the Texas Rangers in four games in the American League Division Series, where Bernie Williams belted two homers in the clincher. Williams also went deep in the 11th inning to win Game 1 of the American League Championship Series against the Orioles, following a bizarrely fortuitous call on a home-run call three innings earlier.

Years before video replay review was instituted by Major League Baseball, a 12-year-old fan from New Jersey named Jeffrey Maier reached over the outfield fence and pulled a fly ball by Jeter into the seats. As Orioles right fielder Tony Tarasco vehemently argued, umpire Richie Garcia ruled the play a game-tying home run, setting up Williams' subsequent heroics. The front page of the *New York Post* dubbed Maier the Yankees' "ANGEL IN THE OUTFIELD."

When the Yankees faced Baltimore in the playoffs again in 2012, I tracked down the 28-year-old Maier for a *New York Daily News* column. "I always chuckle whenever I see it," Maier said of the replays of his contribution to Yankees history. "It's never going away, so when it comes up, you might as well enjoy it. It's a play that—whether or not it matters to me anymore—it's a play that's important to the Yankees and it has a place in the history of the game. I've embraced that."

Torre, who started the year dubbed "Clueless Joe" on the back page of the *Daily News*, finally made it to the Fall Classic for the first time in a career that began in 1960 with the Milwaukee Braves. The Atlanta Braves had won the championship against the Cleveland Indians the previous season, but 1995 turned out to be the lone title for a loaded team with three future Hall of Fame starting pitchers— Greg Maddux, Tom Glavine, and John Smoltz—over an unprecedented 14-year stretch of consecutive playoff appearances (one more than the Yankees would manage from 1995 to 2007).

The Yankees were hammered in the first two games at Yankee Stadium by a 16–1 aggregate, as 19-year-old rookie Andruw Jones blasted homers in his first two World Series at-bats in a 12–1 shelling of Pettitte in the opener. Torre has often retold the story of Steinbrenner barreling into his office between the first two games before assuring The Boss that even if they also dropped Game 2, they'd win the series at home in Game 6 or 7. "Down 2–0, I stood up in the back of the plane and said to the guys, 'Hey, I've been in this position that Atlanta is in, going back to Boston after leaving New York up 2–0," Boggs said of the Boston Red Sox's loss in the 1986 World Series against the Mets. "These guys did not want to come back to New York. I knew what they were thinking. No one knew we'd go in there and take the next three, that was something else. But the information I was throwing out there was we just needed to get the series back to New York, and it's over. You could tell when we got back from Atlanta they knew they let something get away."

With Torre benching O'Neill, Martinez, and Boggs for former Mets slugger Darryl Strawberry and in-season additions Cecil Fielder and Charlie Hayes, respectively, Cone outpitched Glavine to win Game 3.

But lefty starter Kenny Rogers (no relation to the country singer of the same name) put the Yankees in a six-run hole the next night. They halved that deficit with a three-spot in the sixth inning before Leyritz— nicknamed "The King" earlier in his career by Mattingly—did his part to help the Yankees regain the crown while facing fireballing Mark Wohlers. "When we were down 6–0, I remember saying to Mariano Duncan and Pat Kelly, 'Well, at least we didn't get swept,'" said Leyritz, who entered the game after O'Neill batted for Girardi in the sixth. "Sure enough, we put three runs on the board in the sixth, and then in the eighth, I remember standing in the dugout. I only had two bats left because I had broken two bats in batting practice. So I asked Straw if I could use one of his bats. I put some pine tar on it, got it ready. And I remember walking up the steps and saying to Zim, 'So, what's this guy got?' He goes, 'He throws 100 miles an hour, get it ready.'"

Despite the reliever's triple-digit heat, Tim McCarver on the FOX broadcast was incredulous that Wohlers had been throwing so many sliders in that inning. With two runners aboard, the righty reliever threw a couple of breaking pitches early in the ensuing at-bat to Leyritz until the count was even at 2–2. "Sure enough, here comes another slider, and I got just enough of it to hit it out," Leyritz said. "I thought for sure it'd be a fastball. But he hung it just enough. Everybody always asks me what I was thinking going around the bases, and I remember thinking, *If we don't win this game now, it'll be like my '95 home run.* It's a great moment but not impactful enough."

This one maintained its impact, as Boggs drew a bases-loaded walk against Steve Avery in a two-run 10th inning to even the series. "Walking into that clubhouse, to a man, we knew we had just changed the momentum," Leyritz said. "And I think that really gave Andy that little extra for Game 5."

Leyrtiz was Pettitte's personal catcher that season, and the second-year lefty indeed rebounded from his Game 1 shellacking to pen a 1–0 win against Smoltz, one of the most important performances of that run of four Yankee championships in five years. The only run Smoltz allowed was unearned due to an error by Braves centerfielder Marquis Grissom. "Andy got his ass kicked in Game 1, and I called him into my office and asked what the hell that was all about," Torre said. "Andy to this day is such an honest individual, and said, 'Skip, I just felt for the World Series I had to crank it up and be something more than I was.' I said, 'You won 21 games, you're good enough.'"

Pettitte pitched into the ninth inning before giving way to Wetteland for the final two outs. Despite nursing a hamstring injury, O'Neill had been reinserted into the starting lineup for Game 5, while Martinez and Boggs sat for a second straight game. He saved the game with a running catch of Luis Polonia's liner to deep right-center for the final out. "O'Neill almost didn't play that game either," Torre said. "I had called O'Neill, Boggs, and Tino in separately, even though we were facing Smoltz, the righty. Paulie was hurting, and at first I told them none of them were going to play. When they left, Zim was in my office, and he said, 'You know what, O'Neill's been playing on one leg all year. Don't you think we owe it to him?' We called Paul back in, and I told him 'executive privilege.' I have the right to change my mind."

Said O'Neill: "It was one of—if not the best—pitched games I ever was a part of, especially in a game of that importance. I remember getting on the plane that night, just being thankful to be a part of that game. You felt like the tide had turned, and out of all the big games we played over the years, that might have been the most intense and exciting one I ever played in."

The next one was pretty exciting, too. A tense Yankee Stadium erupted and rarely was louder than the third inning of Game 6, when Girardi ripped a triple over Grissom's head against Maddux to drive in O'Neill for a 1–0 lead. Williams added an RBI single, and the Yankees carried a 3–2 lead into the ninth. "My goodness, after Joe hits the triple, it felt like the stadium almost collapsed because people, who were waiting all those years—for that franchise anyway— were screaming and carrying on so loud," Boggs said. "We knew we had it."

Wetteland recorded the final out: a Mark Lemke pop-up to Hayes in foul territory. With tears in his eyes, Torre hugged Zimmer and the rest of the coaches in the dugout, as the dogpile ensued on the mound. "It was such an emotional year. I still have to pinch myself," Torre said. "Those images will stick with me forever."

Among the lasting images was Boggs—who was deathly afraid of horses, having been bitten by one on a farm when he was five years old—climbing atop an NYPD horse and riding around the warning track during the jubilant celebration. "I still can't believe I did that," Boggs said. "We took off down the left-field line, and the next thing I know I'm on the back of a police horse. It was one of those iconic moments that I'm glad always reminds people of '96. That was such a special year and amazing to be a part of."

13

MURDERERS' ROW

Having covered the 1998 Yankees in my first full season as a baseball beat writer, the biggest challenge just about every day was coming up with a creative way to explain how Joe Torre's juggernaut had won yet another game. These were first-world problems, for sure, but it was hard to imagine a team performing better than that one had on a daily basis.

The 1927 Yankees are the one example throughout franchise history—and in baseball history—that probably can top the 1998 version as the best ever. Boasting an intimidating lineup known as Murderers' Row, this pinstriped edition certainly is the most fabled and the most deeply entrenched in folklore, especially with Babe Ruth becoming the first player to reach 60 home runs after pulling away from teammate Lou Gehrig by crushing 17 in September.

At 110–44 in the regular season under manager Miller Huggins, the '27 squad slugged its way to a franchise-record winning percentage (.714), a smidge higher than even the 114-win club registered (.704) over a 162-game slate 71 years later. Second baseman and No. 2 hitter Mark Koenig batted .500 (9-for-18) in a four-game World Series sweep of the Pittsburgh Pirates in 1927. "I don't think it entered any of our minds that we were the best," Koenig said in *Pinstripe Empire: The New York Yankees From Before the Babe to After the Boss*. "We just went on winning."

And winning. And winning.

The legendary everyday lineup featured four future Hall of Famers—Ruth, Gehrig, Tony Lazzeri, and leadoff man Earle Combs—plus sweet-swinging outfielder Bob Meusel. The Yankees dominated the American League in all facets, leading the junior circuit with a .307 team batting average and a 3.20 team ERA, outscoring opponents by 376 runs. The Yankees also established a then-record 158 home runs that season with 107 of them by two players, even though no other team in in the American League finished within 100. The second-place

Philadelphia A's totaled just 56. By contrast, the 2019 Bombers clubbed a team-mark 306 home runs, albeit one behind the Minnesota Twins that season.

The 1927 pitching staff was anchored by Cooperstown-bound starters Herb Pennock and Waite Hoyt and had an out-of-nowhere performance come from 30-year-old rookie Wilcy Moore, who won 19 games and led the American League in ERA (2.28) despite making just 12 starts among 50 appearances.

Huggins' runaway train cruised to a 19-game outdistancing of the A's, shifting the September focus squarely to Ruth's run at the record 59 homers he'd blasted in 1921. Like Mickey Mantle and Roger Maris in '61, Ruth and Gehrig could not have been more different in personality. But the Yankees' No. 3 and No. 4 hitters—hence their eventual uniform numbers first worn in 1929—were neck and neck in home runs for the first five months of the season.

"They didn't get along. Lou thought Ruth was a big mouth, and Ruth thought Gehrig was cheap. They were both right," Lazzeri joked in the book, *Gehrig and the Babe: The Friendship and the Feud*.

After a three-homer game by Gehrig at Fenway Park on June 29, both players had 24. Three days later, it was 26–26. Ahead of a doubleheader in Boston on September 6, it was 44–44. Gehrig actually went up by one in the opener at Fenway Park, but Ruth drew even later in the same game. One inning later Ruth made it 46–45. He clubbed another in the nightcap for a 47–45 lead. Newspapers referred to it as the "Great American Home Run Derby."

Gehrig, however, had pushed Ruth as far as he could. The Iron Horse only went deep twice more over the final three weeks, finishing with a career-best 47 home runs, along with a team-leading 175 RBIs. Ruth still needed 13 in the final 22 games. The Babe's sudden binge continued until he entered the final series of the season against Washington three away with three games to play to reach 60.

No. 58 came in the first inning of the series opener against Washington Senators starter Hod Lisenbee. Later in the game, Ruth represented the first batter faced in the career for rookie reliever Paul Hopkins and rocked a grand slam to match his previous mark. How's that for a future story to tell the grandkids about your big league debut?

Amazingly, one at-bat earlier, Ruth also had tripled off the wall. And in his final trip, his long drive was caught at the wall. Can you imagine if he'd broken the record with a four-homer game? (Of his vast

From left to right, Tony Lazzeri, Babe Ruth, and Lou Gehrig are three of the four Hall of Famers who formed one of the best lineups in baseball history for the 1927 Yankees.

accomplishments, Ruth never managed that feat. Gehrig actually was the only Yankees player to do it—and did so in 1932.)

The record-breaker came the next day against Washington's Tom Zachary, who would join the Yankees the following season. In the eighth inning of a September 30 game with the score tied at 2–2, Ruth hit a fastball into the right-field seats. "Sixty! Let's see some son of a bitch try to top that one!" Ruth shouted after the game, according to *Big Bam: The Life and Times of Babe Ruth*.

Ruth's record would stand for 34 years (no asterisk). He went hitless on the final day of the regular season, but The Babe cracked the lone home run in the ensuing World Series sweep of the Pirates.

Perhaps the most astonishing stat about the 1927 Yanks was that they played the entire year with just 25 men. There were no disabled list replacements, in-season trades, constant shuttling of relievers from the minor leagues, or roster expansion in September. Talk about a different era. And a special team.

Combs, a .325 lifetime hitter and speedy centerfielder voted into the Hall of Fame by the Veterans' Committee in 1970, batted .356 with 231 hits and 137 runs scored atop the lineup. Lazzeri, who wasn't enshrined until 1991, contributed 18 homers and 102 RBIs. Meusel hit .337 and knocked in 103 despite just eight home runs. But the starting rotation of Hoyt, George Pipgras, Pennock, and Moore led the way in October. Pennock carried a perfect game into the eighth inning of Game 3 until Pie Traynor singled with the lefty five outs away from becoming Don Larsen before Don Larsen.

Koenig's .500 average also atoned for the costly error he'd committed in Game 7 the previous year in a World Series loss to the St. Louis Cardinals. "We had them beat before we even started," Koenig said of the Pirates on the 60-year anniversary in 1987. "We beat them when they were sitting in the stands during batting practice, watching Ruth and Gehrig hit balls over the fence. It scared the hell out of them."

The Murderers' Row could be quite menacing. In the book *Pinstripe Empire: The New York Yankees From Before the Babe to After the Boss*, author Marty Appel—a longtime former team employee—wrote that the term originally was coined by a newspaper he did not identify as a way to describe the pre-Ruth Yankees lineup of 1918, referring to Frank

Gilhooley, Roger Peckinpaugh, Home Run Baker, Del Pratt, Wally Pipp, and Ping Bodie.

Much like the 1999 Yankees, the 1928 team also had to live up to the daunting record-setting accomplishments of its predecessors. Huggins used only three pitchers in avenging a 1926 World Series loss to St. Louis with a second straight World Series sweep while outscoring the Cardinals 27–10. "[Gehrig] amassed a .545 batting average, a figure that would usually lead all batters. Uh-uh...Babe Ruth intruded again, hitting an incredible .625," Shirley Povich wrote in *The Washington Post*.

The consecutive sweeps began a string of 12 straight wins in the Fall Classic. Four teams in history won more regular-season games than the '27 team, but only the '98 Yankees won the World Series. The 1906 Chicago Cubs (116), the 1954 Cleveland Indians (111), and the 2001 Mariners (116) all lost in the postseason.

14

THE 1998 YANKEES

Three games into his new job, Brian Cashman was ordered home. It seems silly now to think the 1998 season began for the Yankees with three straight losses and four in the first five games of a season-opening swing out west that unmistakably pushed George Steinbrenner into panic mode 3,000 miles away. Starting his first year as Bob Watson's replacement as the team's general manager, the 30-year-old Cashman was pulled off the trip after two losses in Anaheim and another in Oakland, and The Boss irrationally considered putting former GM Gene "Stick" Michael back in charge.

Forget the Bronx Zoo. This was "Welcome to the Jungle" stuff. "George said to me, 'You're a failure. Get yourself back to New York.' He was all over me," Cashman said. "It was the first week of my first season as GM. Gene Michael confessed later on to me that George called him and said, 'I need you to get back involved, and you need to take this over.' Stick told him, 'Hey, the kid is going to be fine, the team's going to be fine, relax.' So Stick obviously pushed back on him on my behalf, but George obviously was already starting to panic."

There was no need, of course, as Joe Torre and perhaps the most focused assemblage of players in team history overcame that false start and went on to win 114 regular season games—an American League record, though it was broken three years later by the Seattle Mariners (116)—and then the 11 more necessary to win the franchise's second championship in three years.

Yes, it seemed ridiculous—then and now—that even the famously blustering Steinbrenner would overreact in that fashion after three games. But the sting of the previous October and the failed defense of the storybook 1996 World Series title reverberated from Steinbrenner's base in Tampa, Florida, throughout that entire winter. The Yankees had been crushed to be bounced in the 1997 American League Division Series by the Cleveland Indians. First-year closer Mariano Rivera surrendered a game-tying home run to Sandy Alomar

Jr. in the eighth inning of a Game 4 loss, and the Indians went on to take the series the following night. "Even after all of the winning we did," Tino Martinez told me in 2018 for a 20th anniversary story in the *New York Daily News*, "I will never forget that loss."

Veteran infielder Luis Sojo recalled Torre's initial spring-training address as a challenge. "We hadn't played one game, and Joe was talking about the World Series."

But the 1998 season began ominously with two sloppy road losses against the Anaheim Angels and one against the Oakland A's. The first win came in extra innings against the A's on April 5. "One of my prized possessions from that year, which I donated to the Yankees Museum, but Joe sent me the lineup card from the first win in Oakland signed by Joe and all the coaches," Cashman said. "It said, 'Dear Crash, the first of many.' That was so prophetic because of how many games we won that year."

Still, the record stood at 1-4 after a loss the next day. Torre said he felt the need to summon the troops for an early-season team meeting in Seattle, "specially with what was swirling around back in New York."

"We started 1-4, and Mr. Torre's job was on the line," Derek Jeter said in 2018.

Paul O'Neill, who'd been thrown at by Seattle Mariners pitchers the previous night without retaliation, and David Cone were among those who spoke up during the testy conversation. "Obviously, something's up when you have a meeting that early in the year, especially with Joe, who didn't have a lot of them," O'Neill said. "Obviously, it worked because from then on it was a pretty magical ride."

Whether it was the meeting or—far more likely—the abundance of pitching, talent, and depth of that team, the Yankees closed out April with a run of 16 wins in 18 games. They never looked back, running away with the American League East by a whopping 22 games. Jeter finished third in AL MVP voting, establishing himself as one of the game's elite players. With free agency looming, Bernie Williams won the batting title, hitting .339.

In a baseball summer dominated by the storyline of Mark McGwire's and Sammy Sosa's performance-enhancing-drug-fueled assault on Roger Maris' single-season home run record, Tino Martinez led the Yankees with just 28, but 10 players reached double figures in a loaded lineup that plated a Major League Baseball-leading 965 runs. Even Scott Brosius knocked in 98 runs from the bottom of the lineup.

As part of a formidable rotation that also featured lefties Andy Pettitte and David Wells, and (by June) Cuban rookie Orlando "El Duque" Hernandez, David Cone won 20 games for the first time since 1988 with the New York Mets. The minor league addition, Shane Spencer, even provided an unexpected jolt in September with eight home runs, including three grand slams, to force his way into the postseason plans.

The two most defining games of that year came in a span of three days in May. Wells tossed a perfect game against the Minnesota Twins before a crowd of nearly 50,000 to see the game and enjoy the spoils of the Beanie Baby giveaway promotion on a Sunday in New York.

Following a scheduled day off, there also was a vicious bench-clearing brawl against the Baltimore Orioles on May 19 after Orioles closer Armando Benitez fired a 95-mph fastball flush between the 2 and the 4 on Martinez's back after a go-ahead home run by Williams. My opening paragraph in the next day's *Daily News* included the phrase: "From Beanie Babies to a beaning baby..."

Yes, I'm booing myself, too. But the brawl is definitely worth a view on YouTube. "I had no intention of charging the mound, but that was a wild brawl. It felt like all 25 guys on our team were all together," Martinez told me in 2018. "I wouldn't say it was a great moment. It's something you wish wouldn't have happened, but we already knew we were a tight team and had each other's backs, and that definitely proved it. That was one of the craziest fights I've ever been a part of and have ever seen to this day."

Said Wells: "That was an awesome brawl. You had Benitez; he was a knucklehead. I played with him in Baltimore. When he drilled Tino, the thing that really sticks out the most is seeing Graeme Lloyd and Jeff Nelson throwing haymakers as they're running in, the Twin Towers just coming in, throwing punches. Yeah, that was a party."

While the two set-up relievers led the charge out of the bullpen and swung their arms wildly at Benitez, Darryl Strawberry also went after the Baltimore reliever and eventually found him with his fists, as the fight dangerously spilled into the opposing dugout. "I said, 'Oh, this guy's gonna die,'" Wells said. "All of a sudden, all hell broke loose."

"I tried to get Straw out of there, but I didn't have much luck," Torre joked. "I just remember sitting over there with him on their bench and saying, 'What the hell are we doing here?'"

By the time October arrived, the popular Strawberry was unavailable. Three years after Steinbrenner had first taken a chance on the former Mets All-Star after his career had been derailed by substance abuse issues, he hit 24 homers in just 295 at-bats that season. The Yankees announced just ahead of the playoffs that Strawberry was diagnosed with colon cancer, requiring immediate surgery. His departure floored his teammates but served as additional inspiration for a division-series sweep of the Texas Rangers. "That was a gut punch to all of us, such a shock," said veteran designated hitter Chili Davis. "What really motivated us was Straw came in and talked to us and the speech he gave. It was very touching, all about, 'Hey boys, I can't be there with you, but I'm there with you. It's not about doing it for me, but do it for yourselves. Finish what we started.'" Led by future Hall of Fame outfielder Tim Raines, Strawberry's teammates chanted "Darryl, Darryl" during the postgame champagne celebration in Arlington, Texas.

The American League Championship Series provided the desired rematch with Cleveland, but the Yankees slipped into a 2–1 series hole due in part to a massive brain fart by second baseman Chuck Knoblauch in the 12th inning of a 4–1 loss in Game 2 at Yankee Stadium. While blowing a bubble and then arguing with first-base umpire John Shulock, Knoblauch allowed a live ball to roll away, enabling Cleveland's Enrique Wilson to stumble around third base and score the go-ahead run. "I was screaming and yelling at the top of my lungs: 'Get the fucking ball,'" Willie Randolph said. "I still cannot believe Knobby vapor-locked like that. But we got through it."

They did despite Wells also losing Game 3 in Cleveland. Earlier that summer Cashman had resisted Steinbrenner's trade-deadline urgings to obtain Seattle ace Randy Johnson, who instead was dealt to the Houston Astros. "It wasn't just George. It was Joe Torre, too," Cashman said of the Johnson talks. "We actually were playing the Mariners on the night of July 31 deadline, and Randy was supposed to be pitching against us later in that series. Joe called me from Seattle and said, 'Let me show you the lineup I'm using against Johnson.' It was all right-handers. It wasn't your normal Yankees lineup, and he said, 'This is what we'll be facing if we face them in the postseason.' Obviously, they both wanted him, but I was more worried that we had such great chemistry."

That left Game 4 resting in the hands and high leg kick of Hernandez in the first postseason start of his career. That morning, Steinbrenner summoned Torre to his hotel suite.

"That fiasco in Game 2, that was a nightmare," Torre said. "And then after we lost Game 3, I was having a late breakfast with my wife when George asked to have me come up to talk to him.

"He says, 'So what do you think?' I said, 'I can't tell you what to expect from Duque because he hadn't pitched in like two weeks. But I can tell you one thing: he's not gonna be nervous. He's downstairs right now helping clear dishes off the tables.' He was loose as a goose. He pitched lights-out obviously in Game 4, and we were off to the races."

Hernandez had signed a four-year contract worth $6.6 million after defecting from Cuba on a watercraft that has been described as everything from a raft to a ship—but clearly was somewhere in between. El Duque had been a member of the Yankees' rotation since a June start filling in for Cone, who'd purportedly been bitten by his mother's Jack Russell Terrier. Hernandez, 12–4 as a rookie, began building his reputation as one of the great postseason pitchers in baseball history. He went 9–3 with a 2.55 ERA in his October career, beginning with seven scoreless innings against the Indians to even the 1998 ALCS before the Yankees advanced in six. "Out of all of

Duque's big games, and he was a true big-game pitcher," Cashman said. "That was the most important one for us."

Hernandez wasn't the only significant addition the front office had made ahead of that season. Watson previously had acquired third basemen Scott Brosius, who'd batted just .203 in 1997, from Oakland for Kenny Rogers. And three days after replacing the resigning Watson in early February, Cashman traded three prospects, including prized pitcher Eric Milton, to Minnesota for the 29-year-old Knoblauch, a four-time All-Star in his first seven seasons with the Twins. The imported leadoff man averaged 118 runs during his first three seasons with the Yankees, but he would be moved off second base to left field in 2000 due to an odd case of throwing yips—likened to another former Yankees second base predecessor, Steve Sax. (One of Knoblauch's errant throws into the stands struck the mother of TV commentator Keith Olbermann in the head in 2000.) His name also would surface years later in the Mitchell Report on performance-enhancing drugs.

But with the Yankees trailing 5–2 in the seventh inning of the World Series opener against the San Diego Padres, Knoblauch atoned for his ALCS gaffe with a game-tying, three-run homer to left field against Donnie Wall. Later in the inning, the slumping Martinez (5-for-30 in the playoffs) clocked a grand slam into the right-field seats after it appeared he'd been struck out looking on a close pitch from San Diego lefty Mark Langston. "Seven runs in the seventh inning...And the stadium is up for grabs!" Michael Kay hoarsely yelled in the WABC radio booth. "If you listen to the call, my voice is cracking like Peter Brady from *The Brady Bunch*," Kay said. "I just remember the floor shaking, and the beer flying everywhere."

Brosius contributed two homers in Game 3, including a key blast against Hall of Fame closer Trevor Hoffman in the eighth inning. He drove in another run in support of Pettitte's seven-and-one-third shutout innings in the clincher. Brosius batted .471 with six RBIs in the four-game sweep to earn World Series MVP honors. "That's just backyard stuff," Brosius told me in 2018, "dreaming as a kid of doing anything like that in the World Series."

Afterward, former Yankees postseason hero Jim Leyritz, a member of the Padres that season, made a few phone calls to arrange for some of the Yankees to have a celebratory bash at San Diego Chargers star Junior Seau's nearby restaurant. "I did nothing in that series, 0-for-10," Leyritz said. "After it was over, I'm leaving the locker room, and Mr. Steinbrenner sees me and says, 'Hey Leyritz, are you the king of San Diego like you were the king of New York? Where can we celebrate the World Series? These guys need to celebrate.' I called Junior's place and said, 'The Yankees want to come down and celebrate. Can you keep the place open for them?' I actually went down there with them for a bit, hung out with the guys."

The next morning the Yankees flew back to New York. It was a very different cross-country flight for Cashman than the one he'd taken in April.

15

THURMAN MUNSON

More than four decades later, it remains among the saddest moments in New York sports history. Goose Gossage was readying to attend a Waylon Jennings concert, Reggie Jackson was driving his burgundy and silver Rolls-Royce when he heard the news over the radio, Phil Rizzuto and his wife were told by a waiter in a restaurant, Bucky Dent heard it from a parking attendant near the World Trade Center, and Roy White got a phone call from a reporter. Catfish Hunter and Lou Piniella heard it directly from George Steinbrenner. Billy Martin had been fishing on a lake and immediately burst into tears when informed by a team public relations staffer.

I was 11 years old, running through a sprinkler in my backyard on Long Island and not even a Yankees fan, but I was floored when my mother told me and my friends about Thurman Munson. The beloved captain and All-Star catcher of the Yankees died on August 2, 1979, while practicing takeoffs and landings in his private plane at Canton-Akron Airport in his home state of Ohio.

The reverberations were both immediate and lasting for teammates who would try to persevere without their leader and friend—and for a franchise that would preserve his locker as a forever symbol of his impact. "It's been 40 years, and you still see people wearing Thurman Munson jerseys. The fact that people have loved and appreciated him and showed such loyalty means the world to us," Munson's widow, Diana, said at the new Yankee Stadium in 2019 on the 40th anniversary of her husband's death. "We're from Canton, Ohio, but in New York, this for me is coming home, and this is about loving Thurman together. Although sometimes it's difficult, and there have been tears and there will continue to be tears, I think the respect and admiration that people show for Thurman is what cements the kind of person he was and shows people that he wasn't just a ballplayer. He was a family man. He was a businessman. He was a good man. He epitomizes much more than baseball, and I think that shows by the response the fans have. He was impactful."

Diana Munson attends Old Timers' Day each year on Thurman's behalf, joining several other organizational widows. She also returns annually to New York to host the Thurman Munson Awards Dinner to honor her husband, raising nearly $20 million for the AHRC NYC Foundation, which supports programs for children and adults with intellectual and developmental disabilities. "Losing Thurman was just devastating to all of us," former teammate Chris Chambliss said. "I got there in 1974, and it didn't take long to know that Thurman was the heart and soul of that club. He came through the organization, was just this incredible catcher, and probably one of the best clutch hitters I ever played with. Thurman was the real deal."

Bobby Murcer originally had joined the Yankees in 1965. The heir apparent in center field to fellow Oklahoman Mickey Mantle, he made the All-Star team four times before he was traded to the San Francisco Giants for Bobby Bonds in 1975. He'd found his way back to the Yankees in another trade from the Chicago Cubs in late June 1979 and hosted Munson and Piniella at his apartment in Chicago during a weekend series against the White Sox through August 1.

That night Murcer; his wife, Kay; and Piniella drove Munson to Palwaukee Municipal Airport just outside Chicago. They sat on the $1.25 million Cessna jet he'd purchased three weeks earlier—a more powerful upgrade from the propeller plane he'd initially owned—for nearly an hour, listening to Neil Diamond music. Murcer lent Munson $200 for gas and off he flew into the night bound for Canton to spend another off day with his family.

While practicing takeoffs and landings the next morning, Munson came in too low and clipped a tree, falling short of the runway. Two passengers escaped the fiery wreck, but they were unable to help Munson, who was later discovered to be paralyzed by the crash, out of the burning aircraft. The Transportation and Safety Board later determined that pilot error was responsible for the crash. "Those damn little planes. I always told Thurman, 'No way, man, I'm not going up in that thing,'" Gossage said. "I remember I was in the bedroom. My wife was in the bathroom. We were getting ready to go see Waylon

Jennings, and the phone rings. 'Goose, this is George.' I said, 'George who?' It was George Steinbrenner. We knew right away it had to be something really bad. He said, "I have some terrible news: we lost Thurman today.' I knew immediately what he meant."

Fourteen games out of first place after winning the previous two World Series, the Yankees painfully reconvened at Yankee Stadium without Munson the following day. Before their August 3 game against the Baltimore Orioles, Steinbrenner told backup catcher Jerry Narron not to take the field with his teammates during the national anthem so that the catcher's spot could remain empty. Yankees coach Yogi Berra informed Narron when it was appropriate to take his position.

With Jackson, Martin, and several other Yankees in tears along the first-base line, the moment of silence turned into a lengthy ovation and outpouring of emotion from a crowd of more than 51,000, many of whom were wearing No. 15 jerseys. "It had to last 15 to 20 minutes," Narron told WFAN in 2019. "And then Yogi said, 'If you don't go out there, this thing might go on forever.'"

The Yankees sleepwalked through a 1–0 loss that funereal Friday night, but Munson's teammates would experience their own heartfelt release three nights later. They had buried the 32-year-old Munson in Canton before flying back to New York for a nationally televised game against Baltimore. Many of the players' wives remained in Ohio with Diana and her three children. Murcer recorded more than 1,800 hits in his career, but none were more emotional or significant than the ones he rapped on August 6. He drove in all five runs in a 5–4 victory to overcome a four-run deficit with a three-run homer in the seventh and a two-run single down the left-field line in the ninth.

At the funeral services at the Canton Civic Center earlier in the day, a sobbing Murcer read one of the eulogies while Piniella delivered another. Murcer quoted the poet Angelo Patri. "The life of a soul on earth lasts longer than his departure. He lives on in your life and the life of all others who knew him," he said.

On the plane ride home from the funeral, Murcer had persuaded Martin to include him in the lineup. "We were all so young, and that was kind of the first big tragedy that happened to any of us. Honestly, we were all so caught up in the shock of it," Kay Murcer said. "We were with Diana and heard what was happening and how the game ended. I think for Bobby, he was just so emotional and drained. Bobby said he honestly didn't know how he got through the game. But he said he knew when Billy told him he didn't have to play [that] he definitely wanted to play. He said he knew he could not sit out that game."

Joe Torre was managing the New York Mets in 1979, but he was granted permission to accompany the Yankees on their chartered plane to attend Munson's funeral. Torre and Munson had become friendly while running into each other occasionally at a Florida dog track during spring trainings. "It was just so sad," Torre said, adding that he tried to console Martin during the flight. "Billy was crying the whole time. You could tell Thurman really meant so much to him and to that team."

Mets All-Star outfielder Lee Mazzilli had been in the batter's box in the first inning of the opener of a doubleheader against the Philadelphia Phillies on August 2. Aaron Boone's father, Bob, was the opposing catcher. Home-plate umpire Bill Williams called time and pointed to the scoreboard. It read: "Bulletin: Yankee catcher Thurman Munson was killed today in a plane crash, near Canton, Ohio." "I remember Boone saying, 'Oh my God.' It was so eerie, so sad. You could hear a pin drop in Shea Stadium," Mazzilli said. "I stepped out of the box and couldn't believe it. Literally, I didn't know how to react. Thurman and I ran into each a few times. He was this hard-nosed, winning player anybody would want on their team. I stepped back in and hit an RBI double and, even standing on second base, I couldn't believe that's how I found out the news. I will never forget that moment."

Murcer soon would provide another, following a three-run shot in the seventh inning. Dent was on third base and Willie Randolph on second when Murcer slashed an 0–2 pitch from former Yankees lefty Tippy Martinez for a two-run single to left and a dramatic 5–4 victory that legendary broadcaster Howard Cosell summed up for a national audience on ABC: "The New York Yankees, still the world champions, in an absolutely thrilling game. Look at them out there, on a day when they buried their team captain and leader, who tragically died at the age of 32 last Thursday afternoon at the Canton-Akron regional airport. And the hero, Bobby Murcer, one of two eulogists for the Yankees today in Canton, the man who broke up, who couldn't go on. Munson, his leader, his friend, the man who meant so much to Bobby Murcer in the formulation of his own career, and it's almost symbolic. Without being maudlin, they won this game for their team captain. What a finish to a ballgame that became more than an ordinary ballgame, and you know it. Emotion won this game."

Future Yankees broadcaster Ken Singleton played right field that night for the first-place Orioles: "We had a big lead and we were going to the World Series," he recalled years later on the YES Network. "I just remember thinking, *if the Yankees are going to win one against us, this was it.*"

Murcer also would become a beloved Yankees TV analyst before dying in 2008 from brain cancer. He presented the bat he used that night to Diana Munson. Her husband's locker remained untouched until it was moved to the new Yankee Stadium in 2009. "We felt the effects of Thurman's death for years after," Randolph said. "He was our heart and soul. It was the most shocking and stunning day I've ever had on the baseball field. He was this tough, gruff guy, wasn't very warm and fuzzy, but he'd always tell you the truth, and once you were accepted as a friend, he was a friend for life. It was so devastating."

Former Yankees catcher and 1996 World Series hero Jim Leyritz said Munson's legacy was something catchers in the system were taught. Like Munson, Leyritz grew up in Ohio. "It was almost eerie when you walked by his locker in the old stadium. You knew the history and what he meant to the Yankees, and being a kid from Ohio, I definitely knew who Thurman Munson was," Leyritz said. "I grew up rooting for the Reds and became a catcher because of Johnny Bench. But coming up, hearing people like Stick Michael and Buck Showalter talk about Thurman as a player, he reminded me a lot of Pete Rose, who was not the most gifted athlete on those Reds teams, but they played the hardest and left their heart on the field every game. That's what I remember most at Old Timers' Days, hearing from his teammates that's how Thurman was, too. That's the kind of guy and teammate he was. Seeing that locker and knowing what it meant and he meant, it was special."

Derek Jeter's locker at the old Yankee Stadium was closest to Munson's preserved stall and separated only by a storage case for the players' bats. (White had used that stall as Munson's teammate.) Jeter often spoke of his reverence for and bond with Munson, a fellow captain in team lore. Jorge Posada for years displayed a photo and a quote from Munson prominently in his locker about the importance of catchers: "I like hitting fourth and I like the good batting average, but what I do every day behind the plate is a lot more important because it touches so many more people and so many more aspects of the game."

16

WHITEY FORD

Ask any devotee of Sabermetrics, the empirical analysis of statistics at the heart of the numbers revolution that has taken over baseball front offices in the 2000s, and they will tell you that wins and losses no longer matter nearly as much as other metrics in determining a pitcher's value. Although there is overwhelming evidence to support this argument—just ask hard-luck New York Mets ace and two-time Cy Young winner Jacob deGrom—Whitey Ford still deserves full marks for owning a better winning percentage than any pitcher in modern baseball with at least 150 career victories.

He also has registered the most wins in the history of the game's all-time winningest franchise and the most ever in World Series play. That still has to count for something. "I don't care what the situation was, how high the stakes were. The bases could be loaded and the pennant riding on every pitch, it never bothered Whitey," Mickey Mantle said in *Pinstripes and Pennants: The Ultimate New York Yankees Fan Guide*. "He pitched his game. Cool. Crafty. Nerves of steel."

While Joe DiMaggio hailed from the Bay Area, Yogi Berra from St. Louis, and Ford's closest pal and running mate, Mantle, from Oklahoma, Edward Charles Ford represented the quintessential native New Yorker in every imaginable way. By birth, by quick-wittedness, by cocksure attitude, by guile, by toughness, and by loyalty—both to the Yankees organization and to his fun-loving and success-addicted teammates.

Given his nickname because of his blond hair by minor league manager and colorful former Yankees ace Lefty Gomez, Ford pitched 16 seasons for the Yankees. He was a member of 11 American League pennant winners and six World Series titlists, missing out on two more on each list while serving in the United States Army in 1951 and 1952. Ford's 10 wins (with a 2.71 ERA) represent the most in World Series play and three more than Yankees predecessor Red Ruffing and teammate Allie Reynolds, as well St. Louis Cardinals ace Bob Gibson. His big-game prowess earned him "The Chairman of the Board" nickname from catcher Elston Howard. "You kind of took it for granted around the Yankees," Ford wrote in his book *Slick: My Life In and Around Baseball* with Phil Pepe in 1988, "that there was always going to be baseball in October."

Ford was born in 1928 and grew up in Astoria, Queens, but he traveled an hour by bus each way to attend Manhattan's Aviation Career and Technical Education High School because the high school closest to him, William Cullen Bryant High, didn't field a baseball team. A lifelong Yankees fan who idolized DiMaggio, Ford showed up for a tryout camp at Yankee Stadium during his senior season in 1946. He signed shortly thereafter with the Yankees for $7,000—about $500 more than an offer he'd received from the New York Giants.

By 1950, the third of an unprecedented five-year run of championships, Ford made his Bronx debut in a rotation that featured the Big Three of Reynolds, Eddie Lopat, and Vic Raschi. Ford went 9–1 with a 2.81 ERA in 20 games (12 starts) to place as runner-up for American League Rookie of the Year honors to Boston Red Sox first baseman Walt Dropo, who slugged 34 homers and knocked in a league-best 144 runs.

Ford also was a bridesmaid in the Hall of Fame voting in 1973, missing out on first-ballot election by registering 67.1 percent of the vote (75 percent was needed for election) to finish second in that year's balloting behind his contemporary left-hander, Warren Spahn. The blessing of that short-term wait was that Ford fittingly was enshrined the following year alongside Mantle, his teammate for all but one season of his illustrious career. The Yankees also retired his No. 16 in 1974. Ford and Mantle were an inseparable pair who called each other "Slick," a reference to a team meeting called by manager Casey Stengel, in which he took the two of them and Billy Martin to task for too many late nights on the town. "Some of you guys are Whiskey Slick," Stengel was quoted as saying in *Whitey and Mickey: A Joint Autobiography of the Yankee Years.*

Dave Righetti, whose father Leo was a minor leaguer in the Yankees' system in the 1950s, relayed a story about hanging out with the trio of Mickey, Whitey, and Billy over drinks one year during spring training in Fort Lauderdale, Florida. Also among the revelers was Dave

Thomas, the owner of the Wendy's fast-food chain, Righetti said. "Hell, if I didn't drink, drink or smoke, I'd win 20 games every year," Ford said. "It's easy when you don't drink or smoke or horse around."

Ford's father, a former semi-pro ballplayer, worked for Con Edison for several years but later owned a bar with a friend in Astoria. His son, a prototypical crafty lefty, was all business on the mound, however, leaning heavily on his curveball and creativity to keep opposing hitters off balance. Stengel took cautious steps to not overuse Ford in the first half of his career, citing the southpaw's 5'10", 180-pound frame as a reason for using him in more than 225 innings just once in his first nine seasons.

After Stengel was fired in 1960, replacement Ralph Houk employed Ford more heavily, often pitching him on three days' rest. The result was a 25–4 season over a career-high 283 innings in 1961, the summer of the M & M Boys' home run chase, for Ford's only Cy Young Award. He also went 24–7 with a 2.74 ERA in a league-high 269 innings in 1963.

Starting at the age of 32, Ford averaged 260 innings per season from 1961 to 1965 until injuries and age forced his retirement in 1967. That left his final won-loss record at 236–106, a record .690 winning percentage for pitchers with at least 150 wins. Ford also set a record of 33⅓ consecutive scoreless innings in the Fall Classic (eclipsing the previous mark of 29⅔ by Babe Ruth). He was named World Series MVP in 1961. After the 21-year-old rookie tossed eight-and-two-thirds innings without allowing an earned run in his first World Series start in the Game 4 against the Philadelphia Phillies in 1950, Arthur Daily of *The New York Times* wrote that Ford "has the brass of a burglar."

When asked a few weeks earlier by a reporter after a key September start had been the biggest game he'd ever pitched, Ford deadpanned: "Well, no, I remember pitching the Maspeth Ramblers to a 17–11 victory over the Astoria Indians. That was a good one, too."

"Just a great guy, always in a great mood, what a sense of humor," said Roy White, a teammate during Ford's final three seasons. "In those days you didn't hang out with the big guys as a rookie. They had their circle. The one thing about Whitey, I know he mentioned me

Whitey Ford poses in 1960, a year in which he recorded a 3.08 ERA.

in his book as one of the most underappreciated Yankees, so I always appreciated that."

Ford, who celebrated his 91st birthday in October of 2019, endured some painful moments after he retired. He underwent surgery to remove a cancerous tumor from his head in 1995 and again in 2000. His 44-year-old son, Thomas, a former cameraman for WPIX station in New York, died of a heart condition in 1999.

Ford also detailed in his autobiography that he'd doctored the baseball while pitching late in his career, especially as he dealt with hip and elbow injuries and a circulatory condition that required surgery. The eight-time All-Star wrote that he had difficulty mastering the spitball, but he claimed to learn from pitcher Lew Burdette how to strategically apply mud to the ball. He also scuffed the ball with a wedding ring specially made for him by a local jeweler. Ford even would cover the pitching rubber with dirt so he could start his delivery several inches in front of it. "Talk about adding a yard to your fastball," he joked. "I didn't begin cheating until late in my career, when I needed something to help me survive...I didn't cheat when I won the 25 games in 1961. I don't want anybody to get any ideas and take my Cy Young Award away. And I didn't cheat in 1963 when I won 24 games. Well, maybe a little."

When it was over in 1967, Ford continued the quips, saying, "I came in wearing a $50 suit, and I'm going out wearing a $200 suit, so that's pretty good."

The Chairman of the Board was better than pretty good. His lifetime ERA of 2.75 is the lowest by a starting pitcher in the live ball era (since 1920), though Los Angeles Dodgers star Clayton Kershaw had a 2.44 mark in his first 12 seasons through 2019. Ted Williams once called Ford the toughest pitcher he ever faced. His first manager agreed. "If you had one game to win and your life depended on it," Stengel said. "You'd want [Ford] to pitch it."

ELSTON HOWARD

Eight years after Jackie Robinson debuted with the Brooklyn Dodgers, breaking MLB's longstanding color barrier, the Yankees finally began correcting a rare, unspoken stain on their storied history. Elston Howard became the first African American player to don the pinstripes in 1955, making his debut in Boston in the second game of the season on April 14. The Yankees were the 13th of the 16 teams in baseball to begin integrating their roster, but Howard would become a nine-time All-Star, the first black MVP in American League history, and one of the most revered players and coaches in team lore. "Ellie was a great example for everyone—just to watch him and how he conducted himself on and off the field. He showed me how to be a Yankee," said former teammate Roy White. "He showed me how to dress in a proper manner, how to carry myself with a lot of dignity. I always got important advice from Ellie from the time I was a rookie in 1965 until he left in '67, and then when he came back as a Yankee coach. He went through so much discrimination, but he was such a big-time player, and I just thought he was a great man, a great teammate who made sure to teach us about the Yankees and how they did things."

For all of their incomparable success, the Yankees didn't always do things the right way. They had won six World Series from 1947—Robinson's first season in Brooklyn—through 1954, but their acceptance of the changing times and of players of color took far too long to manifest itself. In the book, *Baseball's Great Experiment*, by Jules Tygiel, then-Yankees general manager George Weiss is quoted as saying, "The Yankees are not going to promote a Negro player to the stadium simply in order to be able to say that they have such a player. We are not going to bow to pressure groups on this issue."

Weiss also is quoted in Roger Kahn's 1972 book *The Boys of Summer* suggesting the signing of black players would attract the wrong fans to the Bronx. "We don't want that sort of crowd," Weiss said. "It would offend boxholders from Westchester to have to sit with n----rs."

Weiss unfathomably passed on the opportunity to sign future Hall of Famers such as Willie Mays and Ernie Banks, among countless others, until the Yankees finally relented and bought Howard's contract for $25,000 from the famed Kansas City Monarchs of the Negro Leagues in 1950. Howard, a St. Louis native like Yogi Berra, had turned down scholarship offers two years earlier to play football at Michigan, Michigan State, and Illinois. Other schools unsuccessfully recruited him to play basketball or run track. The outfielder instead signed for $500 per month to play baseball with the Monarchs under legendary player/manager Buck O'Neil.

Howard spent 1951 and 1952 serving in the U.S. Army, though he mostly played on a traveling baseball squad in the South Pacific. In 1953 he was assigned by the Yankees to their top farm team, the Kansas City Blues, alongside another black player, Vic Power, a first baseman from Puerto Rico. It was Power who first appeared poised for a summoning to the Bronx, batting .349, but Weiss instead promoted white first baseman Gus Triandos from a level below. Power remained with Kansas City for the remainder of 1953 and was traded to the Philadelphia A's that winter. Weiss later was quoted in Kahn's book, *The Era: 1947–57*, as saying, "Maybe he can play, but not for us. He's impudent and he goes for white women. Power is not the Yankee type."

Said Power: "They were waiting to see if I could turn white, but I couldn't do it."

With Yankees legend Bill Dickey as his organizational tutor, Howard continued to transition to his new position. In 1954 the converted backstop was named MVP of the International League with a .330 batting average, 22 home runs, and 109 RBIs for the Triple A Toronto Maple Leafs.

Public pressure mounted for the Yankees to finally promote him. They had won 103 games in 1954 but still finished eight games behind the Cleveland Indians and their black All-Star outfielder, Larry Doby, who finished as runner-up to Berra for American League MVP honors. Howard indeed arrived in the majors in 1955, entering the second game of the season as a left fielder in Boston in the sixth inning. He ripped an RBI single to score Mickey Mantle in his first career plate appearance, but his first start—a three-hit showing with two RBIs in his return to Kansas City—wouldn't come for two more weeks.

Howard appeared in 97 games as a rookie, finishing with a .290 batting average and 10 home runs. He also played in all seven World Series games against Robinson and Brooklyn, belting a key home run in Game 1, but Howard also made the final out of a Game 7 defeat.

The discrimination and racial indignities Howard endured only continued. Yankees manager Casey Stengel often referred to him as "Eightball," according to Robert Creamer's book *Stengel: His Life and Times.*

At least Howard's teammates were far more accepting. In her biography of her husband with coauthor and longtime *New York Post* editor Ralph Wimbish, titled *Elston and Me: The Story of the First Black Yankee*, Arlene Howard credited white teammates such as Berra, Phil Rizzuto, Moose Skowron, and Hank Bauer for immediately welcoming him to the clubhouse.

During the 1955 campaign with the team in Chicago, a group of Yankees were eating breakfast before a game against the White Sox. Bauer insisted Howard sit with them. "Elston came in the room, and there was an empty seat right next to me," Bauer said years later. "He saw the seat and hedged a bit. I motioned for him to come sit with us. When he sat down, I told him, 'You play with us, you eat with us. You're one of us.'"

When Bauer died in 2007, Arlene Howard told Wimbish for a *New York Post* story: "Hank was very personable, such a good friend to Elston. He was tough-looking but honest and fair. Back then, when America was such a racist country, I don't think race ever crossed his mind. He thought of you as a person."

Although Howard's teammates accepted him, much of America, particularly in the South, had a long way to go. Each year in spring training, as in many road cities, Howard still was not permitted to stay or dine with the rest of the Yankees. Wimbish's father, a St. Petersburg, Florida, doctor named Ralph Wimbish Sr., was the head of the Florida chapter of the NAACP. He was among those who housed black players or found them accommodations during spring training, when they were unable to stay at team hotels due to segregation laws.

Wimbish Jr. was a copy editor in the sports department of the *Post* during my first seven years in the journalism business. I served as an agate clerk, aggregating numbers for the pages that held the standings, box scores, horse racing charts, and other statistics for various sports. In the office Wimbish often regaled us with fascinating tales about meeting Robinson and Jesse Owens, and of ballplayers such as Howard, Hector Lopez, Bob Gibson, and others staying at his childhood home. "It was pretty cool having your favorite players staying in your bedroom in spring training," Wimbish said. "Elston started coming around when I was five or six. I didn't even realize at the time the reason why he was staying in my bedroom. But I was thrilled to have him there."

Blocked by Berra—think of Steve Young sitting behind Joe Montana, or Aaron Rodgers behind Brett Favre—Howard started at catcher only 49 times over his first three seasons before taking over more regularly for an aging Berra behind the plate with 64 starts in 1958. Of course, that didn't stop Howard from providing a few memorable October moments early in his career.

Against the Milwaukee Braves in the 1957 World Series, Howard blasted a three-run homer off Warren Spahn with two outs in the ninth inning of Game 4 for a 4–4 tie, though the Yankees eventually lost in 10 innings. In Game 7 against the Braves the following year, Howard snapped a 2–2 tie with an RBI single to score Berra in the eighth inning to help complete the first comeback by any team from a 3–1 World Series deficit.

By 1960 Howard was the Yankees' regular catcher, and Berra mostly shifted to the outfield. Largely overlooked in the M & M Boys' home run chase, Howard batted a team-leading and career-best .348 in 1961. Two years later he hit .285 with 28 homers and 85 RBIs—while earning his first of two Gold Glove Awards behind the plate—to become the first black player to be named American League MVP, garnering 15 of 20 first-place votes to easily outdistance Al Kaline of the Detroit Tigers. Howard also finished third the next season, trailing only Baltimore Orioles third baseman Brooks Robinson and Mantle in the balloting.

In all the Yankees reached the World Series nine times in Howard's first 10 seasons, winning four. He batted .261 with five homers and 19 RBIs in 47 postseason games for them.

With Berra and others retired and Mantle fading, however, the Yankees were a second-division club by 1967, finishing 72–90. Howard was traded in August to the Boston Red Sox. While he batted just .147 in 42 games, he was credited with leading a pitching staff fronted by ace Jim Lonborg. Howard wound up in the World Series for the 10th time in his 14 major league seasons, though the Red Sox lost in seven games to the St. Louis Cardinals.

Howard played one more year for Boston before accepting a coaching position to return to the Yankees in 1969. That made him the first African American coach in the American League, though he'd be greatly disappointed to never achieve his goal of becoming baseball's first black manager. (Frank Robinson did so with Cleveland in 1975.) Bill Veeck reportedly wanted to hire Howard in 1968, but his proposed purchase of the Washington Senators didn't go through. Instead, from 1969 to 1978, Howard coached under five managers in New York. He specifically was passed over as a candidate in favor of Bill Virdon in 1974 and never got the chance thereafter. "We talked to George Steinbrenner about that. He changed managers so frequently he said he didn't want to have to fire Elston," Wimbish said. "Elston would argue, 'He wouldn't have needed to fire me.' Elston was not a confrontational individual. He kind of took it in stride, but Arlene would tell you this is what killed him so early. He badly wanted to be a manager and he should have been."

Early in 1979, Howard nearly collapsed at LaGuardia Airport in New York and soon was diagnosed with myocarditis, a heart condition. Unable to continue coaching, Steinbrenner promised him a front-office position as an assistant to the owner. His primary duties were to appear at team functions and scout minor league talent. On December 4, 1980, Howard was admitted to Columbia Presbyterian Hospital in New York. Two weeks later, he was dead at 51.

"I was playing in Japan in 1980, and when I came back, I heard Ellie was in the hospital and I went to see him," White said. "We talked about baseball, and he was talking about how he was disappointed he wasn't getting the chance to manage. That was a dream. He mentioned that several times. But he also was excited when I saw him because he was supposed to be coming out of intensive care, said he was getting much better, and he would be going to a regular room. Four or five days later, he died. It was devastating."

In 1984 the Yankees retired Howard's No. 32 in Monument Park. His baseball legacy also includes being a part of the company that first manufactured weighted baseball doughnuts, which generations of players have used on their bats while in the on-deck circle. Whitey Ford, along with White and Reggie Jackson, spoke at Howard's funeral service. Ford got choked up memorializing his longtime teammate and friend. *The New York Times* columnist Red Smith wrote that day, "The Yankees' organization lost more class on the weekend than George Steinbrenner could buy in 10 years."

Several baseball dignitaries served as honorary pallbearers, including Ford, Berra, Mantle, Dickey, Banks, and fellow Negro Leagues alum Monte Irvin. "Elston meant everything to me, personally," Chris Chambliss said. "He was a real mentor as one of our coaches. Yogi was, too. We always could talk to those guys about what was going on. I was so proud to have him around us during those years in the '70s. I'd hear the stories, and he didn't really try to tell those stories, but other players have told me. I know what guys like Elston went through to make it easier for guys like me. I had it easy in my career compared to them. But that was because of them."

18

JOE TORRE

Joe Torre admittedly didn't know George Steinbrenner particularly well, but that certainly was about to change. As a former manager of the New York Mets, they'd crossed paths occasionally at baseball dinners in New York throughout the years. The Boss even had helped him procure tickets a couple of times for the Super Bowl. Then the confluence of events of a devastating ending to the 1995 baseball season, as well as multiple intermediaries and loyalists acting on Torre's behalf, brought them together later that year. The result was an immediate fairytale return to the World Series in 1996 and four championships in the first five seasons of Torre's dozen years in the Bronx, including a postseason appearance in every one of them.

His managerial tenure in New York didn't end well because they never did with Steinbrenner, but Torre parlayed his success into a spot in Monument Park for his No. 6 and a 2014 induction into the Baseball Hall of Fame in Cooperstown. "First off, I was really tickled to get the opportunity, but I know there were a lot of questions and criticism because of my overall record," Torre said. "I was 100 games under .500 as a manager, but I felt it was an opportunity I couldn't say no to, even though my brother, Frank, had tried to talk me out of it. I just felt it was time to find out if I could do this. I obviously took the job and never looked back, never second-guessed myself. I certainly never was intimidated by George. This was an opportunity I never counted on because I had no connection with the Yankees. But I enjoyed the hell out of it."

Indeed, Torre's career record over 15 seasons managing the Mets, Atlanta Braves, and St. Louis Cardinals had been 894–1,003, and his lone postseason appearance came with Atlanta in 1982 and resulted in elimination via a three-game sweep by St. Louis. The Brooklyn native had participated in more games as a player and manager than anyone in baseball history without getting to a World Series.

Ian O'Connor of the *New York Daily News* wrote a column expressing that the 55-year-old Torre didn't know what he was getting himself into with Steinbrenner, who didn't even attend the introductory press conference. *Daily News* slot editor Anthony Rieber came up with a corresponding back page headline. Riffing off Shoeless Joe Jackson, the newspaper branded Torre "Clueless Joe."

Four months after he'd been canned by the Cardinals, Torre initially interviewed with Steinbrenner's then-son-in-law, Joe Molloy, and outgoing general manager Gene Michael, who was sliding into a scouting and advisory role, for the GM vacancy. Bob Watson ultimately was hired for the position, but less than two weeks after that meeting, Torre received another call from Arthur Richman, the former public relations official from his days with the Mets who had transitioned to a position as a special advisor to Steinbrenner. Richman wanted to know if Torre was interested in being considered to replace Buck Showalter following Steinbrenner's 21st managerial change in 23 years owning the team.

Richman added Torre to a short list of impressive candidates that featured former championship-winning managers Sparky Anderson, Tony La Russa, and Davey Johnson, who'd fronted the Mets to the 1986 World Series title. "I still believe to this day I was on the bottom of the totem pole on that list," Torre said. "But Tony took my old job with St. Louis, and Davey, I think, was already committed to Baltimore. Sparky had retired, especially after the 1994 strike and the replacement year in '95. So I was the only one left. Obviously, it was the best thing that happened in my baseball career."

Torre's even-keeled demeanor and calming influence was evident from the start of 1996. He often served as a deflector from Steinbrenner's tirades and meddling for his players. "Joe was the perfect fit for this team," outfielder Paul O'Neill said. "He understood the pressure of New York, the importance of winning, what it takes to win, and just the ups and downs of the season. He had been an All-Star player. He had been fired as a manager a few times before. I think from what he'd gone through earlier in his career and his life at that point [that] he understood what happens away from the field was so important to what you did on the field. I think that was his biggest strength as a manager. He understood what was going on in your life and how it could affect you as a player."

Torre was named National League MVP in 1971 when he batted .363 with a league-best 137 RBIs for the Cardinals. According to Andy Pettitte, Torre often reminded his players he also once hit below .200 in a season, so he fully understood the fine line between success and failure.

From Derek Jeter's home run on Opening Day in Cleveland, to reclamation project Doc Gooden's no-hitter in May, to David Cone's seven innings of no-hit ball in Oakland in September after missing four months because of a shoulder aneurysm, the season had a storybook quality throughout.

Still, all eyes were on Torre in his long-awaited first World Series. He calmly defused Steinbrenner's venom after losing the first two games of the series at home, and after making a few daring lineup changes in Atlanta, the Yankees won the final four games for their first World Series title since 1978. The emotion of a season that also saw Torre's brother, Rocco, die of a heart attack in June only heightened when Frank Torre underwent a heart transplant on the off day between Game 5 and the Game 6 clincher. Joe Torre broke down in tears during the winning celebration. "It was really an emotional year and it just felt like this completed the circle in my career," Torre said. "I've always said, 'It's no fun watching somebody else eat a hot fudge sundae.' But when you get to the World Series and taste that success, you never get tired of it."

That success would continue. Following a crushing loss to the Cleveland Indians in the 1997 American League Division Series, the Yankees became the first team since the Oakland A's in 1972–74 to capture three straight championships. They won a record 125 games, including the postseason, in 1998. They posted an 11–1 October mark in 1999, which began with Torre missing two months following prostate cancer surgery. And they managed a five-game victory against the crosstown Mets in 2000, giving Torre four rings in his first five seasons at the helm. "I always give credit to Billy Martin as one of the best managers I ever played for—even if for small periods of time," said Willie Randolph, the former Yankees second baseman who served as

Torre's third-base coach. "But there was nobody I've been around in Yankee history in all my time there that was as impressive in that role as Joe Torre."

Hitting coach Chris Chambliss, another key member of the Yankees' championship-winning teams in the 1970s, later played for Torre with Atlanta. He also had been a member of Torre's coaching staff in St. Louis. "There was no bullshit with Joe. None," Chambliss said. "There was never a bunch of junk going on. Joe was such a straightforward guy, knew how to handle guys, and just commanded all that respect."

However, 2000 would be Torre's final championship with the Yankees. They lost in the World Series two of the next three years. All-time saves leader Mariano Rivera blew a ninth-inning lead in Game 7 to the Arizona Diamondbacks in 2001, and then came a six-game loss to the upstart Florida Marlins in 2003 after Aaron Boone's extra-inning home run had knocked out the Boston Red Sox in the American League Championship Series.

With key players such as O'Neill, Cone, Tino Martinez, Scott Brosius, and Joe Girardi gone, the Yankees never rediscovered that postseason success under Torre despite adding high-priced additions such as Alex Rodriguez, Mike Mussina, and Jason Giambi. The Mitchell Report in 2007 also alleged that Roger Clemens, Pettitte, Chuck Knoblauch, and relievers Mike Stanton and Jason Grimsley from the championship teams were among several former Yankees to be involved with performance-enhancing drugs.

Following a first-round playoff loss to the Detroit Tigers in 2007, Torre was summoned to Tampa, Florida, where the Yankees offered him a significant pay cut. Torre called the offer insulting. It all ultimately led Girardi to be hired as his replacement, while Torre signed a three-year contract to manage the Los Angeles Dodgers. In his 2012 book with *Sports Illustrated*'s Tom Verducci titled *The Yankee Years,* Torre stated he believed GM Brian Cashman "betrayed" him during the negotiations. "Joe and George just could never got back on the same page. Joe always handled his contract negotiations directly. This was no different," Cashman said. "At that point George had been trying to walk away from Joe Torre years earlier, and I pretty much always had been standing in the way of that. Bottom line, The Boss had been off of Joe Torre for several years already. He was looking to make a change. It probably would have happened sooner if I wasn't running interference. I know for a fact that it would have."

Torre's book also revealed that Yankees players often referred to Rodriguez as "A-Fraud," and that the third baseman had a jealous obsession with Jeter that bordered on the 1992 suspense flick *Single White Female*.

Once in Los Angeles, Torre led the Dodgers to two straight National League West titles but no World Series appearances before he stepped down, following an 80–82 campaign in 2010. Don Mattingly, the former Yankees All-Star who had served on Torre's coaching staff for six seasons in New York and Los Angeles, replaced him for 2011, his first managerial job.

Torre accepted a position with Major League Baseball in 2011 as the executive vice president for baseball operations, a title he still held in 2019. The new gig also afforded Torre more time to dedicate to the charitable foundation—The Safe at Home Foundation—he had formed at his wife Ali's urging in 2002. Torre revealed that he grew up a product of domestic violence with an abusive father, Joe Torre Sr., a former NYPD officer. The foundation's mission statement was "to provide health services to youth who have been traumatized by exposure to violence including domestic violence, child abuse, teen dating abuse, and sexual assault in order to empower them to live healthy lives free of violence."

As of 2019, 15 centers known as "Margaret's Place," named after his mother, existed in New York, New Jersey, California, and Ali Torre's home state of Ohio. "I never in my wildest dreams thought I'd ever talk about it," Torre said. "I know I felt in my home growing up, when my dad was abusive to my mom, I was responsible for what was going on. There was a lot of whispering going on in my house, and my mom would never share with me things. Even though I saw the results of what my dad did to her, she never talked about it. When we started our foundation in 2002, it was unusual for a man to talk about domestic violence. It's been very satisfying for me to see these kids and talk to them about it. It feels good to connect with young people and help them feel better about themselves. There are a lot of similarities I think in what I did for a living as a manager because I think it's important that players know that you care about them."

Many of Torre's players reciprocate those feelings, a bond shared through such interpersonal experiences, as well as their success together on the diamond. By both measures Torre's place in Yankees history is secured and unquestioned. "I still have to pinch myself," Torre said. "The Yankees represented the elite. There's no question. The expectation, the number of championships, all the names. I didn't feel that I was part of the Ruth and Mickey and Whitey and Yogi and Reggie lineage because I never played here. I managed. But I'm certainly proud of the fact that I was part of something very special. Playing 16 to 17 years of a pretty good playing career is not even close compared to managing this team in my hometown and the success we enjoyed together."

19

CASEY STENGEL

Casey Stengel hardly was a popular choice when he was named manager of the Yankees in 1949. The so-called "Ol' Perfessor" was widely regarded as more of a buffoon than a master strategist at the time of his hiring. After all, in nine years fronting the Brooklyn Dodgers and the Boston Bees/Braves, he never had led a club to anything better than a fifth-place finish. "The Yankees represent an investment of millions of dollars. They don't hand out jobs like this just because they like your company," Stengel said at his introductory press conference. "I got the job because the people here think I can produce for them. I know I can make people laugh, but some of you think I'm a damn fool."

In Stengel's first five seasons in pinstripes, he won five consecutive World Series titles. No one was laughing anymore.

Despite Stengel's unorthodox strategies and often scrambled syntax—a language that would come to be known simply as "Stengelese"—there never would be an era in which one team so dominated. "We thought we got us a clown," pitcher Eddie Lopat said years later. "But it was a treat for him to be with us after all of the donkey clubs he'd been with. He was something."

So, too, were Stengel's clubs in the Bronx. They captured 10 American League flags and seven World Series titles in his dozen years at the helm. Stengel and Joe McCarthy (1933–43) are the only two managers in baseball history to win more than five. It had shocked much of baseball to see him initially ascend to the post, especially after compiling a .439 winning percentage (581–742) previously in his managerial career. It actually sounds reminiscent of the mistreatment Joe Torre received—albeit for different reasons—when he arrived with a .481 career winning percentage in '96 and then went on to win the World Series four times in his first five seasons. "Casey knew his baseball. He only made it look like he was fooling around," Hall of

Fame manager Sparky Anderson said, according to the Hall of Fame's website. "He knew every move that was ever invented, and some that we haven't even caught on to yet."

With Joe DiMaggio limited by a persistent heel injury, the Yankees finished third in the American League in 1948, prompting the firing of popular manager Bucky Harris. He had replaced McCarthy just the previous year and defeated the Dodgers in seven games in the World Series during his first season in the dugout.

Stengel vowed a return to prominence and he did so by implementing facets of the game that would become universally used, such as the reliance on Joe Page as the team's primary relief pitcher in late-inning situations and employing stringent platoons between right-handed and left-handed batters such as Moose Skowron and Joe Collins at first base, Bobby Brown and Gil McDougald at third, and Hank Bauer and Gene Woodling in left field.

Charles Stengel grew up in Missouri and was set to attend Western Dental College in Kansas City, when he was signed by the Dodgers in 1910. During a 14-year playing career, Stengel also had the distinction of registering the first home run in the history of Ebbets Field in 1913 and the first homer in World Series play at Yankee Stadium in 1923, upstaging Babe Ruth by legging out an inside-the-parker in the ninth inning of a Game 1 win for the New York Giants.

Three decades later Stengel was a five-time champion with the Yankees. He also guided them to World Series wins in 1956 and 1958, alternating with October defeats in '55 and '57.

A third-place finish in 1959 and a seven-game loss to the Pittsburgh Pirates in 1960 were enough for owners Dan Topping and Del Webb to dismiss the 70-year-old Stengel and replace him with Ralph Houk. When Topping tried to announce at a testy press conference that Stengel had "retired," Stengel interjected, "I was fired."

Even at his age, he wasn't out of work for long. The expansion Mets hired him to be the face of their franchise, which began play with a bumbling season of 40–120 in 1962. They were lovable losers, and Stengel was game to promote them as only he could. "I've been in this game 100 years, but I see new ways to lose 'em I never knew existed

STENGELESE

Casey Stengel had a way of colorfully describing it all. His pithy observations and quotable soundbites have put him among the game's foremost characters.

- On baseball: "Good pitching will always stop good hitting and vice versa."
- On Yogi Berra: "He'd fall in a sewer and come up with a gold watch."
- On postgame drinks: "Don't drink in the hotel bar. That's where I do my drinking."
- On Mickey Mantle: "He should lead the league in everything. In fact, he should do anything he wants to do."
- On Joe DiMaggio: "I came in here, and a fella asked me to have a drink. I said 'I don't drink.' Then another fella said, 'I hear you and Joe DiMaggio aren't speaking.' And I said, 'I think I'll take that drink.'"
- On his managerial philosophy: "Keep the five guys who hate you away from the five who are undecided."
- On later taking over the expansion 1962 New York Mets: "Can't anybody here play this game?"
- On one of the Mets' prospects: "We have this fine young catcher named Gooseen, who is only 20 years old. In 10 years he has a chance to be 30."

That is not to suggest in any way that everything that came out of Stengel's mouth was funny or acceptable. Stengel also was accused of using racial epithets to describe black players.

In an article for the extremely thorough SABR.org website (Society for American Baseball Research), author Bill Bishop, however, wrote: "Casey did use language that would certainly be considered offensive today but was quite common vernacular in the '50s. He was effusive in his praise of black players like Satchel Paige, Larry Doby, and Howard."

before," Stengel joked during that initial season. Arthur Daley of *The New York Times* wrote that Stengel "gave the Mets the momentum they needed when they needed it most. He was the booster that got them off the ground and on their journey. The smoke screen he generated to accompany the blast-off obscured the flaws and gave the Mets an acceptance and a following they could not have obtained without him."

Stengel finally retired in 1965. One year later he was inducted into the Hall of Fame alongside Ted Williams. In June of 1975, months before he died of cancer at 85, Stengel made one final grand entrance at Shea Stadium by riding into the Mets' annual Old Timers' Day in a chariot dressed in a toga and a gladiator helmet. But Stengel had proven long ago that he was far more than just the butt of a joke.

20

BILLY MARTIN

Unlike Lou Gehrig and Thurman Munson, Billy Martin's status as a tragic hero in Yankees history mostly was self-inflicted. The 1953 World Series MVP was hired and fired as manager five times by George Steinbrenner over a tumultuous 13-year span beginning in 1975. The era was punctuated by clashes with The Boss and star Reggie Jackson, physical altercations with players, and multiple drunken bar fights, dating back to his playing days, until Martin was killed in an alcohol-fueled, single-car crash on Christmas of 1989. "It's like losing a part of our own family," Steinbrenner told the *New York Daily News'* Bill Madden the night Martin died.

Four days after his close friend and former teammate's death, Mickey Mantle said, "We used to tease each other about whose liver was going to go first. I never thought it would end for him this way."

It was Christmas night. I was home on Long Island during my college break when the news flashed across the TV that Martin had died in a single-car wreck.

"Drinking?" my father asked.

"Drinking," my uncle nodded.

It initially was reported that Martin was not driving the pickup truck he owned, which careened off an icy road near Binghamton in upstate New York late that holiday afternoon. But it certainly wasn't hard to picture alcohol being involved in the sad ending to Martin's turbulent life and career with the Yankees.

Local sheriffs charged the supposed driver, a friend named William Reedy, who survived the accident, with driving while intoxicated after the vehicle skidded down a 300-foot embankment. Martin was pronounced dead with a broken neck and internal injuries barely one hour after arriving at the hospital. Reedy, a former tavern owner near Tiger Stadium when Martin managed the Detroit Tigers, later testified that he was not driving, insisting he only told police he had been behind the wheel to prevent Martin from a DWI bust. Reedy still was found guilty of driving under the influence and had his driver's license suspended. He died in 1999 of pancreatic cancer.

"Billy's death really stung. Not that I was surprised, but it was very tragic for it to end that way," Willie Randolph said. "Billy always will have a special place in my heart. He was my first manager, and I felt like he went to bat for me and took me under his wing. There were guys who didn't like him, but Billy was always good to me. But I was there for all the crazy stuff, too, and watched him self-destruct so many times. You always hoped it wouldn't go down like that. You hoped maybe he'd stop all that at some point."

The Oakland product had been playing hard and partying harder since his arrival in the Bronx in 1950. The scrappy second baseman became a favorite of Casey Stengel, whom he previously had played for in the Pacific Coast League. Martin's hard-nosed approach and penchant for timely hits and key defensive plays helped seal the 1952 World Series. He then was named World Series MVP the following October, batting .500 (nearly double his career average) with a then-record 12 hits, two home runs, and eight RBIs. "We was beat by a .257 hitter," Brooklyn Dodgers manager Charlie Dressen lamented in *Baseball Dynasties: The Greatest Teams of All-Time*.

Nicknamed "Billy the Kid," Martin was known to hit more than baseballs during his career. He engaged in a series of on-field fights, including two with St. Louis Browns catcher Clint Courtney in 1952 and 1953. He also regularly hit the town with close pals Mantle and Whitey Ford. The three 20-something teammates made for an unlikely trio: Martin hailed from the West Coast, Mantle came from the Midwest, and Ford was a New York native. "I have no idea why I liked him so much. We never could figure it out," Mantle said of Martin in 1989. "Me and Whitey and Billy were all so different. That's why we got along so well."

That trio—along with teammates Yogi Berra, Johnny Kucks, and Hank Bauer—was involved in an infamous melee at the Copacabana nightclub in Manhattan while celebrating Martin's 29th birthday in May of 1957. The fight reportedly started when the Yankees attempted to quiet hecklers who were shouting racial taunts at performer Sammy Davis Jr. One patron was knocked out in the brawl and he later unsuccessfully sued Bauer for assault. Although the culprit never officially was determined, Yankees general manager George Weiss traded Martin, whom he deemed a bad influence on the others, one month later to the Kansas City A's.

A heartbroken Martin was particularly crushed that Stengel, who he considered a father figure, didn't defend him. They didn't speak for years before reconciling just before Stengel's death in 1975. Martin wouldn't return to the Yankees until Steinbrenner hired him to replace Bill Virdon in 1975. By then he had built a reputation as a fiery and aggressive skipper of the Minnesota Twins, Tigers, and Texas Rangers. Martin led the Twins to the Western Division title in 1969, but he also was involved in a fight with one of his players at a bar in August, punching out 20-game winner Dave Boswell. He was fired after the Baltimore Orioles swept him in the playoffs.

Steinbrenner axed Virdon midseason in 1975 and hired Martin, who had been fired again days earlier by Texas. Martin led the Yankees back to the World Series in 1976, though the Cincinnati Reds swept them in four games, and then to the championship behind Jackson's legend-making "Mr. October" performance in 1977. Of course, Martin and the Yankees' big-ticket free agent signee had feuded that entire year, including the prominent benching and near dugout scuffle in Boston in June.

Upon his ballyhooed arrival as a free agent the following season, new closer Goose Gossage also instantly got off to a rocky start with his manager when he refused to heed Martin's racially charged demand to drill Texas' Billy Sample with a pitch early in spring training. "I told Billy flat out, 'I'm not gonna do it,'" Gossage said. "I knew Billy was testing my loyalty to him. He came out in the outfield during batting practice and said, 'I want you to hit that blankety-blank Sample in the blankety-blank head.' For a minute I thought he was kidding, maybe for a flash, a second, but then I realized he wasn't. I said, 'Billy, I throw 100 miles an hour. I could kill him.' He said, 'I don't give a shit if you kill him.' I said, 'Billy Sample's never done anything to me. I won't do it.' I know he managed there, but whatever Billy had between him and Sample, that's between him and Sample. I had no beef with him. So Billy brought me in to face him in like the seventh inning. Sample comes up, I didn't hit him, and that was the end of our relationship before it even began."

Martin's relationship with Jackson only deteriorated until it resulted in his first firing by The Boss that summer. With the Yankees 14 games behind the Boston Red Sox in the American League East, Martin suspended Jackson for insubordination, essentially for ignoring an order to swing away after initially being given a bunt sign in the 10th inning of a tie game against the Kansas City Royals at Yankee Stadium on July 17. Jackson was eligible to return July 23 in Chicago, but Martin refused to put him in the lineup, playing catcher Thurman Munson in right field instead.

According to Madden's in-depth biography *Steinbrenner: The Last Lion of Baseball,* Martin already was stewing after learning that weekend from Chicago White Sox owner Bill Veeck that The Boss had offered earlier in the year to trade him straight up for Chicago manager Bob Lemon. While awaiting a team flight that night at Chicago's O'Hare Airport, Martin shredded Jackson, saying the team could win without him, to beat reporter Murray Chass of *The New York Times*. A few minutes later, Martin approached Chass and Henry Hecht of the *New York Post* and uttered perhaps the most infamous quote in team history: "The two of them deserve each other," Martin said of Jackson and Steinbrenner. "One's a born liar, and the other's convicted."

In the days before cell phones existed, Chass had to wait until the flight landed in Kansas City to find a pay phone and call Steinbrenner's home in Tampa, Florida, to relay Martin's quotes and score a juicy comment. A furious Steinbrenner dispatched general manager Al Rosen to Kansas City to fire Martin even if the move was couched as a resignation. Martin read a tearful statement, claiming he was partially misquoted. "I owe it to my health and mental well-being to resign at this time and I am very sorry there were things written about George Steinbrenner. He did not deserve them, nor did I say

Though they often clashed, George Steinbrenner (left) and Billy Martin (right) pose during a copacetic period before the 1983 season.

them," Martin said. "George and I have had our differences, and in most cases, we have been able to resolve them."

Lemon, Rosen's former Cleveland Indians teammate, was hired to replace Martin. His calming presence helped the Yankees erase that 14-game deficit and defeat Boston in a one-game playoff on October 2. Days after Martin's ouster, however, Steinbrenner had dropped another bombshell on Old-Timers' Day. Without consulting the front office, Steinbrenner secretly arranged for public-address announcer Bob Sheppard to read a statement that Lemon would move into the front office in 1980 and Martin would return as manager. Martin then emerged wearing his No. 1 jersey to deafening applause. "We were looking at each other like, *You've gotta fucking be kidding me,*" Gossage said. "Forget the Bronx Zoo. The circus was back in town."

Martin actually ripped Jackson again to local reporters about 10 days later, saying he never considered him a superstar, and "there were times I'd put Chicken Stanley ahead of him," referring to light-hitting shortstop Fred Stanley. However, it happened to be the same day the pressmen union at the primary New York newspapers—*The Times*, *Post*, and *Daily News*—went on strike, limiting its coverage and the damage.

Of course, Battling Billy would be axed four more times by Steinbrenner, and most of the firings were shrouded in controversy. It actually led to a series of humorous commercials for Miller Lite, in which they'd argue whether they drank the beer because it was "less filling" or "tastes great." The spots alternately ended with Steinbrenner saying, "Billy, you're fired" or "Billy, you're hired," and Martin each time replied, "Oh no, not again."

The "not again" feeling certainly was a common refrain when it came to Martin's series of prodigious public fights leading to his firing, most of them alcohol-fueled. In 1979 he fought a marshmallow salesman named Joseph Cooper at a hotel in Minneapolis. Free-agent pitching bust Ed Whitson broke Martin's arm in a fight in a scrap in a hotel bar in Baltimore in 1985. Three years later he brawled in the restroom at a topless nightclub named Lace's in Arlington, Texas. He also once fought a newspaper reporter in a bar in Las Vegas.

Somehow, by the 1989 offseason, Steinbrenner and Martin were readying for Billy Part VI. As The Boss always said, the unpredictable manager always "put fannies in the seats." At the Winter Meetings in Nashville, Tennessee, shortly before Martin died, he told future YES broadcaster Michael Kay, then a reporter with the *Daily News*, that Steinbrenner planned to bring him back to replace manager Bucky Dent, who had finished the '89 season (going 18–22) after Dallas Green was fired. Steinbrenner refuted the story to Madden, but it was clear Martin at the very least would have been warming in the bullpen at the first sign of trouble. (Dent ended up being replaced during the 1990 season by Stump Merrill.)

Almost two weeks before he died, Martin nearly was shot in an Indiana bar when a gun fell from a woman's purse and discharged. The manager of the bar told a reporter the bullet came "so, so close" to hitting Martin, who was no stranger to dangerous incidents in watering holes from the beginning to the end of his days with the Yankees.

21

THE CORE FOUR

Each member of the quartet fondly and reverentially referred to by Yankees fans as the Core Four—Derek Jeter, Mariano Rivera, Andy Pettitte, and Jorge Posada—debuted in the Bronx in 1995. They went on to win four championships in five years, beginning the following season under Joe Torre, and another with former teammate Joe Girardi in charge in 2009. Their manager for each of their initial major league stints actually was Buck Showalter, who was let go following a heartbreaking five-game playoff loss to the Seattle Mariners in 1995.

Posada only appeared in one game that season, but he was included on the postseason roster against the Mariners, along with Pettitte and Rivera. The only one of the four who wasn't activated was Jeter, but Showalter had him travel with the team so he could experience postseason play. He would reach the playoffs each of the next 12 years and in 16 of his 20 seasons with the Yankees.

By 2011 Rivera, Jeter, and Posada became the first set of three teammates in Major League Baseball, the NFL, the NBA, or the NHL to play together on the same team for 17 consecutive years. If only Pettitte hadn't left to pitch for his hometown Houston Astros from 2004–06—or briefly retired in 2010 before returning for two final seasons with the Yankees—he would have joined them. "You won't see anything like this happen again," Showalter told the *New York Post* in 2013. "There are too many variables for that to ever happen again. And what you have to remember is the makeup of those guys. The common thread was their agenda. They didn't branch off. They didn't want to disappoint each other. They were guys who never wanted to let their teammates down."

The disappointment was real, however, in June of 1995, when Jeter and Rivera sat in a booth and cried together at a Bennigan's in New Jersey, consoling each other over being sent back to the minors. No one recognized them that day, but that would change the following year and forever thereafter. Jeter snared American League Rookie of the Year honors, and Rivera was converted full time from a starter to the bullpen, where he emerged as a multi-inning weapon at Torre's disposal as a set-up man for John Wetteland during the Yankees' run to the 1996 World Series title.

Pettitte won 21 regular-season games in his second full season and made the most important start of that first championship run, the 1–0 victory against Atlanta Braves pitcher John Smoltz in Game 5 for a 3–2 lead. "Andy was the rock all of '96. I was out with the shoulder aneurysm for four months. Andy won 21 that year, and without him we don't get there," former teammate David Cone said. "We don't start the run in '96 without Andy. That's how important he was. That game he pitched against Smoltz was legendary. John Smoltz was probably the best big-game pitcher of his era and he was on his game that night. It wasn't even his fault he gave up a run because there was a misplay in the outfield. But Andy matched him every step of the way, and it was fitting. He was the best pitcher on our team all year long. Without him we don't get the rings."

Pettitte actually had been lit up in Game 1 of that World Series, but all he wanted was another chance. Aided by the expanded playoff format starting in his rookie season, he went on to record the most wins in postseason history (19). "That was my mentality when I took the mound in Game 5. It wasn't: maybe we can win. It was: this is ours," Pettitte said in a story on Jeter's website, The Players Tribune. "Smoltz was pitching against us, so thank goodness they made an error, and we scored a run on him, but I ended up pitching a good game after that terrible performance in Game 1. Coming back from that was a huge moment in my career. It was fun, man."

Posada considers his two signature coming-of-age moments to be catching David Wells' perfect game in 1998 and being tabbed by Torre to catch Roger Clemens in the 1999 World Series Game 4 clincher against the Braves after splitting time with Girardi most of those two seasons. "It was Jorgie's time," Torre said. "I came up as a catcher, so I knew what that meant to him. And he deserved it."

Posada made his first of five All-Star appearances in 2000 and finished third in the American League MVP voting in 2003 behind future teammate Alex Rodriguez of the Texas Rangers and Carlos Delgado of the Toronto Blue Jays. Posada also delivered a game-tying double against Pedro Martinez in Game 7 of the 2003 American League Championship Series to set up Aaron Boone's series-winning homer in the 11th. "What you didn't realize about those guys before you got here was how into winning they were," said Boone, who returned as the team's manager in 2018. "You knew they were good, but they were even better than you thought."

Personally, Posada was probably my favorite Yankees player to cover in more than two decades writing about baseball for the *New York Daily News*. He was always passionate, honest, accommodating, and available with the media. He also had a heart-tugging personal tale involving his son, Jorge IV, being born with craniosynostosis, a condition in which the skull doesn't develop evenly. Posada finished with 275 career homers and was the second Yankees catcher to belt at least 30 in one season (after Yogi Berra) and later joined by Gary Sanchez. He and Jeter also hold the team record for most games played together as teammates previously held by Lou Gehrig and Tony Lazzeri.

Pettitte ranks first on the Yankees' all-time list in strikeouts (2,020) and third in wins (219). He likely would have caught Whitey Ford (236) and Red Ruffing (231) had he not left for those three seasons in Houston. Pettitte and Rivera also hold the Major League Baseball record for most wins/saves by a starter/reliever duo with 72.

Although Rivera and Jeter were automatics for Hall of Fame induction, it should be no insult to Posada and Pettitte that they have fallen short of the demarcation line for Cooperstown. Judging by the early returns on admitted or confirmed performance-enhancing drug users, Pettitte's case will not be helped by his admission of using HGH after his name appeared in the 2007 Mitchell Report on PEDs. "I hate that any young person or whatever would ever think that I was trying to do something to cheat this game or to cheat other players or whatever," Pettitte said when he retired in 2013. "I know my heart and I'll tell you I've never tried to cheat this game. I've never tried to cheat anything in my life."

The Bronx fans never got cheated watching the Core Four blossom and help lead their team to those first four titles. Even as they fought for that fifth ring nine years after they'd won No. 4, a new generation of Yankees watched them closely and followed their lead. "It was just how hard those guys worked, all of them," CC Sabathia said. "By the time I got here in '09, they already had four rings, but they were working like they had none. That's the kind of thing that rubs off on everybody."

An international signing out of Panama for a mere $2,500 signing bonus and two middling draft picks in the 22nd and 24th rounds, respectively, Rivera, Pettitte, and Posada arrived first in the organization in 1990. Jeter, the sixth overall pick in the amateur draft in 1992, was more of a blue blood. The four of them didn't become teammates until they all reached Triple A Columbus in 1994. Drafted as a second baseman and converted to catcher, Posada first worked with Pettitte at Single A Oneonta in 1991. They teamed up with Jeter at Single A Greensboro the following year.

Posada was the first to officially retire for good in 2011. Pettitte and Rivera departed together in 2013, and finally Jeter retired in 2014. Their uniform numbers—20, 46, 42, and 2—all were retired to Monument Park. Rivera perfectly summed up the Core Four at his Hall of Fame induction in 2019: "These are my brothers."

22

A-ROD

Hal Steinbrenner calls it "the comeback of all comeback stories," and the owner of the Yankees just might be right. It was incredible, unfathomable, and absurd. Consider the miraculous fall and rise of Alex Rodriguez within five years of bottoming out with his season-long 2014 performance-enhancing suspension. He threatened to sue everyone from Major League Baseball to the Yankees and their medical staff, his former manager revealed his teammates referred to him as "A-Fraud," and his general manager pointedly and very publicly told him to "shut the fuck up."

Five years hence, Rodriguez had restored his reputation with the Yankees and his good standing with MLB commissioner Rob Manfred. He became one of the ubiquitous faces of the game as its most prominent television analyst—first on FOX and then on ESPN's showcase Sunday night telecasts. He hosted his own show on CNBC and started hanging out with Mr. Wonderful on *Shark Tank*. He got engaged to Jennifer Lopez and sat behind Lady Gaga and Bradley Cooper at the freaking Oscars. "Yankees, MLB, and everything else, I give him a lot of credit," Steinbrenner told me in 2019. "I was certainly honest with how I felt and what I felt he did to the organization and my family. It was clear right away that he was sincere in the lessons he learned, and what he learned from the whole ordeal, and how he wanted to change his life and be a different person. It was clear and it was believable, and I believed it. I am happy for him."

Obviously, there were $64 million reasons why Steinbrenner and the Yankees stood by Rodriguez once he was reinstated from a year-long suspension for violating MLB's policy on performance-enhancing drugs, specifically stemming from his involvement with Biogenesis, a South Florida anti-aging clinic that provided PEDs to various major league players. The 14-time All-Star still had three years remaining on the 10-year contract he signed after opting out during the 2008 World

Series, and not even the money-printing Yankees were going to eat that sum.

Even after the financial commitment had ended in 2017, Steinbrenner stood by him, keeping him on as a front-office advisor because he believed the transformation was genuine and legitimate. "With all my screw-ups and how badly I acted," Rodriguez said in 2016, "the fact that I'm walking out the door and Hal wants me as part of the family, that's hitting 800 home runs for me."

In an expansive profile in *Sports Illustrated* in 2019, mainly detailing all of the budding financial might of his investment company A-Rod Corp., Rodriguez likened his series of "screw-ups" to falling from the Empire State Building. "Nobody pushed me. I fucking jumped. No parachute. I have no one to blame but myself," he said. "But what's changed is: I got my ass humbled. I paid a deep penalty. I've learned lessons. And I'm different."

Whereas Derek Jeter mostly steered clear of the perils of the New York tabloids—despite dating a bevy of singers, actresses, and models—Rodriguez was a headline writer's dream in every conceivable way from the moment he arrived in New York in 2004. The star shortstops had been close friends when A-Rod played for the Seattle Mariners, but that relationship never was the same after he downplayed Jeter's importance to the Yankees in an *Esquire* interview in 2001 soon after he left the Mariners to sign a 10-year, $252 million deal as a free agent with the Texas Rangers. "Jeter's been blessed with great talent around him. He's never had to lead," Rodriguez said. "He can just go and play and have fun. And he hits second. That's totally different than third and fourth in a lineup. You go into New York, you want to stop Bernie [Williams] and [Paul] O'Neill. You never say, 'Don't let Derek beat you.' He's never your concern."

In his 2007 book, *The Captain*, author Ian O'Connor wrote that Rodriguez drove 90 minutes from the Rangers' training camp in Port Charlotte, Florida, to Jeter's home in Tampa, Florida, to apologize. A furious Jeter made him wait outside the house for several minutes. He barely acknowledged A-Rod as he "begged for forgiveness." By 2004 the estranged friends were coexisting alongside each other on the left side of the Yankees' infield. A trade that would have sent Rodriguez to the Boston Red Sox for Manny Ramirez and Jon Lester fell through over the players' union's concerns about A-Rod's agreement to alter his contract to facilitate the deal.

"I was completely bummed it collapsed," Rodriguez said in a 2019 interview with sports-talk station WEEI in Boston. "It was so depressing, never knowing that the Yankees were even an option at that point, and, of course, a few weeks later, I sat next to Brian Cashman in New York collecting my MVP award...and then a few weeks later, I have my press conference in New York."

The timing of that Baseball Writers Association of America dais meeting between A-Rod and the Yankees' GM couldn't have been more perfect. Third baseman Aaron Boone had blown out his knee playing pickup basketball. Cashman figured it was worth a shot to see if Rodriguez would be willing to make a position change. "He was willing to do whatever he could to come join us," Cashman said. "He was the better shortstop—I think everyone in the industry would recognize that—in terms of both defense and offense. But we weren't going to move our All-Star shortstop who's going to be a first-ballot Hall of Famer. We weren't going to ask that of Jeter to move. Jeter wouldn't have looked or played the same at third or second, even though he probably could have done it. But Alex, you could envision him. Because of that offense, he could be a Mike Schmidt at third base. And that's what he became. He was like, if that's what it takes to be part of a championship team, I'm all in."

That blockbuster move intensified the Yankees-Red Sox rivalry, which hardly needed to be amped up, especially after Boone's Game 7 American League Championship Series-clinching home run the previous October. Obtained in a deal that sent Alfonso Soriano to Texas, A-Rod exchanged blows with Red Sox catcher Jason Varitek after getting hit by a Bronson Arroyo pitch in July of 2004. A few months later, he swatted a ball out of Arroyo's glove in Game 6 of ALCS. The Red Sox became the first team in history to overcome an 0–3 hole on their way to ending their 86-year Curse of the Bambino.

Off the field, controversy also seemed to regularly find Rodriguez. The *New York Post* could have named its Page 6 gossip spread after him. A-Rod dated Madonna, Kate Hudson, and Cameron Diaz, following his divorce from his wife, Cynthia, the mother of his two daughters. He was photographed sunbathing in Central Park before a game. On a road trip in Toronto, he was photographed while still married with a buxom blonde under the *Post* front-page headline "Stray Rod." He posed for one magazine photo shoot kissing himself in a mirror. A *Post* photographer caught him flipping a ball to a female fan and asking for her phone number during a playoff game. *US Weekly* quoted a former fling saying he had a picture of himself as a centaur in his bedroom, a claim he insists is untrue. "I wish that was true because it's such a cool story," he told *The New York Times* magazine in 2019.

While Rodriguez actually produced in his first postseason with the Yankees in 2004, hitting .320 with three homers and eight RBIs in 11 games against the Minnesota Twins and the Red Sox, that wouldn't be the case the following three Octobers. He batted .159 (7-for-44) in 13 games in three consecutive first-round eliminations from 2005 to 2007. Joe Torre even had dropped him to eighth in the batting order for Game 4 of the American League Division Series against the Detroit Tigers in 2006. "Alex's life is baseball, and he enjoys the attention," Torre said in 2019. "When he first came over, I just sort of let him know that he didn't have to do it all here. In Texas, everything pretty much centered around him. That wasn't the case here, but he still wanted to be that guy. I think he put a lot of pressure on himself. There were other playoff games that he didn't do so well. He would come into the office and feel bad about his lack of contribution, but he wanted it so bad, and sometimes that becomes a curse. But I'm happy that he got his ring. I know how much that meant to him."

Following the team's first playoff miss in 14 seasons under new manager Joe Girardi, the '09 season started ominously. Rodriguez publicly acknowledged during a press conference attended by the entire team early in spring training that he'd taken steroids while with the Rangers. The admission confirmed a report by Selena Roberts of *Sports Illustrated* that he'd tested positive for PEDs during MLB's supposedly anonymous survey testing. "I knew we weren't taking tic tacs," Rodriguez said infamously about his steroid use.

A-Rod also missed the start of that season due to right hip surgery, but he ripped a three-run homer on the first pitch of his first at-bat of the season on May 8. He reached benchmark numbers (30 homers and 100 RBIs) in just 124 games. Rodriguez finally delivered as a Yankee in the postseason, hitting .438 with five homers and 12 RBIs through the first two rounds of the playoffs. He also went deep twice in the lone World Series of his career, a six-game win against the Philadelphia Phillies. "Oh man, Alex was unstoppable," Cashman said. "Just huge, impactful moments. Like I said when he retired, I wouldn't have what I have on my hand—this ring from 2009—if it wasn't for Alex and his massive contributions that year."

The postseason disappearing act, however, resumed the following year. A-Rod batted .152 (12-for-72) with zero homers or RBIs in his final four postseasons in pinstripes. Girardi even benched him for three games in 2012 against the Tigers and Baltimore Orioles. "2009 was the best October he had here, and we won the World Series," CC Sabathia said. "If he would've had more of those, we'd have more rings."

Rodriguez underwent his second hip surgery in 2013. On June 25 of that year, he infuriated Cashman by tweeting that he'd been cleared by a personal doctor unaffiliated with the Yankees to begin a minor league rehab assignment. "You know what? When the Yankees want to announce something, we will. Alex should just shut the fuck up," Cashman barked to ESPN reporter Andrew Marchand.

"Andrew can bring that out of you," Cashman jokingly recalled in 2019. "Obviously, I had my clashes with Alex because ultimately he went off-line, and his representation was based on some doctor that didn't speak for the Yankee doctors. I regret using that terminology, but I don't regret pushing back."

It was A-Rod who pushed back hard after MLB announced in August that he would be suspended for 211 games, the longest in history, for violating baseball's PED policy. He was allowed to play while his ban was appealed, however, appearing in 44 games the rest of the season. The suspension later was reduced to 162 games—or the entire 2014 season.

A-Rod kept swinging, especially during a wild in-studio interview with WFAN's Mike Francesa. "Were you guilty of any of these charges?" Francesa asked him.

"No," A-Rod replied.

"Did you do anything wrong?"

"No."

"Did you do any PEDs?"

"No."

"Did you obstruct justice? Any witnesses? Did you do anything that they accuse you of doing?"

"No."

"Nothing?"

"Nothing."

The three-time AL MVP also threatened to sue MLB, the Yankees, and their medical staff, but he never followed through. In November of 2014, the *Miami Herald* first reported that A-Rod had confessed to federal DEA agents and prosecutors earlier that year that he'd purchased and used illegal PEDs from Biogenesis founder Anthony Bosch. He also testified that he paid Bosch and an attorney hush money to keep the transaction quiet. The contrition tour began in a sit-down with Steinbrenner before A-Rod returned to the Yankees during spring training in 2015.

The road to "the comeback of all comeback stories" began that day, too.

23

DONNIE BASEBALL

Whenever you see a top PGA golfer, as Phil Mickelson was early in his career, referred to as "the best player to never win a major," it truly is a backhanded compliment. It's certainly no fault of Don Mattingly's that he almost certainly qualifies under that heading in Yankees lore. The first baseman known fondly as Donnie Baseball—or later Cap to his younger teammates—was an immensely popular and productive player by every measure and a beloved and respected captain in ways that cannot be quantified. "It's a tough pill to swallow, but I've always been pretty realistic about it," said Mattingly, the manager of the Miami Marlins under owner Derek Jeter. "Baseball's a team game, a different game, and I look at the teams we had in that era. It just didn't happen. We had some good teams but obviously didn't have the teams to win. I also know with the Yankees that's how everything is measured and I get that, too. I guess my answer is that everybody wants to accomplish that, but not everybody does."

Mattingly had the misfortune to play for the Yankees during a rare downturn in their storied history. He arrived as an unheralded 19th-round draft pick in 1979, the year after they'd won a second straight World Series. He departed a "what-if" icon after a 1995 return to the playoffs, one year before the Bombers of Joe Torre and Jeter captured their first of four titles in five years. The Yankees appeared in the postseason just once during Mattingly's 14-year career, which began with a seven-game cup of coffee in 1982, the year after they'd lost to the Los Angeles Dodgers in the World Series.

At 6'0" and 175 pounds, he'd never hit more than 10 home runs in any year coming through the farm system, but Mattingly opened eyes by hitting .358 at Class A Greensboro in 1980 and .332 across three levels in parts of five minor league seasons. The power would come, some scouts believed, once he took his pigeon-toed stance and tailor-made lefty swing to the short right-field porch of Yankee Stadium.

In his first full season in the Bronx, Mattingly and high-priced teammate Dave Winfield went down to the final days of the 1984 season, fighting for the American League batting title. Mattingly went 4-for-5 against the Detroit Tigers on the final day of the season to finish at .343—three thousandths of a point ahead of Winfield—with 23 home runs and 110 RBIs. "That year was like a no-lose situation for me," Mattingly said. "I was kind of the underdog, right? Winnie was the guy who came over as the big free agent. I'm the rookie essentially making nothing. It's a battle between two guys, but it's a tougher situation for Winnie. But what I gained from it was a total respect for Winnie in the way he handled it all. He could have made me feel uncomfortable. He never did. He treated me great. I know he wanted to win, too. It could have been uncomfortable."

Earlier that season, which was one year after Darryl Strawberry of the rival New York Mets had been named the National League's top rookie, George Steinbrenner boasted to the media: "You can talk all you want about Strawberry. I'll take Mattingly. He's the best young talent in baseball today."

The following year, Mattingly wasn't just one of the best players in New York. He indeed emerged as one of baseball's breakout stars, winning MVP honors and showing unforeseen power while delivering 35 home runs and 145 RBIs in a potent lineup that featured leadoff man deluxe Rickey Henderson and the bopping bats of Winfield and veteran designated hitter Don Baylor behind him. "How great was Rickey that year?" Mattingly said of Henderson, who finished third in MVP balloting with 24 home runs, 80 stolen bases, and 146 runs scored. "It was a great lineup. That was a year that just came together as probably our best offensive teams during my career."

Following the unceremonious firing of manager Yogi Berra with a 6–10 record on April 28, that 97-win club finished two games behind Toronto in the American League East, barely missing the playoffs. That was the closest the Yankees would come to qualifying until Mattingly's final season in 1995, but he continued a six-year stretch of All-Star appearances the following year as the MVP runner-up to Boston Red Sox pitcher Roger Clemens. He broke the single-season franchise marks for hits (238) and doubles (53), surpassing Earle Combs and

Lou Gehrig, respectively. "I couldn't believe what I was watching with Donnie. It was like watching Stan Musial, basically," said teammate Dale Berra.

From 1984 through 1989, Mattingly averaged .327, 27 home runs, and 114 RBIs, while also earning five Gold Gloves at first base. He was named team captain in 1991. The pinstriped faithful adored the small-town guy from Evansville, Indiana. "I really just loved playing there. Everybody wants if you play well for people to recognize it, but you didn't have to go search for attention there," Mattingly said. "A lot of guys come from a small town, and it can be intimidating being in New York, but the energy there just worked for me. New York to me is a no-excuse town. If you play hard and know how to play, you get attention for the little things: how to get a runner over or playing good defense. Fans recognized the real stuff other than just what ESPN throws at you. New York always appreciated good baseball. And I felt like that was perfect for me."

In 1987 Mattingly blasted six grand slams and tied Dale Long's major league mark with at least one home run in eight consecutive games, which Seattle Mariners outfielder Ken Griffey Jr. later matched. Sadly, that power would not last. Mattingly first experienced disc issues in his lower back that season, though he vehemently denied a report that the injury occurred as a result of wrestling with reliever Bob Shirley in the clubhouse. He even began getting some grief publicly from Steinbrenner, following a contentious arbitration battle in 1988.

A few years later, Mattingly and three teammates were suspended by manager Stump Merrill for not adhering to Steinbrenner's stringent haircut policy. Mattingly and columnists Steve Serby and Mark Kriegel were depicted with clean-shaven heads on the back page of the *New York Post* under the headline "Play Bald!" "Maybe I don't belong in the organization anymore," Mattingly told reporters after sitting out one game against the Kansas City Royals before shearing his locks for charity. "I talked to [general manager Gene Michael] about moving me earlier in the year. He said we'll talk at the end of the year. Maybe this is their way of saying we don't need you anymore."

Don Mattingly hits a home run during 1986, a year in which he had a .352 batting average, 31 home runs, and 113 RBIs.

That same year, Mattingly had appeared with other baseball stars in the classic episode of *The Simpsons* called "Homer at the Bat," in which Homer Simpson's boss, Mr. Burns, remarks, "Hey, Mattingly, for the last time get rid of those sideburns." When Burns kicked Mattingly off his ringer softball team, Mattingly said, "I still like him better than Steinbrenner."

The episode, which also featured Steve Sax and future Yankees Wade Boggs, Darryl Strawberry, and Roger Clemens, actually was taped before Mattingly's hair-today, gone-tomorrow benching. "It's incredible how that was about that," Mattingly said. "It blew up into this big whole thing, and those $2.88 residual checks I still get are awesome. I don't even cash them anymore. I like to think there's a guy keeping the books somewhere, wondering what happened to $2.88."

Back problems limited Mattingly to 102 games in 1990, in which he hit a career-worst .256 with just five home runs. He played more regularly in subsequent years, but his power stroke appeared zapped. He averaged 11 home runs over his final five seasons, likely costing him any chance at the Hall of Fame.

Fans often compared Mattingly's case and statistics to those of Kirby Puckett, the former Minnesota Twins center fielder whose career was cut short by eye problems. Puckett, who actually is credited with giving Mattingly the nickname "Donnie Baseball," was enshrined in his first year of Hall of Fame eligibility in 2001. "My career is what it is," Mattingly said in 2008. "Things happened the way they happened. If my self-worth about who I am is tied to that, there's something wrong."

The Yankees had fully recovered from a last-place finish in 1990 and owned the best record in the American League (70–43) under manager Buck Showalter when a 1994 players' strike resulted in the cancellation of the World Series. A late 25–6 closing kick in '95 earned the Yankees the American League wild-card and a first-round series against Seattle. "We had to win almost every day for like a month," Mattingly said. "The playoffs, getting in, I knew what my situation was. I knew that was gonna be it, and just to get in was a great feeling. The feeling of finally playing in Yankee Stadium in playoff games was indescribable."

The Yankees blew a 2–0 lead and lost in the American League Division Series to the Mariners. Game 5 ended with Edgar Martinez's double in the bottom of the 11th inning to plate Griffey with the winning run. Mattingly batted .417 (10-for-24) with a home run, four doubles, and six RBIs. His Game 2 blast at Yankee Stadium came against Andy Benes, who also was from Evansville. "Don Mattingly is my favorite of all time and he'll never be touched," longtime radio voice Suzyn Waldman said. "His ovation in '95 when he came out before the playoffs—the whole place went nuts. The introduction of Donnie, that's something I still tear up when I think about that."

Longtime teammate Jim Leyritz ended Game 2 with a 15th-inning homer: "We all came into '95, saying, 'Let's get to the World Series.' But I think Buck really made that season about getting Donnie to the playoffs. And then we go to Seattle and lose three straight. My home run became a footnote, and that was it for Donnie. We were all crushed."

Bronx native Michael Kay was a self-described "huge Mattingly guy" even before he became a beat writer for the *New York Post* and the *New York Daily News* in the late 1980s and then transitioned to the radio booth in the early part of the next decade. "For him to have that kind of series after waiting all those years, and when [he] hit the home run, the stadium was literally shaking. That was the Don Mattingly postseason," Kay said. "I felt like I wasn't finished watching him, as they say. That was the only time I've seen an entire team playing for one guy. But one of my most vivid memories of all the time I've been around the Yankees was that flight home from Seattle. The entire team was crying, but they were all consoling him. They weren't crying for themselves. They were just sad. It was amazing. Everyone was hugging him, and they just knew that was it."

Wade Boggs said he and Mattingly cried together in the training room immediately after the Game 5 loss, but he could not talk his teammate out of retiring. "I said, 'You can't go. We're right on the verge of winning it all. Really think it over.' But he said he was going home," Boggs said. "I said, 'We came so close this year and we'll be back again next year.' There was really no talking Donnie out of not coming back. It was a shame. He decided to hang it up, and coincidentally we ended up winning the World Series the next year."

Mattingly didn't officially announce his retirement until January of 1997, but the Yankees moved on and won it all without him in '96. They acquired Tino Martinez from Seattle to replace him at first base, and Joe Torre supplanted Showalter as manager. "A lot of people have the fallacy that it was all about my back, but I was able to manage it by then," Mattingly said. "It was really about my boys being back home in Indiana, getting older, playing ball, and they weren't even coming to New York anymore for the summers. They wanted to play at home, be in leagues, and that's really one of my biggest regrets. That's really what weighed on me. I couldn't put that out of my head. It was not a great existence for me. I still loved playing with the guys, and especially at the end, when I felt like I had figured out everything physically, but I just couldn't get over the family part of it. It was exciting to watch those guys have success the next year, but it was hard from the standpoint that I'd fought for so long to get there. But the reason why I was home was the right reason."

Steinbrenner convinced Mattingly to don pinstripes again as a member of Torre's coaching staff in 2004—first as hitting coach and later as a bench coach—but he was passed over for Joe Girardi when Torre stepped down after the 2007 season. "It wasn't a crusher or anything like that. I understood. I had no managerial experience," Mattingly said. "I probably wasn't ready for it, and at the end of the day, I wasn't ready at all at that time with all the stuff that was going on behind the scenes personally. It was kind of a blessing for me."

Mattingly, who was going through a divorce from his wife, Kim, followed Torre to Los Angeles and received his long-awaited first managerial shot as Torre's replacement in 2011. He led the Dodgers to three straight division titles from 2013 to 2015—something no manager in team history had done. He lost in the National League playoffs each time, however, and the sides parted company following a 2015 National League Division Series loss to the New York Mets.

Mattingly then was hired by the Miami Marlins. Despite a 57–105 record during a painful rebuilding 2019 season, he was granted a two-year contract extension through 2021 by Jeter. "You think you're ready for something. And there's a lot of stuff you learn as you go," Mattingly said. "Look at Joe with the Mets and the Braves and the Cardinals before he got to the Yankees. If I can win my first World Series as a manager, like Joe did, that's what it's all about."

24

SCOOTER

There is not a more endearing figure in Yankees history than Phil Rizzuto, the undersized Italian American kid from Queens who went to work at the big ballpark in the Bronx for 55 years. Holy cow, indeed.

Dubbed "Scooter" by a minor league teammate in the 1930s, Rizzuto was an unlikely centerpiece of the Yankees' five-peat dynasty from 1949 to 1953 before also spending four decades entertaining and charming fans as the beloved, idiosyncratic announcer of thousands of games on WPIX through the 1996 championship season.

I mean, how could a slap-hitting, 5'6" shortstop with a .273 lifetime average and 38 career home runs possibly be the MVP of Joe DiMaggio's Yankees, much less of the entire American League? Rizzuto enjoyed a career season in 1950—Whitey Ford's first with the Yankees—but his .324 batting average, his 125 runs scored, his 36 doubles, and his 92 walks were merely the tangible reasons he took home the prestigious hardware. He also had been runner-up to Boston Red Sox star Ted Williams the previous year. "He's the greatest shortstop I've ever seen," Casey Stengel beamed after the 1950 World Series sweep against the Philadelphia Phillies, according to *The Ultimate Yankee Book: From the Beginning to Today*. "Honus Wagner was a better hitter, but I've seen this kid make plays that Wagner never did."

This glowing compliment actually was quite the reversal for the nutty Ol' Perfessor. Years earlier, Stengel had sent a teenaged Rizzuto dejectedly back home to the Richmond Hill section of Queens following a tryout with the Brooklyn Dodgers, telling him he was too small to play in the majors. In a scene right out of *Goodfellas*, Stengel even told him: "Go get a shoeshine box." "When he became the Yankee manager in 1949, I reminded him of that, but he pretended he didn't remember," Rizzuto said years later. "By '49 I didn't need a shoebox anyway. The clubhouse boy at the stadium shined my Yankee spikes every day."

Rizzuto shined for 13 seasons—despite an interruption for three years of military service during World War II—as the Yankees' dependable defensive wizard after taking over for Frank Crosetti in 1941, winning eight World Series titles. Yankees ace Lefty Gomez called the 150-pound shortstop a "Lilliputian," but Rizzuto proved his big-time worthiness by hitting .307 as a rookie. He also was a more than worthy adversary to Pee Wee Reese, his cross-borough Hall of Fame counterpart with the Brooklyn Dodgers. "The little guy in front of me, he made my job easy," DiMaggio said. "I didn't have to pick up so many ground balls."

No less of an authority than Ty Cobb called Rizzuto "the best bunter I ever saw." "My best pitch is anything the batter grounds, lines, or pops in the direction of Rizzuto," Yankees pitcher Vic Raschi said in *Pride of October: What it Was To Be Young and a Yankee.*

Rizzuto's popularity only grew when he transitioned into the TV booth alongside "Voice of the Yankees" Mel Allen and fellow Hall of Fame broadcaster Red Barber after the front office essentially forced him to retire on Old Timers' Day in 1956. Like Stengel before him, Howard Cosell famously told Rizzuto he'd never last as a broadcaster, saying, "You look like George Burns and you sound like Groucho Marx."

But Rizzuto lasted 40 years, which is longer in the Yankees' booth than anyone in team history, including Allen. It was a second career he lovingly and teasingly shared with nearly two dozen partners. His time with Frank Messer and former St. Louis Cardinals first baseman Bill White from 1971 through 1984 was the most memorable for my generation. "I always tell people there were four male voices heard in my house growing up: my dad, Scooter, Messer, and Bill White," Michael Kay said in 2019. "I just felt like Phil wasn't broadcasting. We were just hanging out with him, sitting in his living room. Because I was such a Yankee freak, I knew what a great player he was. For him to transition into the broadcast booth and do it for so long, I think he might be the most beloved broadcaster of all time. I know everyone loved the wacky stories, but if you listen to some of Phil's big calls, he was a damn good broadcaster, too. He really knew how to tighten it up. But yes, when the game was all over the place, he was going all over the place."

Indeed, Scooter's charming idiosyncrasies and tangents while interacting with his partners were classic. I loved that he almost exclusively referred to his fellow announcers by their last names. He'd say, "Come on, White" or "You know what, Messer?" Later on, Rizzuto similarly would needle "Murcer" or even "Seaver," the New York Mets pitching legend who worked games for Channel 11 for five seasons after his retirement during a rare ugly period for the Yankees between 1989 and 1993. "Bobby just adored Scooter," said Murcer's widow, Kay. "He loved that part of his career so much. Scooter was such a big part of his years there—when he first broke in, not being familiar with broadcasting at all. He was one of the first ones to make that transition. He would crack Bobby up all the time with his stories."

In addition to his trademark phrase "Holy Cow," which he attributed to a high school coach "trying to get me to not swear so much," Rizzuto talked on the air about everything from his golf game, Italian restaurants, or bakeries he'd frequented ("Oh, the cannolis,") and his bride of more than 50 years, Cora. He sent countless birthday wishes to friends and fans. He famously left games early to beat the traffic over the George Washington Bridge to his home in Hillside, New Jersey. He referred to any player making an error as "a huckleberry." He used "WW" in his scorebook for "wasn't watching," a designation often repeated when I sat beside longtime baseball columnist and *New York Daily News* colleague Bill Madden in the Yankee Stadium press box.

Rizzuto became so transcendently popular in his second act that comedian Billy Crystal impersonated him on *Saturday Night Live*, and the rock singer Meat Loaf used his voice in the 1978 hit "Paradise by the Dashboard Light." Rizzuto's play-by-play on the tune was euphemistic for a young man getting to first base, second base, third base, and attempting to "hit a home run" with a woman. "Okay, here we go, we got a real pressure cooker going here. Two down, nobody on, no score, bottom of the ninth," Rizzuto said in the song. "There's the windup, and there it is, a line shot up the middle. Look at him go.

This boy can really fly. He's rounding first and really turning it on now. He's not letting up at all, he's gonna try for second. The ball is bobbled out in center. And here's the throw, and what a throw! He's gonna slide in head first. Here he comes. He's out. No, wait, safe, safe at second base! This kid really makes things happen out there. Batter steps up to the plate. Here's the pitch, he's going. And what a jump he's got. He's trying for third. Here's the throw. It's in the dirt, safe at third. Holy cow, stolen base! He's taking a pretty big lead out there, almost daring 'em to try and pick him off. The pitcher glances over, winds up, and it's bunted, bunted down the third-base line. The suicide squeeze is on. Here he comes, squeeze play, it's gonna be close. Here's the throw, here's the play at the plate. Holy cow, I think he's gonna make it!" Then female singer Ellen Foley, later a cast member of the 1980s sitcom *Night Court*, interjects "Stop right there!"

For years, Rizzuto maintained he didn't realize the intended sexual innuendo of his scripted words. "Phil was no dummy. He knew exactly what was going on and he told me such," Meat Loaf, a lifelong Yankees fan, told ESPN in 2007 after Rizzuto's death "He was just getting some heat from a priest and felt like he had to do something. I totally understood. But I believe Phil was proud of that song and his participation. He was one of the greatest storytellers baseball has ever seen. He would talk about the game, but he'd also talk about Billy Martin's fishing trip or a great restaurant nearby or somebody's 50th birthday. He was very unique."

After years of waiting to be voted in to the Baseball Hall of Fame in Cooperstown, Rizzuto was elected in 1994 by the Veterans' Committee, which included close friends Reese, White, and longtime teammate Yogi Berra. The Yankees had retired his uniform No. 10 in 1985, fittingly presenting him with a (holy) cow. The animal knocked him over, making everyone laugh yet again.

Upset that he'd worked a game in Boston instead of traveling to Dallas for Mickey Mantle's funeral, Rizzuto briefly resigned from WPIX in August 1995. He later admitted he "made a big mistake" and came back for one final season to make it an even 40. Joe Torre's Yankees sent him out with one more championship.

When Rizzuto died in August 2007 of pneumonia at 89, fellow Hall of Fame shortstop Derek Jeter, a rookie in Scooter's final season in the booth, revealed that one of his most prized possessions was an autographed photo of the two of them together. "You always remember the way people treat you, especially when you're coming up," Jeter said. "He was just always positive. It's always great when you have players that you respect and had played the game and been successful, and they go out of their way to tell you nice things."

25

BUCKY "FREAKING" DENT

Bucky Dent's middle name, for the record, is Earl. Everywhere, that is, except Boston.

There, folks still refer to him more than four decades later as Bucky "Bleeping" Dent, Bucky "Freaking" Dent, or something a little more inflammatory. "I just go with the initial F," Dent said with a laugh in 2019.

Dent's three-run home run into the netting above Fenway Park's Green Monster in the seventh inning put the Yankees ahead in a one-game divisional tiebreaker in 1978 and catapulted them to their second straight championship, and Dent was named World Series MVP. That's quite the star turn for a light-hitting shortstop who totaled just 40 home runs over a 12-year career. "First of all, it changed my life dramatically," Dent said of his blast against the Boston Red Sox. "Sports is a game of moments. I think every kid dreams in the backyard of hitting a home run like that. I know that was my dream growing up. I wanted to be Mickey Mantle. To be up in that spot, it seemed like the whole world was watching. You had Boston, you had New York. One of my closest friends after I hit the home run called me up and said, 'Your life will never be the same.' I didn't really understand what he meant, but now I do 40-something years later."

Aaron Boone similarly would dash Boston's hopes a quarter-century later, forever earning himself the same middle name or initial in Beantown because of his game-winning home run in the 11th inning of Game 7 of the 2003 American League Championship Series. Dent's homer wasn't quite that dramatic, though the circumstances of the entire '78 season certainly were startling for a Yankees squad looking to defend its 1977 World Series title.

With imported closer Goose Gossage not living up to his free-agent contract and with '77 October hero Reggie Jackson still feuding with manager Billy Martin, the turmoil rolled to a full boil, and the Yankees slipped to 14 games behind Boston in the American

League East by July 19. Two days earlier, Jackson was suspended for disobeying the manager's order to swing away after initially being given a bunt sign in Kansas City. Martin was out as manager later that week following a verbal jab at Jackson and George Steinbrenner.

Third-base coach Dick Howser took over for one game before Steinbrenner brought back former pitching coach Bob Lemon, who'd been fired earlier in July as manager of the Chicago White Sox. "It's very simple. All the turmoil was gone," Chris Chambliss said. "Billy made those quotes about Reggie and George, and it was this here-we-go-again kind of thing. But the addition of Lem was just the perfect personality and calming influence. He just let everybody play. There was not a lot of junk with him."

Lemon's arrival spurred a 48–20 surge through the end of the season, including a four-game sweep of the Red Sox at Fenway by a 42–9 aggregate score from September 7 to 10 referred to by the New York papers as "The Boston Massacre." The Yankees then flushed a one-game lead on the final day of the regular season. Catfish Hunter was knocked out in the second inning of a 9–2 loss in Cleveland, and Boston defeated the Toronto Blue Jays 2–0 behind a two-hitter from Luis Tiant to force the first one-game playoff in the American League since the Red Sox lost to the Indians in 1948.

Ace lefty Ron Guidry started for the Yankees on three days' rest and hurled six-and-one-third innings of two-run ball despite giving up a second-inning homer by Carl Yastrzemski to improve to 25–3 in a Cy Young-winning season. Boston starter Mike Torrez had been a Yankees pitcher most of the previous season following a trade from the Oakland A's and won 14 games and went the distance in the Game 6 World Series clincher against the Los Angeles Dodgers.

Torrez, who signed with Boston as a free agent, had held his former mates scoreless before Chambliss and Roy White stroked one-out singles to start the go-ahead rally in the seventh.

Pinch-hitter Jim Spencer flied out, and Dent fouled a 1–0 pitch off his left foot, causing a brief delay.

While Dent was being attended to by a trainer, the batboy brought him a new bat borrowed from teammate Mickey Rivers. Russell Earl "Bucky" Dent choked up and got the next pitch up in the air. Here's the call from Yankees announcer Bill White: "Deep to left...Yastrzemski will not get it. It's a home run!"

Years later, various Red Sox, including Tiant and Fred Lynn, have charged that Rivers' bat was corked, a notion both "Mick the Quick" and Dent vehemently have denied for decades.

"That's something we made up to mess with them," Dent said.

(A brief aside on the colorful Rivers: in spring training one year probably around 2010 or so, I approached him for what my sports editor wanted as a "Where Are They Now?" piece for the Sunday paper. Rivers' reply? "Where am I now? Tell your boss I'm right here." And then he laughed hysterically and walked away.)

Anyway, Dent and Torrez remained friendly throughout the years, making appearances together, and Dent often greets his former teammate with "Hey, the bat was corked!"

Torrez's standard reply is: "I knew it!"

"I never saw the ball go in the net. I was running hard because I didn't hit a lot of home runs and I didn't think it was high enough," Dent said of his homer. "When I rounded first, I saw the umpire signal it was a home run and I saw Yastrzemski's knees buckle at the wall, but we knew that game was far from over. We still had three more innings in Boston against that lineup at Fenway in a park that anything can happen."

After his epic blast, Dent circled the bases with only his fifth homer of the season. The Yankees tacked on to their 3–2 lead with two more runs on a Thurman Munson double later in the inning and a solo homer by Jackson against reliever Bob Stanley in the eighth.

Gossage surrendered run-scoring singles to Yastrzemski and Lynn in the bottom half, and two runners reached against Goose while nursing the 5–4 lead in the ninth inning. But Lou Piniella barely snared a Jim Rice liner he'd lost in the sun for the second out, and Yastrzemski popped up to Graig Nettles to seal the division crown. "Yaz comes up, and, Jesus, that's what I went to bed the night before thinking, *I'm gonna be facing Yaz for the final out*," Gossage said. "It was eerie almost, the power of suggestion. That was the last thing I wanted, but I was preparing myself for it. Nettles squeezing it was the first deep breath I took all day. I'd never been in a game of that magnitude. Yankees-Red Sox, you couldn't write a better script or a better scenario. We hated them, and they hated us. And Bucky, are you kidding me? Of all the guys!"

Indeed, Dent was an unlikely hero. The Yankees had acquired him from the White Sox for Oscar Gamble and future Cy Young winner LaMarr Hoyt two days before Opening Day in 1977. Dent had run into Steinbrenner a few years earlier at a Chicago Bulls game he was attending with then-agent Nick Buoniconti, the former Miami Dolphins linebacker. Dent claims The Boss told him, "I've been trying to get you, kid."

"It took a few years, but there I was," Dent joked. "I went from a last-place team in '76 to a team that had a chance to win the World Series. That's always your dream as a player. For me, to play in New York, the Yankees. Mantle was my hero growing up. To win two world championships in a row, I was pretty lucky."

After a third consecutive elimination of the Kansas City Royals in the ALCS, Dent also went 10-for-24 (.417) with seven RBIs to earn MVP honors in the World Series rematch against the Dodgers. Manning second base for injured Willie Randolph, reserve infielder Brian Doyle batted .438 (7-for-16), and Jackson belted a World Series-sealing home run in the Game 6 clincher. Gossage was on the mound for the final out.

Dent didn't agree with Goose's assessment that "everything after the Red Sox game was anticlimactic," but he's definitely more remembered, especially in Boston, for that shot into the netting at Fenway. "Boston-New York, it's definitely a fun love-hate relationship on both sides," Dent said. "Yankee fans, there isn't a day that goes by that somebody from New York tells me, 'I was however many years old, and that game changed my life. I love you.' Red Sox fans also say I changed their lives, but it's 'I hate you.' And it's Bucky F-ing Dent. They still call me that up there. It's like a badge of honor I can wear, I guess, and still do proudly."

26

AARON "BLEEPING" BOONE

For the longest time, Aaron Boone did not fondly recall one of the most memorable home runs any Yankees batter—any baseball player really—ever has belted. The Yankees did not win the World Series in 2003, falling in six games to the Florida Marlins a couple of weeks after Boone had propelled them there with a game-winning blast against Boston Red Sox knuckleballer Tim Wakefield in the 11th inning of Game 7 of the American League Championship Series. "Now, I definitely appreciate it more and I'm far more grateful of the moment," Boone said in 2019 during his second season back in the Bronx as the Yankees' manager. "But for a long while, I definitely distanced myself from it. Because the vivid memory for me, almost like I'm in a dream, it's just silence in the stadium with this October fall air and the Marlins' voices off in the distance celebrating. I'll never forget that feeling because you never know how many chances you're going to get. But as time's gone on, I really am grateful and appreciative of it."

Boone was a third-generation major leaguer. His grandfather, Ray, was a two-time All-Star third baseman who won a World Series title as a rookie with the Cleveland Indians in 1948. His father, Bob, won seven Gold Gloves as a catcher during a 19-year career and won a championship with the 1980 Philadelphia Phillies. His brother Bret, who was in the FOX booth the night of the homer, was a three-time All-Star infielder during a 14-year career.

Aaron Boone had made the lone All-Star appearance of his dozen seasons in the majors in 2003 for the Cincinnati Reds before the Yankees acquired the 30-year-old third baseman at the July 31 trade deadline. Boone met the Yankees in Oakland the next day, but he didn't have much of an offensive impact the rest of the season, batting .254 with six home runs in 54 games. To open that postseason, he was just 5-for-31 without a homer in a four-game ousting of the Minnesota

Twins in the American League Division Series and the first six games against the Red Sox.

In Game 3 of the ALCS, the longtime rivals had engaged in a wild brawl at Fenway Park. Manny Ramirez took steps toward the mound after a marginally high-and-tight pitch from Roger Clemens in the fourth inning. In the top half of the inning, Red Sox ace Pedro Martinez had drilled Yankees outfielder Karim Garcia with a pitch and then pointed at his own head as an apparent warning while Jorge Posada, David Wells, and other Yankees jawed with him from the visiting dugout.

Martinez also tossed 72-year-old Yankees bench coach Don Zimmer, who had managed the Red Sox in 1978 when Bucky Dent forever earned "Freaking" as his middle name, to the ground during the ensuing bench-clearing melee. Zimmer was removed from the ballpark on a stretcher. "The whole thing with Zim was sad," Joe Torre said. "We were headed out of the dugout, and I looked over at my left and I wanted to say, 'Zim, no.' Because I know he was pissed at Pedro and his antics, but I knew it wouldn't have done any good. You weren't going to keep Zimmer on the bench. He ran over there, and Pedro was just sort of like a matador, and *ole'd* him. It was like everything stopped when he wound up on the ground. In the end Zim was just mortified by the whole thing. He apologized for embarrassing baseball. It was really sad more than anything."

After the teams alternated wins through the first six games, the struggling Boone was benched by Torre for Game 7 in favor of utilityman Enrique Wilson, who had strong career numbers against Martinez. "It was hard. I was obviously frustrated and disappointed I wasn't in the lineup," Boone said. "Then early on, it's not looking too good, and it's like, man, here's this opportunity, and you're not able to make an impact. Nothing was going well, and then the comeback started."

Wilson actually committed a key throwing error that helped Martinez carry a 4–0 lead into the fifth inning, and then Jason Giambi hit the first of two solo home runs that resulted in a 5–2 game heading to the bottom of the eighth. "We thought, *Okay, now we're in striking distance,*" Giambi said. "Pedro's tough, especially if you give him a lead like that. But the guys on the bench started saying, 'Now we have a chance.'"

One of those guys was Boone, who thought to himself that he'd better be prepared for any opportunity that came up. His teammates made sure he would receive one. Derek Jeter stroked a one-out double and scored on a single to center by Bernie Williams. Boston manager Grady Little visited the mound with lefty reliever Alan Embree, and righty Mike Timlin was warmed and ready in the bullpen. Martinez later admitted he was gassed, but, of course, he told his manager he could continue. Little stuck with his tiring ace, and Hideki Matsui ripped an 0–2 fastball for a ground-rule double. On Martinez's 123rd and final pitch of the night, Posada looped a two-run double to shallow center to knot the score.

Boone actually entered the game in that inning as a pinch-runner for Ruben Sierra, who'd been intentionally walked while batting for Wilson. While Mariano Rivera worked three scoreless innings for the Yankees, Wakefield had thrown a spotless 10th, retiring Matsui, Posada, and Giambi in order. The knuckleball specialist had pitched effectively in winning Games 1 and 4, but Boone would tag him with the Game 7 loss as the first batter in the 11th inning. "I was considering taking a strike or taking a pitch just to see one. And as I'm walking to the plate, I thought, *You know what? Forget that. Just get a good pitch to hit and hammer it*," Boone said. "Whether it's the first pitch or the seventh pitch, get a good pitch without overthinking it. It happened to be a first pitch. It was up, and I got it."

Not that he'd envisioned Boone's heroics, but Torre claimed the previous night he'd dreamt that Manny Ramirez would be running dejectedly off the field. "Boonie was a mess, man," Torre said. "He was trying so hard. He was just swinging as soon as the pitcher let the ball go. Now facing Wakefield, I remember saying to him, 'Just try to hit a single to right, but that doesn't mean you're not gonna hit a home run to left. Knuckleball. Be flat-footed, be patient.' First pitch, there it was: a knuckleball up high, and he knocked it out of the park. And there was Manny trotting off the field."

And there was Boone, as unlikely as it would have seemed a few hours earlier, trotting around the bases. "The memory itself is very fuzzy," he said. "There's moments in your life that you can remember photographically—exact feeling, where you were, who was there, what you were saying. That was not one of them. I remember consciously thinking, *Look around, drink this in, try and soak it in as best you can.* But it's all a blur, a very fuzzy memory. I learn more just seeing the video of it and I pick out somebody in the crowd or a player and watch the different reactions. That's been the most fun for me."

By the time Boone passed second base, Rivera already was kneeling and kissing the mound. Boone high-fived third-base coach Willie Randolph and jumped into a pile of jubilant teammates led by Jeter, who waited for him at home plate. "Movie script stuff," Brian Cashman said. "Honestly, it was such a scary night. We were on the verge of getting beat. It was like a tale of two games. The first half we are being dominated and shut down by one of the great pitchers in the game. The second half we're coming back and then somehow having this extraordinary comeback being finished off by a walk-off homer by a guy who had really struggled for us."

In Boynton Beach, Florida, 1978 homer hero Bucky "Freaking" Dent had dozed off moments before Boone's blast. His wife Marianne's screams jarred him from his sleep. "As the game is going on, I was thinking, *Who's going to do it?*" Dent said. "Who's got a B in their name? Bernie? Maybe Boone? Who's got a B in their name to keep it going against the B for Boston? There was Babe, Bucky, Buckner, and now Boone."

Cashman and first-base coach Lee Mazzilli both likened the high-leverage comeback to quarterback Tom Brady leading the New England Patriots back from a 25-point deficit to defeat the Atlanta Falcons in overtime in Super Bowl LI in 2017. "It's like the Yogi line, 'It ain't over 'til it's over,'" Mazzilli said. "With Brady, with us, with both teams actually, it wasn't ever over."

Eleven days later after Boone's blast, the Red Sox announced that Little's contract for the 2004 season would not be renewed. And the following season, the Red Sox and first-year manager Terry Francona became the first team in baseball history to overcome a three-game hole in a seven-game series, vanquishing the Yankees in the 2004 ALCS before finally halting their franchise's 86-year Curse of the

Bambino drought with a World Series victory against the St. Louis Cardinals.

Much earlier in 2004, though, Cashman received an unexpected phone call while vacationing with his family in Anguilla. It was a call that altered the next decade of team history.

Boone, who had agreed to a one-year contract worth $5.75 million earlier in the offseason, had agent Adam Katz phone Cashman to confirm that he'd torn the anterior cruciate ligament in his left knee while playing pickup basketball at a health club near his family's home in Southern California. "It was a Friday night. My brother-in-law was in town, staying with us. And he was going to play hoops," Boone said. "I hadn't done my cardio that day, and we weren't doing anything, so I said, 'Sure, I'll go.' We weren't more than a few minutes into the game, and it's not like I was even really mixing it up or doing anything reckless or anything. It was 5-on-5, and there was a ball saved out of bounds. It's thrown over my head, and I'm running the other way and get it at the free-throw line. I'm kind of extended out like I'm catching a pass in football, and this guy just comes in and wipes me out, undercuts me. It was just some guy. I didn't even know him, but it was violent."

Boone had torn his ACL a few years earlier in 2000, but he immediately believed this injury was "even worse, totally different." "I actually hobbled out of there, drove away, and kind of cried myself home," Boone said. He was examined the next day by the Anaheim Angels' team orthopedist, Dr. Lewis Yocum, who confirmed his initial fears. "I heard him say 'ACL,' and I was like, 'Oh no,'" Boone said.

The standard Yankees contract prohibited participation in even the most mundane activities, such as bowling, billiards, table tennis, and shuffleboard. Boone insisted he never considered making up another cover story to tell the Yankees. "I don't live my life that way," he said. Getting seriously injured playing basketball, though, led the Yankees to void Boone's contract; he said he received "basically a million bucks" in termination pay.

Later that year, Boone signed a two-year deal with the Indians, but his injury led the Yankees to the franchise-altering acquisition of Alex Rodriguez, a lightning rod for controversy in the Bronx over the next decade. A-Rod also replaced Boone as the lead analyst on ESPN's *Sunday Night Baseball* once the latter left the booth to accept the job as Joe Girardi's managerial replacement in 2018. "Maybe he'll be the next manager," Boone joked about A-Rod. "I met his daughters, and he was telling his daughter the story. 'I became a Yankee because he got hurt. Now, I have the Sunday night job that he had.' I said to her, 'So that means your dad is going to manage the Yankees next.'"

Boone, of course, had no immediate plans to relinquish the post. The Yankees won 100 games in his first season at the helm before losing to Boston in the division series, and the Red Sox won their fourth title since 2003 later that fall. They improved to 103–59 in 2019 before losing to the Houston Astros in the ALCS. "As soon as Cash called me about the job, I said, 'Hell yeah, I'm all in,'" Boone said. "The ultimate in sports is the New York Yankees. They transcend sports. To be back in the organization now, to be entrenched in it, to see how healthy and strong we are as an organization makes you proud to be a part of it."

27

DAVID WELLS' PERFECT GAME

An unapologetically hard-partying, authority-challenging, beer-swilling, weight-battling, history-revering yet unmistakably talented left-hander, David Wells began 1998, the winningest season in Yankees history, with a 5.23 ERA over his first nine starts. But on May 17, a Sunday game against the Minnesota Twins, more than four decades after Don Larsen's 1956 World Series gem against the Brooklyn Dodgers, Wells joined the initial "imperfect man" as the only Yankees to that point in their history ever to throw a perfect game. His buddy David Cone would join them barely one year later. The other mindboggling factoid about Wells joining Larsen was that they both were alumni of the same high school, Point Loma High, in San Diego.

If anything the legend of Wells' perfect game only grew when he revealed in his autobiography a few years later he'd pitched that day "half-drunk," or at least with a "skull-rattling" hangover from a late Saturday night on the town. "Perfect games aren't easy to come by. There's only 23 of them," Wells said 20 years later in 2018. "You would never in a million years think that you're going out hungover as shit and go out and throw a perfect game. You've got to be lucky to do those things. To me, it's just amazing that it can happen, especially in the state of mind that I was in. For the first few innings, I was like, 'Holy shit, how am I going to do this?' It was a rough night. As Joe Torre always said, 'That's Boomer being Boomer.' I think I overdid it. But it worked out, right?"

His fellow pitcher thought it was a watershed moment. "I remember thinking and telling him right away that this is going to turn his season and his entire career around," Cone said. "It was such a defining moment for him. He was such a history buff. He was a memorabilia collector and he was so into Yankees history and memorabilia, especially anything to do with Babe Ruth. I think he understood what all of that meant. The historical nature of doing something like this at Yankee Stadium, it just lifted him to a whole new level."

Cone and Paul O'Neill both said they believed Wells was the "best pitcher in the league" the remainder of 1998. Indeed, Wells finished that season on an 18–3 run with a 2.93 ERA beginning on that date, including a 4–0 mark in five starts during the Yankees' 11–2 postseason run. Wells has claimed his pregame bullpen session on May 17 was "horseshit," but pitching coach Mel Stottlemyre felt differently and simply told Torre "wow" before the first pitch. "That doesn't normally mean a perfect game or even a win, but it did this time," Torre said. "Boomer was outstanding. That's something he can take with him wherever he goes."

Following the historic season and a World Series sweep of his hometown San Diego Padres, Wells took that memory with him to Toronto as the main piece in a three-player package for Blue Jays pitcher Roger Clemens during the first week of spring training of 1999. "Boomer was floored by it," Cone said. "He had essentially made it through the winter and got to camp. I was really surprised, even though it was Roger Clemens, the best pitcher of our generation. That's all the front office needed to say at that point, but we all were stunned, and Boomer was absolutely crushed."

Wells found his way back to the Yankees by 2002, winning a team-high 19 games, but his recollections of his shining moment turned much of the clubhouse and his manager against him the following spring. In addition to discussing his hangover in his biography, *Perfect I'm Not: Boomer on Beer, Brawls, Backaches and Baseball,* Wells also alleged that at least 25 percent of major league players were using steroids, and amphetamines and other stimulants were made available in the Yankees' clubhouse. He also took shots at current and former teammates throughout the book.

Fined $100,000 by general manager Brian Cashman in March, Wells then issued a statement essentially claiming he'd been misquoted in his own autobiography, which was coauthored by Chris Kreski. "When I took the mound the day of my perfect game, I was ready to pitch," Wells said. "I certainly was not drunk. Anyone who knows me, knows I only intended to write this book in the spirit of fun. I am sorry the book hasn't been taken in that vein."

Of course, Wells has claimed in various interviews thereafter that he had been drinking heavily the night before his gem at a *Saturday Night Live* after-party, hanging out with the likes of Jimmy Fallon, Will Forte, and Fred Armisen until nearly 5:30 AM. That really must have been some afterparty, considering the *SNL* season finale hosted by actor David Duchovny had aired the previous weekend on May 9. Also the three actors that Wells mentions were not yet members of the cast during the 1997–98 television season. Whatever the story, when Wells addressed and apologized to his teammates in March 2004, several of them pointedly reminded him about being disloyal to the sanctity of the clubhouse. Years later, he took issue with Torre "for doing the same shit" and "airing dirty laundry" from the clubhouse in his 2009 book, *The Yankee Years*. Wells called his former manager a "punk" and a "coward" and publicly threatened to "knock him out."

During his first stint with the Yankees, Wells had been fined for wearing a Babe Ruth game-worn hat he'd previously purchased for $35,000 in the first inning of a game against the Cleveland Indians on June 28, 1997. The leather band inside the cap was inscribed "G. Ruth," and historians dated the authenticated size-7⅜ hat to the 1930s. Torre wasn't amused then either. He made the hefty lefty remove it, fining him $2,500 for wearing the non-regulation heirloom. Wells later claimed he paid the fine with 2,500 dollar bills. Wells reportedly sold the cap at auction in 2012 for more than $537,000.

The price Wells could fetch for his own memorabilia was forever changed that Sunday afternoon in 1998 against the Twins. The previous week, he had been called out publicly by Torre for being "out of shape" and "a little overweight" after practically flushing all of a nine-run lead without getting out of the third inning in an eventual 15–13 win in Texas.

The Twins' starting pitcher that day was LaTroy Hawkins, whose 21-year major-league career through 2015 included a half-season with the Yankees in 2008. "Even being on the losing end, it was cool to be a part of any time baseball history is made," Hawkins said. "By the end I secretly found myself rooting for it."

By the seventh inning, a TV camera showed Cone in the dugout with his Yankees jacket buttoned up above his mouth, but he sensed that someone needed to needle the increasingly nervous starting pitcher. While everyone else avoided Wells, Cone told him to try throwing a knuckleball because "your stuff sucks." "I'm sure I was getting blamed if he didn't finish it," Cone joked.

The superstitious Wells has said he also tried to tune out hearing radio announcers John Sterling and Michael Kay discussing the perfect

Bernie Williams, Willie Banks, and Darryl Strawberry carry David Wells off the field after the pitcher, who has claimed he was hungover from partying, throws a perfect game in 1998.

game on the radio while the Yankees batted in the middle innings. "Maybe it's the old reporter in me, but I've always believed that you say what's happening," Kay said. "That's how Vin Scully always has done it. If it's good enough for him, it's good enough for me."

Wells threw 79 strikes among his 120 pitches and had 11 strikeouts in his performance, which ended with Pat Meares' routine fly ball to O'Neill in right. "That was an easy play and that's what you want. A perfect game is much more stressful than a no-hitter because any little thing can mess it up," O'Neill said. "Going through it with Wells and Coney and even before them Tom Browning in Cincinnati, it's an amazing day to play baseball and be a part of it. I'm sure it's more stressful for the pitcher, but it's extremely stressful for the players, too, because you don't want to be that one guy that does something wrong."

Sterling's radio call on WABC-AM was just right: "The 0–1, swung on, he's gonna get it. Popped up to right field, O'Neill near the line. He…makes the catch! David Wells! David Wells has pitched a perfect game. Twenty-seven up, 27 down. Baseball immortality for David Wells!"

Three days shy of his 35th birthday, Wells raised both arms in the air as he waited for the ball to descend into O'Neill's glove. He then emphatically pumped his left fist toward the ground as his teammates mobbed him. O'Neill handed Wells the ball from the final out after joking that he'd throw it into the stands. Darryl Strawberry, Bernie Williams, and Willie Banks carried their teammate off the field to a raucous ovation from a crowd of more than 49,000 buoyed by a Beanie Baby promotional giveaway.

By the time Wells finally made it into the clubhouse, three magnums of champagne already were waiting in front of his locker. I also vividly remember actor and Yankees fan Billy Crystal standing outside Torre's office looking to get his ticket stub signed by Wells. "I got here late. What happened?" Crystal quipped.

What happened next was a phone call set up by former sportswriter and current George Steinbrenner adviser Arthur Richman. He arranged a conversation between Larsen and Wells, who'd graduated from Point Loma 35 years apart and thrown perfect games 42 years apart.

"I'm honored to share this with you, Don," Wells said. "I mean, two guys from the same high school doing this? What were the odds? Who would ever believe it?"

The following day, Larsen told *The New York Times* that Wells "will think about this every day of his life just like I do."

"Nobody can take this away from me ever. No matter what happens," Wells said, fighting back tears. "I just wish a few other people were here to see it." Wells' mother, Eugenia Ann, aka "Attitude Annie," rode with the Hells Angels for years before her death in 1997. Wells enjoyed telling stories of the notorious biker gang coming to his Little League games, offering cash as incentives for strikeouts and victories. "It's easy to dedicate a game when something goes good, but I dedicate every game to my mom," Wells said. "My family is always with me in heart, mind, and soul."

Minutes earlier Cone had sat in the dugout alone with Wells and pointed to the scoreboard. "Enjoy the moment," Cone said. "You'll never see that again."

He almost was wrong. More than three months later on September 2, Wells nearly pitched another perfect game in Oakland. He retired the first 19 batters before A's slugger Jason Giambi ended the bid with a two-out single in the seventh inning of a two-hit shutout. Wells actually said afterward that he was "relieved" not to have duplicated the feat because of all the attention his earlier masterpiece had received. "Everyone wants a piece of you," he said.

The Hall of Fame certainly wanted their piece of Wells, but he refused the museum's customary request for game-used gear. Wells kept it all except for loaning the Yankees his glove to display at Yankee Stadium. The entire Twins lineup also signed the pitching rubber for him.

The 239-game winner later served for four seasons (2015–18) as the head baseball coach at Point Loma, his and Larsen's alma mater, while donating and raising $2 million for a field that was named in his honor. Wells told reporters in 2015 that he was hoping the job would lead to one with a major league team—perhaps even the Yankees. It had not. "I would have never in a million years thought I'd be doing this," Wells said. "I've been trying for the last seven years to get into the big leagues and failed miserably. I think they look at the fact when I played, I was outspoken. But if I'm going to take a job, I'll be serious about it. I'm not the guy who played. I don't think they've gotten over that yet."

No, not all endings are perfect. Wells certainly was not either. For one day in May of 1998, he was as flawless as any pitcher in the history of the game.

28

DAVID CONE'S PERFECT GAME

The aging All-Star pitcher had accomplished so much in a distinguished career that clearly was coming to a close, but there he stood on the mound at Yankee Stadium a few outs from baseball immortality. That was the setting for the 1999 movie, *For Love of the Game*, in which Kevin Costner's character, 40-year-old Billy Chapel, completed a perfect game for the Detroit Tigers against the mighty Yankees in the final game of the season and in the final start of his career.

In 1999 a real-life Hollywood ending similarly played out in the Bronx with a script that may have been even more unfathomable. Barely one year after David Wells had joined 1956 World Series legend Don Larsen as the only Yankees in history to author perfectos, 36-year-old David Cone threw his own 27-up, 27-down masterpiece. Incredibly, Larsen and his 1956 World Series batterymate Yogi Berra were in attendance. "Kevin Costner actually wrote me a congratulatory note, a really nice note telling me that I did exactly what he was trying to capture in *For Love of the Game*," Cone said in 2019, 20 years after his own defining pinstriped moment. "I never expected to hear from him, but I think the similarities really struck him. That he took the time to reach out was really cool."

Just about all of the circumstances of July 18, 1999 were cool and beyond—both for Cone and a Yankees fanbase that finally had welcomed Berra back to Yankee Stadium on Opening Day for his first appearance since George Steinbrenner had fired him 16 games into the 1985 season. That Sunday afternoon game in July against the Montreal Expos was dubbed Yogi Berra Day, and Larsen threw out the ceremonial first pitch to the Hall of Fame catcher. Berra even used Joe Girardi's mitt during the festivities. "So you've got Larsen touching Cone's glove, and Dad touching Girardi's glove, and then another perfect game? How can that possibly happen?" Yogi's son, Dale Berra, said. "Stunning day. We were all sitting in George Steinbrenner's box, just amazed, completely blown away."

As Cone eventually would be, though he at first was only embarrassed for making a mistake in his initial exchange with Larsen that afternoon. "Don was at the mound, and I said to him, 'So, are you going to go run and jump in Yogi's arms again?' And he goes, 'You got it wrong, kid. He jumped in mine,'" Cone said. "I considered myself a history buff, too. So much for that."

History would soon be on Cone's side. Just not mine. I had covered Wells' perfecto the previous year as the beat writer for the *New York Daily News*. It was one of six no-hitters I have worked during my writing career. That includes Roy Halladay's gem for the Philadelphia Phillies against the Cincinnati Reds in the 2010 National League Division Series, joining Larsen as the only pitchers with no-hitters in postseason history.

I had a scheduled day off for Cone's perfecto, obliviously spending the day at a Long Island beach with my family. We didn't learn what was happening until late in the game, when I was alerted by nearby sunbathers listening to John Sterling's and Michael Kay's radio call. As temperatures soared to 98 degrees, Cone went to work. None of the Expos ever had faced him before, but the second batter of the game, Terry Jones, ripped what Cone thought "for sure was a triple" only to watch Paul O'Neill make a tumbling catch in right-center field.

Ricky Ledee and Derek Jeter homered in a five-run second inning, but after Cone retired the first nine batters on 32 pitches, a rain delay arrived, lasting 33 minutes. Cone stayed loose by throwing with batboy Luis Castillo, known as "Squeegee," in the narrow hallway outside the clubhouse. Cone worried if it lasted much longer "especially at my age," Joe Torre wouldn't allow him to continue when the game resumed. "I was going to leave that up to Coney," Torre said. "At that point of his career, that's his call."

The game also marked the 59th birthday for Torre, who previously had attended Larsen's perfect game as a teenager. As he noted in 2019, "there couldn't have been many" others who were present for all three in Yankees history.

When Cone returned from the delay, his stuff appeared even sharper, Joe Girardi told him years later. But as the innings wore on, most of his teammates, even Girardi, superstitiously steered clear of Cone in the dugout. He had been the one to break the ice with Wells the previous year, jokingly telling his pal to try a knuckleball. Veteran designated hitter Chili Davis served that role for Cone, grabbing a catcher's mitt to warm him up before the top of the seventh. "When he warmed me up, I was kind of lobbing it in there, waiting for Girardi to get his equipment on," Cone said. "I didn't really let anything go, and Chili took offense to that. He said, 'Hey, I can catch your shit. Let it go.' Just the way he said it and looked at me with this smirk on his face made me laugh, and that was what I needed."

Scott Brosius made a nifty stab of Wilton Guerrero's grounder headed for the shortstop hole in the seventh. Chuck Knoblauch, whose throwing yips became more pronounced that season, made a perfect throw to Tino Martinez after a backhanded play up the middle to nail Jose Vidro in the eighth. "When Knobby made that play," Cone said, "I thought, *Okay, maybe this is my day*."

Cone gave himself a pep talk in the clubhouse bathroom. "Out loud I was telling myself, *Three more outs, you've got this. You've waited your whole life for this*," Cone said. "You try to talk yourself into staying positive, but there's all these negative thoughts that come in like, *What if you hang a slider, or what if you blow it? How are you going to react if you do?* You try to push that thought out of your mind. I've said this before, but I could feel my hair growing as I walked out to pitch the ninth inning. The crowd's reaction, the adrenaline rush that you feel, it's like nothing I've ever felt before or since."

Hearts stopped briefly until Ledee came up with a wobbly grab of pinch-hitter Ryan McGuire's sun-splashed liner to left for the second out of the ninth. Cone was one out away. "Hanging slider to McGuire, I figured that was it," Cone said. "That ball caught Ricky, not the other way around."

With a crowd of nearly 42,000 on its feet, including Larsen and Berra, Cone's 1–1 slider to Orlando Cabrera was popped up to Brosius in foul territory. Cone dropped to his knees with his hands on his head in disbelief. Girardi was the first to arrive, pulling the pitcher on top of him. They had their moment frozen in time—just like Berra jumping into Larsen's arms.

With Berra's No. 8 painted behind home plate, Cone remarkably had thrown 88 pitches.

"To this day, I still can't believe they were there," Cone said. "Whatever you believe in—the stars aligning, the baseball gods—everything was tested, every fiber of my being was tested that day because of everything that happened. At the end of the day, I feel like the most incredible stat of the whole day was the 88 pitches. Yogi wore No. 8. Go figure. If you're a numerologist or whatever you believe in, it was on display that day."

Davis, Knoblauch, and Girardi carried Cone off the field. When he got to the top of the ramp, the 69-year-old Larsen was waiting outside the clubhouse. "I hugged Don like he was my own dad," said Cone, whose parents Ed and Joan Cone had tuned into the game on FOX in the latter innings. The former World Series hero had watched closely. "I shook hands with David before I threw the pitch to Yogi, and we sat and watched the game. Usually, I'm gone after three or four innings with something to do," Larsen told MLB.com in 2019. "As time went on, they made us both stay. We both stayed and watched him do his marvelous performance."

After Cone phoned his parents in Kansas City, he soon received another call from Wells in Boston, where the Toronto Blue Jays were facing the Boston Red Sox. He wanted to find a way to get to New York that night to celebrate, the way Cone had with him the previous year.

"He had to pitch the next night, so there was no way to get that done," Cone said. "But that was Boomer, always trying to make things happen."

A bleary-eyed Cone made it to City Hall the next morning to receive a key to the city from mayor Rudy Giuliani. The Yankees would repeat as champions that October and again in 2000, but that latter season was Cone's last in pinstripes. Cone went 4–14 with a 6.91 ERA in 2000, though he did record an important out against the New York Mets' Mike Piazza in the World Series. "Those were the final pitches I threw as a Yankee," Cone said. "That season was devastating for me. I just could not figure out what was going wrong. Obviously, now I look back and can just see that I was a pitcher in decline. My skills were diminishing before my eyes. My slider sort of quit sliding, my fastball lost a couple of ticks in velocity. Even when I did have a decent game going, there was always one pitch or inning that got away from me, that one big inning that a lot of declining pitchers talk about. As a pitcher you're kind of in denial. You're the last one to know when your stuff doesn't work anymore. That was kind of the case for me. I was in denial all year long."

Cone hooked on the following year with the Red Sox, which he admits "was really weird," and then pitched five games back with the Mets in 2003. He returned in 2008 as a full-time broadcaster with the YES Network, using his insights and embrace of analytics to become one of baseball's top analysts.

29

THE 2000 SUBWAY SERIES

Joe Torre thought Mike Piazza had gotten all of it. Who knows how the only World Series ever played between the Yankees and the crosstown New York Mets would have turned out if Piazza, who had been embroiled in a vortex of controversy months and days earlier involving opposing pitcher Roger Clemens, had taken Mariano Rivera's ninth-inning cutter over the wall in center field at Shea Stadium in Game 5 of the 2000 Fall Classic?

Torre certainly knew what it would have meant if Bernie Williams had not hauled in that final out of the Yankees' 4–2 series-sealing win and what it would have meant if the Mets had completed that comeback and possibly found a way to overcome a 3–1 series deficit. "God, I didn't want to have to face them," Torre said. "Of course, when it was determined that it was going to be against the Mets, you'd go to drop off your dry cleaning, and it was all anyone was talking about. All the pressure and stress was ratcheted up pretty well in the organization and in the city. Right down to that last out, when Piazza got it up in the air, I thought it was a home run. I screamed, 'No, no!' But then I see Bernie just settling under it on the warning track and I couldn't believe it. It never felt so good to be wrong."

Even having won the World Series in three of the previous four years, the 2000 Subway Series assuredly was "going to be a different animal" for the Yankees, Brian Cashman said.

From 1921 through 1956, the Yankees faced either the New York Giants or the Brooklyn Dodgers in the World Series 13 times, winning 10 of them. The two National League rivals had left the city for the promise of riches in California in 1958, and this marked the first time the Yankees squared off in October against the 1962 expansion team from Queens. "You couldn't get away from it. It was everywhere in the city," said Paul O'Neill, who had played the night his father had died during the 1999 World Series clincher. "After '99 I was just hoping I could get back to a World Series where I could enjoy it again. But I think the pressure was really on us in 2000. It was kind of a no-win situation. If we win, we're supposed to win. If we don't, we never hear the end of it."

The Yankees barely were above .500 (37–35) when Cashman swung a trade on June 29, acquiring lefty-swinging outfielder David Justice from the Cleveland Indians for Ricky Ledee and pitchers Jake Westbrook and Zach Day. Justice, whose Atlanta Braves and Indians teams had appeared in postseason play seven times during the 1990s, batted .305 with 20 home runs, 60 RBIs, and a .977 OPS (on-base percentage plus slugging percentage) in 78 games thereafter with the Yankees. Thus, long before the Yankees had a Judge patrolling right field, they had a Justice.

"George and everybody else had their eyes on us getting Juan Gonzalez, Moises Alou, or Sammy Sosa," Cashman said. "Instead, we swung a deal directly with Cleveland. We surprised everybody when we acquired Justice, who fit perfectly into our culture and our ballpark and had an MVP-level performance the rest of the way. He basically catapulted us to greatness once again."

That wasn't exactly true, as the Yanks slogged through a 3–15 conclusion to the regular season to finish with 87 wins, their lowest total over a 17-year span from 1996 through 2012.

"We really stumbled into the postseason that year," Torre said. "I remember having a meeting in Baltimore when we clinched the division, even though we didn't win, but because Boston had lost. I said, 'You guys should just drink the champagne before the game,' because they were so uptight trying to get things done."

Cashman's other key summertime acquisition had been lefthanded pitcher Denny Neagle, who arrived from the Cincinnati Reds for four prospects. That package included Drew Henson, a two-sport star whose football claim to fame was sharing snaps at quarterback as a sophomore at Michigan with a senior named Tom Brady. Henson returned to the Yankees less than a year later and signed a $17 million contract to concentrate on baseball, but he never amounted to much professionally in either sport, appearing in eight games in the major leagues and later nine in the NFL. Neagle didn't have much positive impact on the Yankees either, posting a 5.81 ERA over 16 games the rest of that season.

The Yankees needed the full five games to vanquish the Oakland A's in the American League Division Series, as Clemens lost Game 1 and Game 4. The 11-time All-Star redeemed himself in a six-game elimination of the Seattle Mariners in the American League Championship Series, striking out 15 in a scintillating one-hit shutout in Game 4 for a 3–1 series lead. Justice was named series MVP after posting eight RBIs over the six games.

That left the Mets led by manager Bobby Valentine and their star catcher, Piazza, in their franchise's first World Series appearance since their 1986 championship run as the team standing in the way of the Yankees' third consecutive title. "The Boss told me flat-out: 'You better win or else,'" Cashman said. "It felt like if we lost to the Mets, it would've taken away from our previous championships like they didn't count. I'd never been scared of losing before, but I was scared of losing to them. It was miserable actually. It was a no-win situation."

Part of that misery was because Steinbrenner also had been engaged in summer-long renegotiation with Charles Dolan over the team's MSG Network television rights, which ultimately led to the formation of the YES (Yankees Entertainment and Sports) Network in 2002. "George was riding us so hard because of that. Plus the media clearly was getting tired of the '96-through-'99 Yankees story," Cashman said. "They were looking for something new and fresh, and here come the Mets pushing their way to the table."

The Yankees took Game 1 on a blown save by Mets closer Armando Benitez in the ninth inning. O'Neill started the rally with a 10-pitch walk. Acquired in June from the Dodgers in exchange for Jim Leyritz, Jose Vizcaino drove in the winning run with a 12th-inning single for his fourth hit of the game.

The ongoing war between Clemens and Piazza was renewed the next night with one of the most bizarre storylines in World Series history. Clemens had beaned Piazza in the helmet on July 8 at Yankee Stadium during the back end of a rare day/night doubleheader with one game played in each team's home ballpark. Piazza had smoked Clemens for three homers among five hits in eight at-bats since The

Rocket had joined the Yankees the previous season. In the first inning of Game 2, Clemens broke Piazza's bat with a pitch, and the barrel landed at the pitcher's feet. Clemens then oddly hurled it back in the batter's path while Piazza jogged toward first base, emptying both dugouts. "What is wrong with you?" Piazza yelled.

Clemens insisted he initially thought the shard was the ball, but FOX broadcaster Tim McCarver immediately dubbed it intentional, calling the pitcher's actions "foolish" and "a blatant act." Piazza has maintained for years that he agreed with the latter take. "The same thing I said at the time, I say now; Clemens was certainly not trying to hit him with the bat," Torre, who had served since 2011 as MLB's executive vice president for baseball operations, said in 2019. "Of course, that was only blown up from what happened right before the All-Star break when Roger hit Piazza in the head. This just put the cherry on top. Everything against the Mets was always magnified, and all of a sudden, you add this on top of it? It's crazy."

Yankees coach Willie Randolph, who would later manage the Mets, had been at the plate for the A's when a livid Clemens was ejected by umpire Terry Cooney for arguing balls and strikes in Game 4 of the 1990 ALCS with the Boston Red Sox. Randolph's time managing the Mets from 2005 through 2008 also may have altered his perspective on the 2000 Clemens-Piazza incident. "I feel Roger lost his cool, lost his composure. It was a total snappage," Randolph said. "Piazza pretty much owned Roger for a while there, and Roger was such a competitor. It was almost like in basketball, blocking someone's shot and yelling, 'In your face!' I actually couldn't believe Piazza didn't charge the mound, but I give him credit for keeping his cool. He meant so much to his team. He couldn't get ejected there, so I thought he showed great restraint. And Roger, I don't think he was trying to hit Mike with the bat. I think it was more of a 'Take that, I finally got you this time.'"

Clemens, who later was fined $50,000 by Major League Baseball, ended up hurling eight shutout innings that night for the Yankees' second straight win. He didn't appear again in the series and wouldn't have to bat against the Mets until Shawn Estes comically threw a fastball behind him during an interleague game in 2002. Estes and Piazza both hit homers against him in that game.

Clemens later was named in the Mitchell Report on performance-enhancing drugs and failed to gain election into the Hall of Fame from the Baseball Writers Association of America ballot in his first seven tries on the ballot through 2019.

On the undercard to the Clemens vs. Piazza title bout, Steinbrenner also personally ratcheted up the rivalry when he had moving vans bring in furniture from the Yankee Stadium clubhouse into the cramped visiting clubhouse at Shea Stadium. During Game 4 a water pipe had burst, flooding the remodeled locker room, and players returned to find The Boss helping bail water from the area. "You just knew George was going to inject himself into that series somehow," Randolph said.

"George didn't like anything about Shea Stadium. He didn't think it was worthy of a major league facility. He especially didn't think the visiting clubhouse was worthy of the New York Yankees," Cashman said. "Then there was this water breakage, and he set up camp in our clubhouse, which I don't think was really a healthy environment for our players to be coming in and out of there while he was there. Thankfully, we won in five, but coming in and out of that clubhouse with him in there all the time was pretty intense. It was funny, but it was not a fun scene."

Derek Jeter, the eventual series MVP, ripped a first-pitch home run to lead off Game 4. David Cone, who had been shelled for a 6.91 ERA during the regular season, came out of the bullpen to replace Neagle in the fifth inning and retired Piazza on a pop-up for the final out.

"I obviously had a vested interest in that World Series. I had played for the Mets for six years and I was on the outside looking in, wondering if I'd even get a chance to make an appearance," Cone said. "I was desperate to do so. I was thankful that Joe gave me that chance, that one chance."

Backup infielder Luis Sojo then notched the game-winning single up the middle against Al Leiter in the top of the ninth inning of Game 5. Sojo, a popular reserve on the previous three championship teams, had departed as a free agent and started the 2000 season with the

Pittsburgh Pirates before being reacquired via waivers in August. He had popped out with the bases loaded ahead of Vizcaino's game-winning hit in Game 1. "I wasn't one of the main guys on those teams, but to come through at that particular time was the highlight for my career," Sojo said. "I just remember Jeter saying, 'We've been in the World Series so many times, but this is the one we gotta win. Yankee fans would be all over us for the rest of our life if we don't beat the Mets.'"

Not to mention Steinbrenner, who for years had treated annual exhibitions against the Mets known as the Mayor's Trophy game, as well as the early years of interleague play, which began in 1997, as end-of-the-world events. "That to me was the most nerve-wracking series I've ever been a part of, and I wasn't even playing," Randolph said. "Being in New York and understanding the bragging rights and the first Subway Series since the Dodgers and the Giants left town, that was not as much fun as it should have been. We knew if we didn't win their fans and our fans would never let us hear the end of it."

30

THE COLONELS

It seems unfathomable that Colonel Jacob Ruppert had to wait until nearly a century after he purchased the Yankees and almost 75 years after he died to be recognized by the Baseball Hall of Fame. Although late Yankees owner George Steinbrenner similarly continued to be overlooked as of 2019, Ruppert—the man who brought Babe Ruth to New York, oversaw the construction of Yankee Stadium, and presided over their first seven World Series-winning teams—finally was enshrined posthumously in 2013 after decades of surprising omittance.

In fact, the top four members of the Yankees' brain trust from that golden era of the 1920s and beyond reside together now in Cooperstown. General manager Ed Barrow was the first to get the call in 1953, seven-time World Series winning manager Joe McCarthy joined him four years later, and his predecessor, Miller Huggins, was inducted in 1964. "Growing up, I was under the impression that he was inducted sometime in the 1940s or 1950s, but I guess it never happened," K. Jacob Ruppert, the former owner's great-grand-nephew, said when Ruppert's induction was announced in December of 2012. "Some things in history aren't appreciated. If it's not in the here and now, it's off the radar screen. But his mark is now indelible."

A four-term former U.S. Congressman who inherited his family's brewery business, Ruppert transformed the Yankees from perennial American League also-rans (four winning seasons in 12 prior years) into baseball's dominant superpower soon after he and partner Tillinghast L'Hommedieu Huston purchased the Yankees from previous owners, Frank J. Farrell and William S. Devery, in 1915 for a mere $463,000. Ruppert also had been a colonel in the National Guard, and Huston had been a U.S. Army engineer and colonel, so they fondly were referred to as "The Colonels" in the local press. Ruppert bought out his partner's share for $1.5 million, a tidy return on investment for Huston to take into retirement, in 1922.

By then, of course, Ruppert had purchased Babe Ruth from the Boston Red Sox for $125,000 and was on the verge of opening Yankee Stadium in the Bronx in 1923, which coincided with the Yankees' first of four World Series wins in a 10-year span. The Yankees won four more titles beginning in 1936, but Ruppert only was alive for three of them after dying of phlebitis in 1939.

The Ruppert estate maintained ownership until 1945 before selling to lawyer Larry MacPhail, tin magnate Dan Topping, and real-estate developer Del Webb. The latter two bought out MacPhail in 1947 and owned the team until 1964, when they sold to CBS.

Former Yankees general manager Bob Watson was a member of the Hall of Fame's 16-person pre-integration panel that elected Ruppert, longtime umpire Hank O'Day, and 19th century catcher Deacon White in December 2012. "We were surprised to learn he wasn't in," Watson said of Ruppert.

The Yankees finished above .500 only once in Ruppert's first three seasons as owner. He hired Huggins, the diminutive former player/manager of the St. Louis Cardinals, at the behest of American League president Ban Johnson in 1918. After Huggins posted a record of 80–58 in 1919, Ruppert swung the deal for Ruth, changing the course of team history, baseball history, and American history. After years of salary disputes, fines, and suspensions over his unruly behavior, the retired Ruth showed up to Ruppert's bedside 20 years later just before the Colonel died at Lenox Hill Hospital, according to the book, *The Colonel and Hug: The Partnership that Transformed the New York Yankees*. "It was the only time in his life he ever called me 'Babe' to my face," Ruth said. "I couldn't help crying when I went out."

Late in the 1929 season, Ruth had been heartbroken when Huggins died unexpectedly at 50 years old. The Yankees and their Murderers' Row lineup were coming off back-to-back World Series sweeps of the Pittsburgh Pirates and St. Louis Cardinals. "Hug was the only man who knew how to keep me in line," Ruth said.

Huggins' team went on to win 302 regular season games, three American League pennants, and two championships from 1926 to 1928. But in 1929 Huggins checked into St. Vincent's Medical Center in Greenwich Village on September 20 with influenza and a high fever.

He died five days later after developing an infection following a blood transfusion. "Hug was more like a father to me than anything else," Lou Gehrig said, according to the Hall of Fame's website. "I'd call him the squarest shooter I ever knew in baseball."

When McCarthy won his first title with the Yankees in 1932, Huggins became the first person to have a monument erected at Yankee Stadium. That was before Gehrig, Ruth, or even Ruppert, who was feted in 1940.

Barrow had won a World Series championship with the 1918 Red Sox in his debut managerial campaign and he made a bigger impact on baseball history the following season, converting Ruth from a pitcher to a full-time outfielder. Hired as Ruppert's top executive in 1921, Barrow soon followed Ruth to the Yankees. "There has never been a smarter baseball man than Mr. Barrow," Branch Rickey said in the book, *Ed Barrow: The Bulldog Who Built the First Yankees Dynasty*. "He knows what a club needs to achieve balance, what a club needs to become a pennant winner. I perhaps can judge the part, but Mr. Barrow can judge the whole."

In addition to Ruth, either Ruppert, Barrow, or both acquired future Hall of Famers Gehrig, Earle Combs, Tony Lazzeri, Bill Dickey, Joe DiMaggio, Waite Hoyt, Herb Pennock, Lefty Gomez, Red Ruffing, Joe Gordon, Phil Rizzuto, and Yogi Berra. Barrow, who also was credited with having the Yankees become the first team to add full-time uniform numbers, retired as team president of in 1946. He was honored with a plaque in Monument Park in 1954 and a spot in the Hall of Fame the following year. Ruppert finally joined Barrow, McCarthy, Huggins, and all of those legendary players in the Hall of Fame in 2013.

31

THE CHAMBLISS HOME RUN

A new generation of New York baseball fans, many of whom probably had heard their fathers talk about Bobby Thomson's famed "shot heard 'round the world" for the New York Giants a quarter-century earlier, stormed the Yankee Stadium infield as Chris Chambliss rounded the bases after belting a pennant-winning home run in the ninth inning against the Kansas City Royals in Game 5 of the 1976 American League Championship Series.

The Yankees were on their way back to the World Series for the first time in a dozen years, assuming Chambliss could navigate his way around, over, and through thousands of euphoric fans dangerously impeding his path to home plate. "Getting around the bases was quite an adventure, to say the least. The thrill of a lifetime—but also scary as hell," Chambliss said. "I was a running back in high school, so I knew how to lower my shoulder and get through some people. I still like to watch that video once in a while."

Teammate Roy White likened Chambliss breaking tackles to Jim Brown, but the Yankees simply were elated he'd conjured images of Thomson, whose home run against Brooklyn hurler Ralph Branca in 1951 had catapulted the Giants to the National League pennant. Just as the Giants lost to the mighty Yankees thereafter in the Fall Classic, the Bombers dropped the 1976 World Series to Pete Rose, Johnny Bench, and Cincinnati's famed Big Red Machine in a demoralizing four-game sweep. The Chambliss homer, though, set the stage for the following two years, serving as an impetus for George Steinbrenner to pursue and land marquee free agent Reggie Jackson as the final piece to a back-to-back championship puzzle.

Notably, the moment also came in the first year back at the remodeled Yankee Stadium after the Yankees had spent the 1974–75 seasons as co-tenants with the New York Mets in Queens. "Playing at Shea was definitely weird," Chambliss said. "In those days the planes from LaGuardia used to come down really low over the stadium. It was a real distraction. We were all excited to get back to the Bronx for '76. For me that finally made me feel like an official Yankee."

Chambliss, the son of a Navy chaplain, had been acquired from the Cleveland Indians a few weeks into the 1974 season, along with versatile reliever Dick Tidrow, for a four-player package that featured pitcher Fritz Peterson, who gained notoriety for trading wives and families with teammate Mike Kekich earlier in the decade.

The 11-year World Series drought had been the Yankees' longest—at the time anyway—since Babe Ruth was acquired and it included a bottoming out in the form of a 70–89 last-place finish in 1966 and a 72–90 mark (ninth place out of 10) the following year. Dubbed for the light-hitting middle infielder who posted an anemic .621 OPS (on-base percentage plus slugging percentage) over more than 1,200 games with the Yankees in that span, those years became known as "the Horace Clarke era."

The Chambliss trade gave the Yankees' lineup the winners of three consecutive American League Rookies of the Year awards in Lou Piniella (1969), Thurman Munson (1970), and Chambliss (1971). In 1975 they also had landed baseball's first marquee free agent, pitcher Jim "Catfish" Hunter, a four-time 20-game winner and three-time World Series champion with the Oakland A's, on a five-year contract worth $3.75 million. Catfish went 23–14 and hurled 328 innings for the Yankees in 1975 and he won 17 more with a 3.53 ERA over 298 innings the following year.

In Billy Martin's first full season managing his former team, he led the Yankees to a 97–62 record and their first American League East crown and playoff appearance since divisional play had been enacted in 1969. Munson was named league MVP, batting .302 with 105 RBIs to become the Yankees' first winner since Roger Maris (twice), Mickey Mantle, and Elston Howard had copped the honor over four consecutive seasons from 1960 to 1963. Third baseman Graig Nettles led the league with 32 home runs. Chambliss, mostly batting cleanup, made the All-Star team for the first time in his career, finishing with 17 homers and 96 RBIs. "That was a really huge year for all of us. With Billy, going into the fixed-up stadium, it meant everything to my career," Chambliss said. "I hit fourth that year. This was before Reggie

Besieged by celebrating fans, Chris Chambliss tries to circle the bases, following his walk-off home run to send the Yankees to the 1976 World Series.

got there, and I had Mickey Rivers, Roy White, and Thurman hitting ahead of me, all .300 hitters. I had a lot of opportunities for RBIs."

The '76 ALCS against Kansas City marked the first of four meetings between the teams in postseason play over the next five years. The sides alternated wins in the first four games. The Yankees took Game 1 on the road behind Hunter and Game 3, in which Chambliss ripped a key home run, at Yankee Stadium. Martin brought Hunter back on three days' rest in Game 4, and the Royals knocked him out after three innings in a series-tying 7–4 win.

Game 5 provided a fittingly thrilling conclusion. Yankees starter Ed Figueroa, a 19-game winner obtained with Rivers in the fruitful deal that sent Bobby Bonds (Barry's dad) to the California Angels, was tagged for a two-run homer by John Mayberry in the first inning, but the righty carried a 6–3 lead into the eighth. After Al Cowens laced a leadoff single, Martin turned to lefty reliever Grant Jackson. Two batters later, All-Star third baseman George Brett atoned for a costly error earlier in the game by clobbering a three-run homer to right for a 6–6 tie.

The capacity crowd was silenced but only temporarily.

Hard-throwing reliever Mark Littell had worked a scoreless bottom half and he was back on the mound for the ninth. But the inning was delayed as rowdy Yankee Stadium fans began pelting the field with toilet paper, beer bottles, and other debris. Legendary public-address announcer Bob Sheppard implored the crowd to behave: "Please do not litter the field. Please do not throw bottles on the field. The Yankees request good sportsmanship on the part of all."

Chambliss noted the temperature had been dropping as the game progressed, and "it couldn't have been more than 40 degrees" while he loosened in the on-deck circle. He knew Littell "had to feel it," too. Chambliss was hitting .500 (10-for-20) for the series as he strode to the plate. Reggie Jackson, working the ABC broadcast booth with Keith Jackson and Howard Cosell after spending the season with the Baltimore Orioles following a salary-dump trade from Oakland, quipped that "Chambliss is so hot he's got his shirt unbuttoned. He's in heat!"

"There was a lot of excitement, but the at-bat was delayed for almost 10 minutes because the ground crew had to clean up all the junk the fans were throwing," Chambliss said. "We had to stand around a little bit there, but so did Littell. My approach was simple, nothing complicated. Littell had two really good pitches: a fastball he threw hard and a nasty slider. There wasn't much guessing going on except that you're trying to get around on the fastball. The very first pitch, I got a fastball up and when I hit it I had no idea it was going to go out. It wasn't one where you feel that. Man, it was up in the air a long time. Hal McRae was their right fielder, and he's right at the fence, and he jumps to try and catch it. When he comes down and doesn't have it, that's the only time that I knew it was out."

Chambliss thrust both arms in the air midway down the first-base line, but his adventure was just beginning. "I've watched it so many times and I feel like I see new things all the time," Chambliss said. "Touching first, there was one real good shot. Somebody had an angle from left field, where I touched first, and a fan came up right behind me and took the base and sprinted away. And then I hit second base and tripped, went down to a knee. From then on I'm worried about people jumping on top of me. I got up, and somebody tried to steal the helmet, which I was lucky enough to pull off and keep. I held it like a football, and that's what it felt like the rest of the way. Third base was just an absolute mob of people. There were so many people near third. I had no chance of touching that base. So I just turned left and I'm just looking to get to the first-base dugout. I did it by knocking over a few folks over."

White was right. Chambliss leveled a few fans like Brown used to do to opposing linebackers. Willie Randolph joked that he gladly served as the pulling guard while knocking a few fans to the deck to create holes for Chambliss. "People were just mobbing him," Randolph said. "I just remember thinking, *God, if I don't make a path for him to get to home plate, this is going down.* It was crazy."

Chambliss eventually made his way to the champagne celebration, but there was one problem. "I got into the clubhouse, and everyone kept saying, 'Did you even touch home plate?'" Chambliss said. "Of course, I knew I hadn't. So what I did was I put a jacket on and took a couple of cops with me, and we made our way back out to the field to go up to the home-plate area. People were still everywhere, but with the jacket on, no one seemed to notice it was me. Of course, when we got up there, we looked down, and the plate was already gone by then. I don't know how they got it out, but it was gone. Someone dug it out and took it. So I just stomped my foot there, and we made our way back to the dugout."

Given the unique circumstances, Major League Baseball informed Chambliss that the home run would have counted anyway. He also was relieved to learn that Nettles had the presence of mind to immediately grab the bat Chambliss had dropped before the jubilant mob arrived. The series-winning baseball also was retrieved easily by Yankee

Stadium security; it landed just beyond the outfield fence but shy of the retaining wall of the right-field bleachers.

According to Chambliss, he noticed another thing as he returned to the vacated plate. "So many people on the field were holding these big patches of grass, too," he said. "Remember we still had a World Series to play."

The subsequent sweep by the Cincinnati Reds, which included Bench belting two home runs in Game 4 to seal it, couldn't fully diminish the feeling of what Chambliss still describes as the "signature moment" of his career. "It meant everything. We were real proud of that. When you're there, you understand," Chambliss said. "Roy White was really the only connection to the mid-1960s when he first came up. We were really proud to be there. It was our first exposure to it. And then we won the next two, so I definitely like to think my home run helped that happen."

32

THE FIVE-PEAT

They would come to be known as the "October 12." The dozen Yankees shared the unprecedented distinction of winning five consecutive championships together—between 1949 and 1953—for the remainder of their lives. That stretch of franchise dominance marks the only sequence in baseball history a team has won five World Series titles in succession, a feat almost certainly to never be duplicated.

Extra layers of playoffs were added in subsequent years. The league championship series in 1969 expanded the postseason to four teams, the division series in 1995 made it eight teams, and the wild-card game pushed the number of playoff participants to 10 in 2012.

Since the Yankees won three straight titles from 1998 to 2000, no team in Major League Baseball even repeated as champions over the next 19 seasons. The Yankees added one more trophy to their vaunted case (No. 27 in 2009) during that span, but even that squad couldn't replicate the October 12's success. "We won five straight World Series in a row. The feat is unthinkable, and given today's baseball, unrepeatable," Phil Rizzuto wrote in his 1994 book, *The October Twelve*. "The 12 players won more than five World Series rings. What they won is not worn on a finger. It is carried in the heart. It was a great joy and good fortune to be included in the limited partnership that won five straight American League pennants and then beat the National League five times, again in a row. The National League sent the Dodgers three times and the Phillies and Giants once each. The American League sent us five times, and we came back with all the marbles each time: 1949, 1950, 1951, 1952, 1953. Old Blue Eyes would call them, 'very good years.' And they were."

Of course, Frank Sinatra also crooned the standard, "New York, New York," the city about which he said, "If you can make it there, you can make it anywhere."

These dozen Yankees made it to the top of the heap in their sport five consecutive times. They were: Hank Bauer, Yogi Berra, Bobby Brown, Jerry Coleman, Joe Collins, Eddie Lopat, Johnny Mize, Vic Raschi, Allie Reynolds, Rizzuto, Charlie Silvera, and Gene Woodling.

A dozen teammates earned rings to fill an entire hand in a five-year span. Of course, Berra doubled that total in his Hall of Fame career. He owns Major League Baseball records of 10 championships over 14 World Series appearances. Joe DiMaggio won nine, while Bill Dickey, Frank Crosetti, Lou Gehrig, and Rizzuto took home eight. Mickey Mantle, who arrived in 1951 for the second part of the 1949–1953 quintet, was in the next cluster to win seven. Tommy Henrich did so as well; he bookended "The Mick" there for the first two of that stretch.

The Yankees seemed to have the Brooklyn Dodgers defeated in the 1947 World Series when Bill Bevens nearly threw a no-hitter in Game 4 at Ebbets Field. Cookie Lavagetto broke it up with a two-run double with two outs in the ninth inning in an eventual 3–2 win for Brooklyn.

The Cleveland Indians edged the Yankees by two-and-a-half games for the American League pennant in 1948 and ousted the Boston Braves in the World Series, or else those Yankees might have claimed *seven* titles in a row.

The historic run started in '49, Casey Stengel's first year as manager. He replaced scapegoated dugout boss Bucky Harris. Reynolds outdueled stellar Brooklyn rookie Don Newcombe, their latest find from the Negro Leagues, in a 1–0 shutout in Game 1 of the World Series. Led by Brown's .500 average, the Yankees split the first two at home but took all three games in Brooklyn. That series also was notable because lights were turned on at Ebbets Field in the ninth inning of Game 5, and for the first time, a World Series game was completed after dark.

The following year marked a four-game sweep of the Philadelphia Phillies' "Whiz Kids" behind Raschi and Reynolds and a 9–1 rookie named Whitey Ford. Coleman was the MVP, but the aging DiMaggio belted an upper-deck homer off Robin Roberts in the 10th inning of Game 2 at Shibe Park (later renamed Connie Mack Stadium), and Berra went deep in support of Ford in the clincher.

DiMaggio announced his retirement after the 1951 World Series, a six-game win against the New York Giants, who got there on Bobby Thomson's famed "Shot Heard 'Round the World" pennant-winning home run against the Dodgers' Ralph Branca. That fall marked the only time in their careers that The Yankee Clipper shared a field with rookies Mantle and Willie Mays. The fourth and fifth titles in a row were highlighted by sparkplug second baseman Billy Martin, who made a running catch of Brooklyn's Jackie Robinson's windblown pop-up with the bases loaded for the final out of the seventh inning to save Game 7 in 1952. The following October, Billy The Kid was named MVP for batting .500 (12-for-24), including the game-winning RBI single off Clem Labine in the ninth inning of the Game 6 sealer. Mantle also had clubbed a grand slam off Russ Meyer in Game 5. "Five straight, and while it was a new record, every one of us, and the front office, was perhaps even more confident, thought we would do it again in 1954," Rizzuto wrote. "However, when the Cleveland Indians win 111 games, just what is a Stengel to do?"

Indeed, the Yankees went 103–51 in 1954, but they still finished eight games behind the Indians, who then lost to Mays and the Giants in the Fall Classic. The Yankees' miraculous run had ended, and one by one, the October 12 was dismantled, though a few would earn rings again in 1956 or 1958 or—in Berra's case—straight through to 1961 and 1962 for an even 10 in all.

Yankees pitcher and 1983 no-hit author Dave Righetti felt a special connection to those teams because his father, Leo, had been a former minor leaguer in the Yankees' system and teammates with some of those players from the 1949–1953 dynasty. "To me there were two big deals early in my career: make the Opening Day roster, so you'd get your picture taken, and to be there on Old Timers' Day. That was it," Righetti said. "I had it a little different, my dad being an ex-Yankee minor leaguer. Plus, the Italian thing and being from San Francisco with DiMaggio and then Yogi and Tony Lazzeri and Crosetti. Lazzeri lived down the street from my grandmother on the same street.

"So when I walked in the clubhouse on Old Timers' Day to see guys like Vic Raschi and Allie and Lopat and Lefty Gomez, who managed my dad in the minors, it was amazing. Jerry Coleman and my dad were real close, too. They had been teammates. I really felt a kinship. Ron Guidry would always have Allie Reynolds dressing at his locker, and Vic Raschi always used mine. These guys were kind of the magnets of those teams, and here would be Lopat and, of course, Whitey, and these guys would start telling their stories. Come on. That one group won five in a row. Are you kidding? It was so cool and, the way they treated you, it made you feel like you were a part of them. Can you imagine what it was like to win five in a row?"

33

BRIAN CASHMAN

In George Steinbrenner's first quarter-century as principal owner of the Yankees, he changed general managers 13 times. Some people don't change their smoke detector batteries that frequently. A dozen men held that post in that span. Gene Michael, who took the job twice, recommended 30-year-old assistant GM Brian Cashman to replace Bob Watson, who was resigning barely two weeks before the start of spring training in 1998.

Twenty-two seasons later, Cashman is still there with no sign of stopping. He survived Steinbrenner's wrath for a full decade where the previous 12 Angry Men could not before The Boss' less-meddlesome children took over the operation in 2009. Cashman has navigated the New York media with aplomb for more than two decades. He fought for himself within the multi-voice structure of the organization, attaining the relative autonomy over baseball operations he craved. He has shown remarkable adaptability, embracing the wave of analytics that forever altered his job description.

Most important, Cashman had helmed the Yankees to nothing but winning seasons, and helped add five championships to the 22 that came before his arrival—even if that never seemed to be enough for a fanbase that expected to win it all every year. Cashman was asked to explain his longevity. "Simply winning. We've won a lot," he said. "Timing is everything. I always use a surfing analogy. You have to pick the right wave to ride, and since that wave came in for me, I'm still riding it. We're not winning the World Series every year, but we've always been competitive—with very few exceptions—on a year-in and year-out basis. I feel like that has more to do with my staying power than anything."

His father, John, held a friendly business relationship with Steinbrenner as the manager of Castleton Farm raising harness racing standardbreds in Lexington, Kentucky. Brian Cashman's time with the Yankees began as a college intern in 1986. He was hired full time three years later upon graduating from Catholic University, where he played second base and set the Division III school's single-season record for hits (since broken). He previously had attended Georgetown Prep, where he was classmates with Supreme Court justice Neil Gorsuch (and two years behind another, Brett Kavanaugh).

Cashman ascended to the post of assistant GM in 1992, earning his first World Series ring four years later. He was just 30 years old, the second youngest GM in baseball at the time, when he replaced Watson in February of '98. "I never wanted to be GM, never expected to be GM, never thought that was ever a possibility," Cashman said. "If anything, I remember saying I would never want that job, seeing how my predecessors were dealing with the various pressures and stresses of the day. Watching that play out, I also saw what I thought were big mistakes—whether it was lying to the press or reacting to the pressure of The Boss. Those were the experiences I knew I had to take and learn from when I unexpectedly landed the job."

Nothing can prepare you for landing squarely in Steinbrenner's crosshairs, as Cashman quickly learned when The Boss ordered him home from his initial road trip as GM after the Yankees began what ultimately turned out to be a legendary 1998 season with an 0–3 record.

"He would order you to do certain things, and you had choices to do them or not, and I saw the consequences of those decisions, the domino effect," Cashman said. "In the chair I was sitting in at the time, I always just looked at my superior as general manager as unfortunate, as a bad place to be. But when I got there, I suddenly was faced with those decisions. You get to the point—Gene Michael taught me this— that you just have to fight for yourself. George constantly would exert pressure on you on a daily basis. You either could just take it and crawl into a fetal position and then you become his toy—and you're probably a goner already—or you push back and make sure he knows you're not going to be played that way."

Michael also taught Cashman the importance of "protecting the Yankees brand," that his decisions needed to be "based on the best interests of the franchise in the present and the future."

Three days after his introductory press conference as GM, Cashman swung his first significant move that helped vault the Yankees to three World Series rings in his first three years on the job, acquiring Chuck Knoblauch from the Minnesota Twins. He later boldly executed a deal to augment that championship core, acquiring Roger Clemens (1999) and David Justice (2000), among others.

Even that level of success, though, was not always enough. After the Yankees lost the 2003 World Series to the Florida Marlins, Steinbrenner forbade Cashman from attending the Winter Meetings in New Orleans and personally commandeered negotiations that resulted in the signing of free-agent slugger Gary Sheffield. "It was probably the first time in history a team didn't have its general manager onsite at the Winter Meetings to talk trades or anything. He benched me," Cashman said of Steinbrenner. "I had a contract option that year and I had many opportunities to be the GM somewhere else. Literally, tampering does exist in this game. We all know it. But I remember during those Winter Meetings, getting a call from George King of the [New York] Post, telling me my option was just picked up by Mr. Steinbrenner. So he was mad at me and didn't want me to lead the baseball ops at that point. But at the same time, he didn't want me to go anywhere else. I was building a snowman in the backyard with my daughter and I said I didn't have any comment because I didn't even know if it was accurate or not. Then I got confirmation that he actually did it, which was interesting in the fact that I heard that he'd heard other teams were circling the wagons because they were expecting a change. So The Boss was not going to let me go, but that didn't prohibit him from being pissed either."

Later that winter, of course, Cashman spearheaded the Yankees' trade for Alex Rodriguez, sending Alfonso Soriano to the Texas Rangers. By 2005 he sought to bridge the divide between Steinbrenner's infamous "baseball people" in Tampa, Florida, led by Mark Newman, and the New York office. He was granted relative autonomy over baseball operations.

By 2016 the arrivals of homegrown players such as Aaron Judge, Gary Sanchez, Luis Severino, and earlier Dellin Betances—all of whom made the All-Star team the following year—restored faith in the minor league system.

That is not to suggest that all of Cashman's moves over more than two decades have been so fruitful, particularly when it comes to starting pitching. Sure, 2019 Hall of Fame inductee Mike Mussina and CC Sabathia were free-agent home runs. The latter unquestionably was one of the keys to the Yankees winning the 2009 World Series, their lone title since the team's previous dynasty died in a seven-game loss to the Arizona Diamondbacks in 2001. The misses on the pitching end thereafter have been pronounced from Carl Pavano to Jaret Wright to Kei Igawa to late-career Randy Johnson to Sonny Gray, to name just a few. Of course, misfires are bound to happen over the course of any front-office career of that length.

When Cashman was first hired, Wally Matthews, then of the *Post*, referred to him in print as "Doogie Howser, GM," a play on the popular TV sitcom *Doogie Howser, MD* about a teenaged doctor portrayed by Neil Patrick Harris. Twenty years later in a story for the *Post*, Oakland A's GM Billy Beane of *Moneyball* fame told Bob Klapisch that Cashman "probably belongs in the Hall of Fame" for his success and staying power in the Bronx. "He's a shark, swimming around with that dorsal fin just above the water level," Beane said. "Brian is one of the best who's ever done this job and he does it without an ego. Think about it: never negotiated his contracts in public, never threatened to leave the Yankees, even though he could've made more money if he used that leverage. He's been in the shadow of Steinbrenner, Torre, Jeter, A-Rod and yet he's still here after all these years."

Indeed by 2019, Cashman was one of the industry's elder statesmen. Only Beane, who was named Oakland GM in 1997, had been in the same position longer. Brian Sabean, a former coworker in the Yankees' system, also had been in the San Francisco Giants' front office since 1996. He spent the first 18 as GM before a promotion to executive vice president of baseball operations.

Cashman's front-office career, though, has not been without controversy. He sparred with Derek Jeter's camp during contract negotiations in 2010, telling the Hall of Fame-bound star shortstop to find a better deal elsewhere if he was insulted by what the Yankees were offering.

In an ESPN.com story, he told Rodriguez to "shut the fuck up" over the performance-enhancing-drug-stained star's rehabilitation from an injury.

Cashman, a self-described adrenaline junkie, also made headlines over the years for putting himself at personal risk while taking part in various charitable endeavors. Each year since 2010, he has rappelled from a 350-foot building in Stamford, Connecticut, as part of the city's Christmas celebration. In spring training of 2013, Cashman suffered a broken leg while skydiving with members of the U.S. Army parachute team to raise awareness for the Wounded Warrior Project. In November of 2014, he slept on a New York City sidewalk to help raise awareness of youth homelessness.

With a contract running through 2022, Cashman was on track to become the longest tenured general manager in team annals. Hall of Fame executive Ed Barrow, the manager of the Boston Red Sox when Babe Ruth was sold against Barrow's wishes to the Yankees, switched sides and presided over the franchise from 1921 through 1944, signing or acquiring the likes of Lou Gehrig, Joe DiMaggio, Phil Rizzuto, and countless other stars of that era.

"Brian is the kind of guy that is not afraid to push back when he gets pushed. And that is the kind of person George always appreciated and respected," Hal Steinbrenner said. "He's obviously very respected across the game and within our organization. Through the years he's done a great job of adapting to analytics and every change in our industry and our world that starts to manifest itself. He's always all over it. I think we do it as well as anybody. As far as Brian and I, we've known each other a long time and we've certainly had our ups and downs, but we talk about everything, virtually every move that gets made. He and I are a lot alike in that we don't like to leave stones unturned and we don't like making quick decisions if we don't have to. It's been a strong relationship for a long time."

34

GOOSE GOSSAGE

Just how he fired 100-mph fastballs up and in to opposing batters in the Bronx and for eight other teams in a 22-year major league career, Rich "Goose" Gossage still delivers them high and hard to the flippers of bats, to the steroids users, to those who believe closers of today are comparable to those of his era, and to the analytics crowd in front offices across baseball, especially Yankees general manager Brian Cashman.

Of course, all of it also landed Gossage in the hottest water and officially on the outside of the Yankees' family and inner circle, getting him excluded from future Old Timers' Day festivities and from serving as a spring training instructor for the Yankees. "Hell no, that doesn't hurt me," Gossage said in 2019. "I was put on Earth to be a baseball player. I studied the game and I was coached and I got tough love. I got an arm around me when I needed it and I got a foot in my ass when I needed one. But that mentality is gone now, and it ain't coming back. Everyone has to be told how great they are today. I call it 'The Revenge of the Nerds.' But they can call me the old guy yelling at the clouds all they want. I'll take that. That doesn't bother me at all. If anything, that's like a badge of honor."

All legs and arms with a menacing delivery and a Fu Manchu moustache, the hard-throwing Gossage joined the Yankees amid great fanfare and controversy, inking a six-year deal worth $3.6 million as a free agent a few weeks after his new team had won the 1977 World Series. Yankees closer Sparky Lyle had won the American League Cy Young Award that season, going 13–5 with a 2.17 ERA and 26 saves in 137 innings all out of the bullpen.

Gossage at first believed he'd signed up for more of a tandem closing arrangement with Lyle before he said George Steinbrenner "made it clear he handed me this man's job on a silver platter." That later prompted teammate Graig Nettles to famously quip that Lyle had gone "from Cy Young to Sayonara."

Lyle, who kept a diary during the 1978 season for what would become a best-selling book with Peter Golenbock titled *The Bronx Zoo*, demanded a larger salary or a trade. After not appearing in a single game in the '78 World Series, Lyle was dealt to the Texas Rangers for Dave Righetti. Sayonara, Bronx Zoo, indeed.

Gossage instantly got off to a rocky start with his manager when he refused to heed Billy Martin's racially-charged demand to drill Texas' Billy Sample with a pitch early in spring training. It wasn't the end, however, of what the nine-time All-Star described as "a really shitty beginning" to his pinstriped tenure. He proceeded to cough up at least one run in each of his first four relief appearances in April and seven of his first 11, only contributing further to a hangover start for the Yankees, who trailed the Boston Red Sox by 14 games in the American League East by July 19. "There's no rhyme or reason how that happened. I had envisioned that I would come over and join Sparky and be the best lefty-righty combo ever coming out of the bullpen," Gossage said. "That's how I envisioned it, but it didn't work out that way. George gave me his job on a silver platter, and I proceeded to just blow up my first couple of months there. We didn't play the greatest baseball, but I almost singlehandedly dug us that deep hole. That 14-game deficit was because of *moi*. There's no question about it."

Gossage's teammates attempted to lighten the mood for their tightly wound new closer. Following one tough road loss to the Toronto Blue Jays, Catfish Hunter, Lou Piniella, Nettles, and Thurman Munson took him out to dinner. His catcher, the captain, tried other tactics, too. "I'd come into a game, and Munson would go, 'Well, how are you gonna lose this one?'" Gossage said. "The first time he said it to me, Billy hands me the ball and leaves, and Thurman says it. I'm screaming at him, 'Get back behind the plate, you little fucker!' And he's walking back to the plate, laughing his ass off, going 'I guess we'll find out.' And then I would proceed to fuck it up."

Gossage had blown 10 of 30 save opportunities by the end of August, but he finished the regular season with a league-high 26 saves and, following a lights-out September, a solid 2.01 overall ERA in 63 appearances. "I had put so much pressure on myself. Growing up a Yankee fan all my life—my mom and dad, my whole family, were huge Yankee fans—and just putting on the pinstripes blew my mind," Gossage said. "Now you add to that coming over to take the job of a Cy Young Award winner, I mean, come on. I had absolutely zero envisions of taking Sparky's job. And Billy and I didn't get along at all. We got off on the wrong foot from the first day of spring training, and there was terrible chemistry there with us. But also I was just trying so hard early on. I was my own worst enemy."

Martin was replaced by Bob Lemon in August, and by October Gossage was on the mound to record the final out of the one-game playoff victory over Boston, the American League Championship Series against the Kansas City Royals, and the World Series against the Los Angeles Dodgers.

He endured some other turbulent moments—most notably injuring his thumb in a clubhouse fight with teammate Cliff Johnson in 1979. And he was inconsolable after coughing up a three-run homer to George Brett to seal the Royals' sweep of the Yankees in the 1980 ALCS. But Gossage compiled a 2.10 ERA with 150 saves over the course of his six-year deal with the Yankees, including another trip to the World Series in 1981, a six-game defeat to the Dodgers. Gossage signed with the San Diego Padres for 1984 and appeared in another World Series, losing to the Detroit Tigers, and lasted another decade in the majors. It took nine tries on the Hall of Fame ballot, but Gossage finally exceeded the required 75 percent threshold (receiving 85.8 percent) for induction into Cooperstown in 2008.

In the years since, he has remained an outspoken critic about just about everything involving the modern game, even suggesting Mariano Rivera—the first player in history to garner 100 percent of the Hall of Fame vote—had it easier than him by usually throwing no more than one inning of relief. Following a few public tirades to reporters directed at the Yankees' front office while a spring training instructor in Tampa, Florida, Gossage was banned from team activities in 2018, including Old Timers' Day. "I have no connection to that stadium. I had my career. I was lucky to do what I did," Gossage said. "Of course, I miss the guys, being around the guys. Old Timers' Day is fun. That was my favorite day of the whole season when I played, having all those guys around, in the clubhouse. That was always my greatest day when I played,

Menacing closer Rich "Goose" Gossage, who saved 151 games for the Yankees, poses with his namesake.

sharing a locker room with the Yankee greats: Mickey Mantle and Joe D. and Whitey and Yogi and Larsen and on and on. Somebody would be dressing at your locker, doubled up. It was one of the greatest thrills of being a Yankee, sharing a locker with any one of those guys. But no more. So I don't mind not coming back there one fucking bit."

Gossage then proceeded to trash Cashman again, saying he has "zero respect for the game" while clustering the longtime Yankee GM with other "front-office nerds." In the past, he has said Cashman has "no balls" and "is a disgrace to the Yankees." "All GMs, they're all in one pile," Gossage said. "These guys who all won their rotisserie leagues in Harvard and whatever colleges, smart guys that know nothing about the game, the game we gave up a long time ago. They want to control every aspect of the game rather than letting it come to you and then adjust to it, like it was done for over 100 years. It's a video game now. The product they're putting on the field is a joke. These kids don't even know how to play the game."

Cashman simply sighed when Gossage's latest quotes were relayed to him. "At the end of the day, everybody knows how that played out," Cashman said. "Nobody wanted him here. [Former manager] Joe Girardi didn't want him anymore, our clubhouse guys, our traveling secretary, our media relations director. It's because of all the excess problems and turmoil and chaos and the lack of work that's provided. So I went to our ownership in the end and said, 'Hey, we have these issues with Goose. Nobody wants him back. But I know he's a Hall of Famer. He went in as a Yankee. What are your thoughts?' I told Hal I'd be willing to try to broker a deal if he's willing to come in and be a contributor and stop gaslighting our personnel. My job as head of baseball operations is to protect and create a safe work environment for everyone. That doesn't happen when he's being hostile to a large population of our employees. In his old-world order, that's appropriate. It's not appropriate to be doing what he does and saying what he does about our coworkers here that work hard and are massively contributing to our winning efforts."

Cashman contends that he had "a good, honest conversation with Goose about everything" in 2017 and that the former pitcher promised to "behave" at spring training. It didn't last long. "The first day he showed up, he gaslighted people in the papers, so that was it," Cashman said. "Bottom line is we were the only team willing to take him to camp. I went around talking to other people, teams he played for and had ties with. 'Why don't you bring him to camp?' I talked to Bruce Bochy. I talked even to Derek Jeter. 'Why don't you take him to Marlins camp?' No one is taking him to camp. There's a good reason for that. In the end I'm his target, but I was his last supporter. That's the God's honest truth. He has in his own mind what takes place and he's entitled to his opinions, but that's it. At the end of the day, all you can do is treat people fair and honest and direct, and that's what I did. He hung himself."

Gossage, though, remains content. "I loved playing for the Yankees, but I'm fine with not being there anymore. I know I didn't really leave them any choice," Gossage said, before adding the perfect kicker with a hearty laugh: "Now get off my lawn. That's actually my favorite one."

35

YANKEES ANNOUNCERS

"How about that?" "Holy Cow!" "Now batting, Numbah Two." "It is high, it is far, it is gone. See ya!" The Yankees have been blessed with some of the most distinct voices and broadcasters—and their signature calls—in baseball history. From the earliest days of the original voice of the team, Mel Allen, to four decades of inviting Phil Rizzuto into our living rooms every night to the more recent stylings of the current generation led by Michael Kay and John Sterling and Suzyn Waldman, to a new wave of well-versed retired players that take a backseat to none. "Sometimes I can't believe it that I have this job," said Kay, a former newspaper reporter who transitioned into the radio booth and then to the TV side, where he's served as the YES Network's lead play-by-play announcer since its inception in 2002. "Whenever somebody introduces me as the 'voice of the Yankees on TV,' and John as 'the voice of the Yankees on radio,' I always go, 'No, the voice of the Yankees always will be Mel Allen.'"

Allen, the smooth-sounding kid from Alabama, was 26 years old when he was hired to replace Garnett Marks as Arch McDonald's partner on WABC broadcasts in 1939 after Marks reportedly was fired for mockingly mispronouncing the sponsor Ivory Soap as "Ovary" Soap. By the next season, Allen was the Yankees' lead play-by-play man for their home games. He also handled those same duties for the New York Giants before taking a three-year respite from the gig in 1943 to serve as an announcer for Armed Services Radio during World War II.

When he returned from the war, Yankees games had switched to WINS on the radio dial and by 1947 occasionally appeared on that crazy new medium—television—on WPIX in New York. Allen notably punctuated calls by saying "How about that?" His references, which were paid endorsements, to Yankees home runs as "Ballantine Blasts," and "White Owl Wallop" became part of the vernacular for New York baseball fans during his three decades in the booth. He'd also start each broadcast with "Hello, everybody, this is Mel Allen."

"It was just the sound of the voice," fellow Hall of Fame broadcaster Bob Costas said of Allen. "The really good baseball announcers of my youth—and even before that—gave the game a kind of a melody. A disproportionate amount of them had southern accents—Mel, Red Barber, Ernie Harwell, Lindsey Nelson—kind of a pleasing lilt to the voice. That's what baseball sounded like to me. In fairness, there was so much less bells and whistles, no strike zone box, a bunch of replays. They really had the room to set the scene, to paint the picture, to tell the story."

Of course, the legendary voices of the Yankees and the sounds of their stadiums were not reserved for the broadcast booths. There also was Bob Sheppard, the mellifluous voice that actor Billy Crystal once said always reminded him of what he'd imagined the voice of God sounded like. Sheppard was the Yankees' public-address announcer from 1951 through 2007 and introduced everyone from Joe DiMaggio and Mickey Mantle to "Numbah Two, Derek Jeter. Numbah Two." He also served in the same capacity for the NFL's New York Giants for 50 years.

Even after Sheppard retired from the Yankees, Jeter used his introduction before every game and plate appearance. "A public-address announcer should be clear, concise, correct," said Sheppard, who died in 2010 at 99. "He should not be colorful, cute, or comic."

Allen regularly used to tear up when recounting the story that Lou Gehrig, soon after his forced retirement in 1939, approached him the next season and said, "Mel, I never got a chance to listen to your games before because I was playing every day, but I want you to know they're the only thing that keeps me going."

Allen worked with various retired stars of the day, such as Dizzy Dean and Joe DiMaggio and Joe Garagiola before Rizzuto shifted to the booth upon retirement in 1957. That began a delicious four-decade run for Scooter. Allen also briefly was paired with Russ Hodges, who went on to belt out his "The Giants win the pennant" call upon Bobby Thomson's 1951 home run against the Brooklyn Dodgers. Barber even moved over from the Brooklyn booth in 1954 and worked alongside him until Allen abruptly was let go by the Yankees a decade later. "He gave the Yankees his life," Barber said. "And they broke his heart."

Later generations of baseball fans knew Allen as the host of popular Saturday afternoon highlight show *This Week in Baseball*. He's also remembered for a hilarious baseball scene from the 1988 movie *The Naked Gun* when he uttered his trademark "How about that?" In all, he called 20 World Series but also 14 Rose Bowls and various other college football contests. "Mel had a fabulous voice and just a fantastic way about him. Boy, could he talk," John Sterling said. "Of course, I loved all the calls: the Ballantine Blast, the White Owl Wallop, Gene Woodling, the Fairlawn Favorite, Tommy Henrich, Ol' Reliable. I also loved Russ Hodges and Vin Scully. But I didn't love Barber. Isn't that funny? When Barber came over from Brooklyn, I never really accepted him as the Yankee broadcaster."

One radio voice who had to fight for acceptance, former WFAN and MSG Network reporter Suzyn Waldman, moved into the radio booth as a game analyst when Kay shifted to the YES booth in 2002. With her endearing Boston accent and strong opinions shooting through the New York airwaves, Waldman became the first voice to appear on WFAN and the first woman to regularly hold a radio analyst position for a major league team. "I've always been very aware of where I'm sitting," Waldman said. "I know I'm there, but once you start thinking you've become something, then you're not."

In 2019 Waldman relayed the horrifying details of the vile harassment and death threats she has endured and put up with from listeners over the years to reporter Laura Albanese of *Newsday*. George Steinbrenner tested her often in her early days around the team, but he also made sure to ensure team security maintained her safety. "In the beginning he would do things to see how much I would take to see if I really wanted to do this or not," Waldman said. "He tested me a lot. I've said 1,000 times he told me, 'I'm gonna make a statement about women in sports one of these days, Waldman, and I hope you can take it.' So I think he was trying to see if I'd push back. Well, I'm still here."

As is Sterling, whose true ironman streak calling 5,059 consecutive games (playoffs included) since he debuted in 1987—more than double those of Gehrig and Cal Ripken Jr.—ended when he took four games off with an illness in early July of 2019. Fans either love or hate, applaud or mock Sterling's signature home-run calls for each Yankees

player, such as "El Capitan" for Derek Jeter, "Bern Baby Bern" for
Bernie Williams, "Hip, Hip, Jorge" for Jorge Posada, or "An A-Bomb
from A-Rod" for Alex Rodriguez. It's gotten to the point that fans will
offer suggestions on Twitter any time a new player joins the Yankees'
lineup. They are treasured parts of Yankee folklore, as are his other
signature calls. After a home run, he says, "It is high, it is far, it is gone."
Following any Yankees victory, he says: "Ballgame over, theeeeee
Yankees win!"

New York Daily News media columnist Bob Raissman even dubbed
the team of Waldman and Sterling "Ma and Pa Pinstripe." More people
told me over the years that they heard me on the air with them during
the sponsored "Daily News Fifth Inning" than have ever told me they'd
read something I'd written.

As a beat writer for the *Daily News* and *New York Post* for five
years beginning in 1987, Kay jumped at the chance to join the radio
lineup alongside Sterling in 1992. "At Fordham I was both the sports
director of the radio station and the sports editor of the newspaper.
But since I was nine years old, all I wanted to be was the Yankees
announcer," Kay said. "That was the goal, but I had a really thick Bronx
accent. I figured the next best thing was covering the Yankees for the
newspaper. Traveling around for those five years, you lose your accent
a little bit. First, I got an opportunity doing the pre and postgame for
MSG. And then the job opened up next to John."

Kay, the nephew of actor Danny Aiello, who died in 2019, and
Sterling immediately formed a great team. "[We] got each other from
the very beginning," Kay said. "John has his little quirks and oddities,
and I accepted that. He accepted what I was about. When I first
started, I was really the newspaper man on radio. I wasn't polished
as a broadcaster, but I got to the ballpark at the same time I did as a
writer. I worked the clubhouse like I always did. I just happened to have
a different job. It was a good match. To do four championships in five
years, I think that helped establish us and entrenched us as part of the
whole firmament."

Having been with YES since 2002—while also hosting a popular
sports talk show on ESPN Radio—an entire generation of Yankees
fans has grown up listening to Kay, along with former players and

current YES analysts Paul O'Neill, David Cone, John Flaherty, and Ken Singleton. "I always tell people that O'Neill is the modern-day Rizzuto," Kay said. "They love him like Keith Hernandez with the Mets. He just says what he thinks. There's no filter, and he's more about fun than breaking down X's and O's. You hope that people like to listen to us, and they have fun. Cone is great because he's also a connection to the Yankees championship years and he's also embraced analytics like no other former player/broadcaster has. I believe he's the best analyst in baseball right now, including the national guys."

Through the 2019 season, only Rizzuto (40 years), Sterling (31), and Allen (30) have announced Yankees games longer than Kay's 28.

Costas grew up a Mantle-era diehard in Commack, Long Island. He's broadcasted dozens of national games at the different iterations of Yankee Stadium for NBC and MLB Network over the years, but filling in for one 2019 doubleheader while Kay briefly was sidelined due to throat surgery was a personal thrill. "Even for just one day being the so-called 'voice of the Yankees,' that was kind of a bucket list thing for me," Costas said. "With the doubleheader we were able to do some nostalgic stuff about being a Yankee fan as a kid in the '50s and '60s, so there was a reverential mention of Mel and Red. I just felt like I had to do that. They truly were the reasons I and so many people got into this business in the first place."

36

TWO SPECIAL NIGHTS IN THE 2001 WORLD SERIES

The Yankees have won an unrivaled 27 World Series titles and reached 40 in all. None of their losses in the Fall Classic were as memorable or as heart-tugging as this one—not even Bill Mazeroski of the Pittsburgh Pirates ending Game 7 in 1960 with a walk-off home run against Ralph Terry. Leading up to the 2001 World Series against the Arizona Diamondbacks, there was an inspirational but unmistakably eerie pall, following the terrorist attacks of September 11.

Even while ultimately losing in seven games to the Randy Johnson and Curt Schilling led Diamondbacks, the Yankees astonishingly stole both Game 4 and Game 5 in miraculous fashion, twice ripping tying home runs in the ninth inning—by Tino Martinez and Scott Brosius—before winning each night in extra innings. "That's what I remember most from that World Series. I remember the home games," said Paul O'Neill, who retired after that season. "I knew I was going to be done playing, but I don't even really remember the outcome of the other games in that World Series as vividly as I remember those three nights here when you think about everything that had happened in the city and the country. They were the craziest, most exciting games I've ever been a part of. It was such a weird time in our lives, such a sad feeling everywhere you went. It was almost embarrassing to talk about baseball with everything that was going on. But then you realized the importance it had to people that had been through all of it, that it was still so meaningful to them. They needed something. But the people inspired us, as much as the other way around."

The Yankees surely did their small part to provide normalcy and relief for a suffering city and country as did the crosstown New York Mets. All-Star catcher Mike Piazza had provided the first uplifting moment in the first sporting event in New York, following the attacks, with a clutch home run against the Atlanta Braves at Shea Stadium, which also served as a staging area for supplies and provisions for the massive recovery efforts at Ground Zero.

The Yankees wouldn't play again until September 18 in Chicago and they didn't return to Yankee Stadium until a week later against the Tampa Bay Devil Rays. In the interim they made several visits to firehouses and armories near Ground Zero to spend time with and speak to first responders and family members of victims awaiting word about their loved ones. Joe Torre recalled being particularly struck by the scene of Bernie Williams approaching one distraught woman. "I don't know what to say," Williams told her. "But you look like you need a hug."

In turn, New York threw its collective arms around the Yankees as the 2001 postseason commenced. The end of the regular season had stretched an extra week to October 7 due to all of the cancellations, meaning the World Series was slated to reach November for the first time in baseball history.

A five-game elimination of the Oakland A's—with Derek Jeter's flip play sparking the comeback from 0–2 down—set up an American League Championship Series matchup with the Lou Piniella-managed Seattle Mariners. They had broken the Yankees' 1998 single-season American League record for wins by two with 116 behind MVP-winning rookie Ichiro Suzuki, following Alex Rodriguez's free-agent departure for the Texas Rangers the previous offseason.

The Yankees' pitching depth and big-game experience prevailed, and they took the series in five games to keep alive their hopes to become the first team to win four straight World Series championship since the 1949–53 Yankees won five in a row nearly a half-century earlier. Alfonso Soriano belted a two-run homer in the bottom of the ninth to win Game 4, and Andy Pettitte won his second game of the series one night later to seal the series.

The night of Game 3, a taped message from Torre was shown at The Concert for New York City at Madison Square Garden, which was held for first responders and their families. The event was organized by Paul McCartney and featured heavyweight musical acts such as The Who, David Bowie, The Rolling Stones, Eric Clapton, Elton John, Billy Joel, Jay-Z, Destiny's Child, and the Backstreet Boys. "I just told them how proud and grateful I was for what they did for our city," Torre said, "and that we'd be doing everything we could to get back to the World Series."

An expansion team that impressively reached the World Series in just their fourth year of existence, the Diamondbacks were next. Former Yankees manager Buck Showalter had skippered Arizona during its first three seasons, including a 100–62 record in 1999, but he was fired following a 15-win regression in 2000 and replaced by Bob Brenly. Johnson was the most dominant pitcher in the National League, winning his third of four consecutive Cy Young awards in 2001. Schilling finished second in the voting that season in his first year in Arizona, following a trade from the Philadelphia Phillies. The formidable 1–2 punch typically shoved through the first two games, as Arizona outscored the Yankees by a combined score of 13–1.

Back in New York, the emotions and tensions were high and raw barely one month after 9/11, beginning when president George W. Bush whipped a perfect strike to backup Yankees catcher Todd Greene for the ceremonial first pitch. President Bush later revealed that Jeter had warned him to throw the pitch from the top of the mound or risk being booed by the fans. "And don't bounce it," Jeter added playfully.

"Greatest thing I've ever seen, that strike right down the middle of the plate," Yankees first-base coach Lee Mazzilli said. "Top of the mound, all the special ops guys lined up everywhere. He comes out and throws that strike. It was like, okay, here we go.'" Chants of "USA, USA" reverberated through Yankee Stadium to start Game 3. Roger Clemens threw seven innings of one-run ball with nine strikeouts, and Mariano Rivera hurled the final two for a 2–1 victory.

Working on three days' rest on Halloween, Schilling limited the Yankees to little more than a solo homer by Shane Spencer, and the Diamondbacks took a 3–1 lead into the eighth inning of Game 4. Korean-born closer Byung Hyun-Kim was summoned by Brenly for a six-out save, and no one was questioning the move when the 22-year-old Kim struck out the side in the eighth.

O'Neill reached on a one-out single in the ninth, and after Williams was retired for the second out, Martinez clocked the first pitch he saw into the right-field bleachers for a two-run homer and a 3–3 tie. Kim's third inning of work began with two quick outs in the 10th, but the clock struck midnight as Jeter strode to the plate, marking the first time a World Series game was played beyond October. "Attention fans: Welcome to November baseball," the scoreboard showed.

Jeter had tried to bunt against Kim in the ninth and had been just 1-for-11 to start the series. Kim had been pitching from the windup as Jeter worked the count full, but he oddly switched to the stretch position. Moments before the full-count pitch, the FOX broadcast showed a fan holding a makeshift sign that read: "Mr. November." Jeter used his patented inside-out swing and drove Kim's 3–2 fastball to the opposite field and over the wall in right. Sheer bedlam in the Bronx ensued. At the conclusion of his frantic call on WABC radio, Michael Kay screamed: "The entire Yankee team mobs him at home plate as he leaps onto the dish with a 4–3 Yankee win! A game-winning walk-off home run by Derek Jeter! He is…Mr. November!"

It marked the first time in World Series history that any team had belted a ninth-inning homer to tie the score and then an extra-inning homer to win the game. And on cue, like Yogi famously said, the next night incredibly was: "Déjà vu all over again."

Mike Mussina was tagged for solo home runs by Steve Finley and Rod Barajas in the fifth inning, and Arizona's Miguel Batista carried a 2–0 shutout before departing with two outs in the eighth. Brenly then entrusted Kim, who had to be gassed after working three innings the night before, again with a two-run lead in the ninth. The same situation unfathomably fostered the same result, as Jorge Posada doubled, and Brosius clocked a first-pitch two-run homer into the seats in left with two outs to tie the score. "Two nights in a row? I really can't believe what I'm seeing now," Torre said. As Brosius rounded the bases, Martinez turned to Williams on the bench and similarly said, "You've got to be kidding me."

"The whole way around the bases, I just kept saying to myself, 'No way, no way is this happening again,'" Brosius told me in 2018. "That kind of stuff just doesn't happen. But it did."

Soriano's RBI single against Albie Lopez in the 12th inning scored Chuck Knoblauch for a 3–2 win and a 3–2 series lead, heading back to Phoenix. "It was absurd, like Lazerus coming back from the dead,"

Cashman said. "If you watched that play out in a movie script, you wouldn't believe it."

Adding to the drama, the delirious Yankee Stadium crowd, knowing this would be the retiring O'Neill's final home game in pinstripes, loudly chanted his name for several innings.

"I still get goose bumps, chills, when I watch it or think about it," O'Neill said. "Everything you do on a baseball field, you can prepare for and practice for and do it. How do you prepare for something like that? That meant so much to me. That only happens in New York."

George Steinbrenner had long ago branded O'Neill with the nickname "The Warrior" for his hard-nosed playing style and a water cooler-smashing intensity that fully endeared him to the fanbase, particularly the regulars in the right-field bleachers. "It was embarrassing at the time," O'Neill said, "but I came to really embrace it that Mr. Steinbrenner had that much respect for me."

Regrettably for the Yankees, a storybook finish would not be part of this script. The Diamondbacks pounded Pettitte for six runs in two-plus innings back home in a 15–2 win in Game 6 to force a decisive game.

The Yankees liked their chances with the mighty Rivera on the mound with a 2–1 lead in the ninth after the strength of six-and-one-third innings from Clemens. Plus, Soriano hit a solo blast off of a tiring Schilling in the eighth. But it wasn't to be. Mark Grace stroked a leadoff single, Rivera committed a rare throwing error on a bunt attempt, and Tony Womack ripped a run-scoring double down the right-field line. And finally, Luis Gonzalez, a childhood friend of Martinez's from Tampa, Florida—dunked a bloop single barely over a drawn-in infield into short left field to send the Yankees to one of the most crushing World Series defeats in their history.

"I did everything I could," a despondent Rivera said afterward.

It wasn't enough, even though those two special nights bridging October and November helped heal a city devastated by that terrible morning in September. "Forty-five years in the game, that was probably the hardest pill to swallow for any loss," Mazzilli said. "I completely believed we were destined to win after 9/11. New York was meant to have a championship that year. Even to this day, I look back and wonder what that would have been like."

Third-base coach Willie Randolph, like Mazzilli, grew up in Brooklyn. He had what he described as "the best seat in the house" to the Yankees' late-game heroics, but he knew who the real heroes were during those devastating weeks in New York. "I believe it was the best medicine for the people, the city. It was just surreal. It gave me goose bumps to experience something like that," Randolph said. "I'll never forget it. None of us will. But more than that, we'll never forget going down to those precincts and firehouses, talking to all of these people and their families. I'm a New Yorker and I was hurting tremendously, too. I could sit here all day and talk about all the special moments— good and bad—I've seen with the Yankees. I remember so vividly how disappointed I was that, if not for a little blooper that barely made the outfield grass, it could have been such a storybook ending. That would have been the ultimate."

37

THE 2009 YANKEES

Make no mistake about it: the Yankees were broken. General manager Brian Cashman knew he had to import several players capable of fixing them on and off the field as the Yankees transitioned from George Steinbrenner to son Hal and shifted across 161st Street to a new stadium for the 2009 season, especially on the heels of their first playoff miss after 14 consecutive appearances.

Cashman landed each of the top three players available on the free-agent market that winter—starting pitchers CC Sabathia and A.J. Burnett and first baseman Mark Teixeira—with an authorized $423 million outlay from the new Boss. The influx of All-Star talent—and more importantly, a cultural reset that the newcomers helped foster in a fractured clubhouse—resulted in the Yankees' 27th championship, a six-game knockout of the Philadelphia Phillies in manager Joe Girardi's second season after replacing Joe Torre. "It really came together right away. Right from the start, I felt like we had the best team in the league," Sabathia said a decade later in 2019. "Honestly, I didn't have to do anything. I was just kind of myself. With A.J. and Tex and Swish, it helped tremendously. I don't know exactly what it was like before I got here. I can only speak to once I was here, but that was a fun group, a fun clubhouse, to be around that whole year."

Cashman has been on the job since 1998, winning titles in each of his first three seasons, plus another in an assistant GM role in 1996. His assessment? "We definitely had a clubhouse divided," he said. The onetime friendship of Alex Rodriguez and Derek Jeter had deteriorated to little more than a coexisting business relationship at that point, causing a clear fracture between the aging old guard that had won four rings from 1996 to 2000 and those who still hadn't proven their championship worthiness over most of the next decade. The homegrown pitchers entrusted to seize spots in the starting rotation the previous year—namely Ian Kennedy and Phil Hughes—had been complete washouts with an 0–8 combined record in injury-plagued

2008 seasons. Reliable veteran Mike Mussina also had retired, following the first 20-win campaign of a career that ultimately would land him in the Hall of Fame in 2019.

Cashman was looking to make two significant additions at the top of his rotation for 2009, and his foremost target was Sabathia. The 2007 American League Cy Young winner with the Cleveland Indians had proven to be a big-game workhorse during the '08 postseason, following a trade to the Milwaukee Brewers. He thrived while making every October start on three days' rest.

The Yankees' pursuit of Sabathia, though, was based on more than simple numbers. It was as much about his leadership skills and a reputation as a unifier. Cashman convinced Sabathia with a seven-year deal worth $161 million by including an opt-out clause after the third year if he and his wife, Amber, decided New York was not for them. "First and foremost, we needed a premier starting pitcher. We had gone with the young guys the year before, and I knew I needed to find one, and CC certainly checked that box," Cashman said. "In terms of his reputation, we did a deep dive on who he was and the type of person he was, and he checked all of those boxes, too. He already had heard the reputation of our clubhouse. He knew Alex and Jeter didn't get along. He knew some of our pitchers didn't like throwing to Jorge Posada. We had gone through a few years with a bunch of hired guns. We weren't really a team anymore but a collection of great individuals who had accomplished a lot—some here and some elsewhere.

"I told CC in no uncertain terms, 'I'm signing you to change it and affect that end of it, as much as perform.' I didn't shy away from that, and it's exactly why we paid him what we did. All those guys, I empowered them and said, 'Take this thing over,' and that's exactly what they did."

Burnett was inked days later, agreeing to a five-year, $82.5 million deal after dominating the Yankees for the previous few seasons with the Toronto Blue Jays. After that exorbitant pitching outlay and, especially since Cashman had picked up Swisher in a trade with the Chicago White Sox earlier that winter, the surprise landing of Teixeira in December for another $180 million commitment over eight years showed Cashman, Hal Steinbrenner, and the Yankees truly meant business—and clearly were still open for business.

Still, many wondered why this year's splurge would be different from much of the previous decade. The Yankees had spent and spent on a series of high-priced mercenaries while trying to add World Series No. 27 without success. Productive stars such as Rodriguez, Jason Giambi, Mussina, Gary Sheffield, Bobby Abreu, Johnny Damon, and Hideki Matsui, as well as pitchers Carl Pavano, Jaret Wright, Kevin Brown, Randy Johnson, and Japanese lefty Kei Igawa failed to deliver that championship.

After A-Rod's performance-enhancing-drug admission and hip surgery in the spring, the Yankees were just 15–17 on May 12. But a 16–4 run moved them into first place by early June.

By then Burnett already had established a new tradition of smashing a towel of whipped cream in the face of any teammate who managed a walk-off RBI. The Yankees had 15 of those instances that season on their way to a 103–59 record to win the American League East by eight games over the Boston Red Sox. "That team from Day One really was together," Robinson Cano said. "The older guys won their three or four championships already, and you could see their hunger every day to win another one. But the new guys that year, they gave us some fresh blood that we needed."

The 2009 newcomers also executed Cashman's directive to unify the fractured clubhouse.

Rodriguez's girlfriend at the time, actress Kate Hudson, threw a well-attended 34th birthday bash for him in July at a mansion he rented in nearby Rye, New York, about 20 miles from Yankee Stadium. According to the book *Mission 27* by my longtime *New York Daily News* colleague, Mark Feinsand, and MLB.com beat writer Bryan Hoch, "virtually the entire team—players, coaches, support staff, wives, and girlfriends"—attended the festivities. Even Jay-Z, whose song "New York State of Mind" with Alicia Keys became a rally anthem at Yankee Stadium that season, made an appearance. (They later performed it together before Game 2 of the World Series.)

In formal dress attire, most of the party—led by A-Rod and including even Joe Girardi—ended up in the swimming pool fully clothed by the end of the night. "It just showed how loose we were, how together we were," Sabathia told me in 2019. "It's just not the kind of stuff that happens all the time, where guys jump in a pool at a party with their nice clothes on, especially led by Alex. It was pretty cool to see everyone having fun together."

Teixeira led the league in home runs (39) and RBIs (122) and finished second to Minnesota Twins catcher Joe Mauer in MVP voting. Jeter slotted right behind him, batting .334 with 107 runs and an OPS (on-base percentage plus slugging percentage) of .871. Despite the late start and the controversy over his PED usage, A-Rod reached 30 homers and 100 RBIs in only 444 at-bats. Five other players—Matsui, Posada, Cano, Swisher, and Damon—posted at least 20 and 80 apiece in those categories.

Sabathia, Burnett, Core Four holdover Andy Pettitte, and Joba Chamberlain all made at least 31 starts that season, and Sabathia went 19–8 with a 3.37 ERA and 197 strikeouts in 230 innings to finish fourth in AL Cy Young voting. He stayed another decade in pinstripes, reaching 250 career wins and 3,000 career strikeouts before retiring in 2019. Girardi, wearing uniform No. 27 those first two years as manager to signify the goal of the franchise's 27th title, was able to navigate to the postseason finish line by using just three starting pitchers: Sabathia, Burnett, and Pettitte. Sabathia went 3–1 in five postseason starts and was named MVP of the American League Championship Series. After they'd dropped the World Series opener, Burnett lifted up the Yankees by throwing seven stellar innings of one-run ball to outpitch old foe Pedro Martinez in Game 2, and Pettitte won the clinching game in each postseason series.

Still, the most unavoidable story of that postseason was Rodriguez, especially following his steroids admission and his past postseason failings. A-Rod absolutely carried the Yankees' offense through the first two rounds of the '09 playoffs, however, crushing five home runs in nine games against the Twins and the Los Angeles Angels of Anaheim to reach the World Series for the only time in his career. His two-run blast in the ninth inning against Minnesota closer Joe Nathan tied Game 2 of the American League Division Series before Teixeira won it with another homer in the 11th. Rodriguez drove in six more runs in as many games against the Phillies, but Matsui emerged as the World Series MVP, the first in history to be of Japanese descent. He batted .615 (8-for-13) with three homers and eight RBIs, and six of those came in the clinching game.

Game 6 would be Matsui's final game with the Yankees. He was not retained as a free agent and signed with the Angels that winter. He also played for the Oakland A's and Tampa Bay Rays before retiring in 2012. Nicknamed Godzilla as the top power hitter in Japanese baseball for the Yomiuri Giants—regarded as the Yankees of Japan—Matsui was signed ahead of the 2003 season two years after countryman Ichiro Suzuki had won AL MVP and Rookie of the Year honors for the Seattle Mariners. "It's been a long time, and I'm starting to forget a lot of things," the 45-year-old Matsui joked through a translator in 2019. "I was just lucky to be surrounded by so many great teammates. Winning [the World Series MVP] was all about the teammates that I had."

Another key play in the '09 World Series came from Damon to help win Game 4. Mike Vaccaro of the *New York Post* likened his double stolen base in the ninth inning to Enos Slaughter's fabled "mad dash" in the 1946 World Series for the St. Louis Cardinals. In a 4–4 game, Damon stroked a two-out single against Phillies closer Brad Lidge. With the infielders positioned in an over-shift to the right side against Teixeira, Damon stole second. After a pop-up slide, he took off for an unoccupied third base, making it easily. Teixeira was hit by a pitch, Rodriguez ripped a run-scoring double, and Posada's single drove in two more before Mariano Rivera closed it out in the bottom half. "When they shifted against Tex, we always knew when we had that opportunity. Scoring from third base was a lot easier than scoring from second," Damon said. "It presented itself to me, and I was able to take advantage of it. I really felt like that World Series was the validation for my time in New York."

Damon, the self-proclaimed leader of the Red Sox's "idiots," had been a key member of the Boston team that overcame an 0–3 hole against the Yankees in the 2004 ALCS. He switched sides and landed a four-year, $52 million deal with New York in 2006.

Brett Gardner, still a productive member of the Yankees through 2019, was a rookie reserve outfielder for most of the '09 season. He started in center field for an injured Melky Cabrera in the clinching game against the Phillies. "The team chemistry from Day One of that season was really good," Gardner said in 2019. "Guys like CC and A.J. and Tex were very accomplished star players. Coming over, you don't really know what to expect, especially with the names we already had on that team. It was one of those things that everyone bought in and was on board. It just worked."

It did—just as Cashman had hoped the previous winter. "I couldn't envision how it would come together, especially manifesting itself with the pies in the face and all that stuff," Cashman said. "But when it started playing out, I remember thinking this was exactly what I was talking about."

38

BILL DICKEY

Of all the Hall of Fame ballplayers who have donned Yankees pinstripes, none bridged the eras of superstars quite like Bill Dickey. He palled around with Babe Ruth. He roomed with Lou Gehrig. He batted behind Joe DiMaggio. He briefly replaced Joe McCarthy as manager. He served on Casey Stengel's coaching staff. He mentored Yogi Berra and tutored Elston Howard.

The 11-time All-Star catcher also was a key cog for seven World Series champions, including the game's first four-peat dynasty. "I loved to make a great defensive play. I'd rather do that than hit a home run," Dickey said, according to Baseball Almanac. "A catcher must want to catch. He must make up his mind that it isn't the terrible job it is painted and that he isn't going to say every day, 'Why, oh why, with so many other positions in baseball, did I take up this one?'"

The left-handed-hitting Dickey batted better than .300 11 times over 17 seasons with the Yankees, finishing with a career mark of .313, the same as Mike Piazza. Of all players whose primary position was catcher, only Mickey Cochrane (.320) posted a higher career batting average. Dickey also compiled a .382 lifetime on-base percentage.

Still, it was Dickey's prowess behind the plate—his game-calling ability catered to each starter and his control of the opposing running game—that separated him as one of baseball's elite all-around backstops. "The best [catcher] I ever saw," Cleveland Indians fireballing legend Bob Feller said, according to the Hall of Fame's website. "[I] could have won 35 games a year if Bill Dickey was my catcher."

The Yankees charged Dickey with mentoring a raw Berra, who was groomed to replace him full time behind the plate beginning in 1947. The No. 8 would be retired in honor of both men in 1972. "Bill learned me all his experience," Berra said.

The same could be said—though in more grammatically correct fashion—for Howard, who initially signed as an outfielder out of the Negro Leagues before he was converted to catcher under Dickey's

FOUR CONSECUTIVE TITLES

Here's the breakdown of the four consecutive titles from 1936 to 1939.

1936: New York Yankees defeat the New York Giants in six games.
Carl Hubbell ended the Yankees' 12-game World Series winning streak
with a 6–1 win in Game 1, but Tony Lazzeri bopped a grand slam in an
18–4 win in Game 2. The Bombers plated seven runs in the ninth inning
of a 13–5 win in the Game 6 clincher. Joe DiMaggio hit .346 in his first
of 10 World Series appearances.

1937: New York Yankees defeat the New York Giants in five games.
There was no sophomore jinx for Joe D that season (.346, 46, 167),
and Lou Gehrig registered 159 RBIs, while Bill Dickey had 29 homers
and drove in 133. In his final World Series as a Yankees player (he later
made it with the Chicago Cubs), Lazzeri capped his 12-year pinstripe
career by hitting .400 and had at least one hit in each game. Behind
starters Lefty Gomez, Red Ruffing, and Monte Pearson, the Yankees
won the first three games by a 21–3 aggregate. Carl Hubbell prevented
a sweep in Game 4, but Gomez closed it out the next afternoon.

1938: New York Yankees defeat the Chicago Cubs in four games.
Red Ruffing hurled two complete games, and Monte Pearson went
the distance in Game 3. Bill Dickey rapped four hits in support of Red
Ruffing's 3–1 win in the opener, and Joe Gordon homered and added
a two-run single in Game 3. Frank Crosetti ripped a two-run homer off
Dizzy Dean in Game 2 and added four RBIs in the 8–3 series sealer. It
marked the final Fall Classic for Lou Gehrig and his sixth championship
ring. Dickey was devastated by the death of his closest friend in 1941
and he insisted he play himself in *Pride of the Yankees*.

1939: New York Yankees defeat the Cincinnati Reds in four games.
Three months after Lou Gehrig's poignant farewell speech, the
Yankees finished the regular season with a .702 winning percentage
(106–45). It's still their third highest figure ever behind 1927 (.714) and
1998 (.704). They batted just .206 collectively against the Cincinnati
Reds, but Charlie Keller hit .438 with three homers. Once again, the
New York arms dominated, compiling a 1.22 staff ERA.

tutelage in the early 1950s. "You've got to have Bill work with you to understand how much he can help you," Howard said. "Without Bill, I'm nobody, nobody at all. He made me a catcher. When I start to slip and get careless, there's old Bill to give me a hand."

The Yankees, whose careers Dickey helped, weren't reserved to his pinstriped catching successors. Red Ruffing certainly wasn't on a Hall of Fame track before the Yankees acquired him from the Boston Red Sox in 1930. In six previous seasons with the Red Sox, he sported a record of 39–96 with a 4.61 ERA. Dickey helped turn around Ruffing's career and he totaled 231 victories, including four straight 20-win campaigns from 1936 to 1939. He also posted a 7–2 mark in World Series play, earning himself a spot in Cooperstown in 1967. The Yankees dedicated a long overdue plaque to Ruffing in Monument Park in 2004. "If I were asked to choose the best I've ever caught," Dickey said, "I would have to say it's Ruffing."

Vernon "Lefty" Gomez, Ruffing's fellow ace during that era, also could make a case for that designation. Gomez went 163–84 (of 189 career wins) with a 3.17 ERA over a nine-year stretch from 1931 to 1939. He also was a perfect 6–0 with a 2.87 ERA in seven World Series starts in pinstripes. The flighty Lefty's other nicknames were Goofy and Yankee Doodle Zany.

"I've never had a bad night in my life," Gomez said, "but I've had a few bad mornings."

Gomez, who was inducted into the Hall of Fame by the Veterans Committee in 1972, also wasn't afraid to needle the stoic DiMaggio. "I roomed with Joe and made him famous," Gomez said. "No one knew he could go back on a ball until he played with me."

Brooklyn Dodgers catcher Mickey Owen dropped a called third strike that would have ended Game 4 of the 1941 World Series, enabling Tommy Henrich to take first base and the Yankees to embark on a winning four-run rally. That five-game vanquishing of the Dodgers pushed the Yankees' record to an incredible 32–4 in World Series games since 1927. Twenty-four of those wins came with Dickey as their starting catcher, beginning with the 1932 sweep of the Chicago Cubs.

In 1943 Dickey also helped avenge the Yankees' lone World Series defeat—a five-game loss to the St. Louis Cardinals the previous

October—among the eight in which he appeared. The Arkansas product batted .351 in 85 regular-season games that season and he delivered a key two-run homer off Mort Cooper for the only runs in the Yankees' 2–0 Game 5 clincher against the Cardinals. Right-hander Spud Chandler, who led the American League with 20 wins and a 1.64 ERA in 30 starts that season, tossed two complete games in October for the Yankees, including a shutout in the finale.

Because of World War II, both clubs played without star players who were serving in the military, including DiMaggio, Henrich, Ruffing, and Phil Rizzuto for the Yankees. Immediately following the '43 Series, the 36-year-old Dickey joined the Navy and became a lieutenant commander for the remainder of the war. When he returned from the service in 1946, the 40-year-old backstop was relegated to part-time duty.

Early that season, however, McCarthy quit in a dispute with club owner Larry MacPhail. Dickey took over as player/manager for 105 games (57–48). He would come back to join Stengel's first coaching staff in 1949 primarily to work with Berra and a few years later with Howard. Dickey immediately predicted Berra would be the best catcher in the American League within two years. He was right. "I always say I owe everything I did in baseball to Bill Dickey," Berra said. "He was a great man."

39

RON GUIDRY'S 1978 SEASON

Known both as Gator and Louisiana Lightning, the 160-pound lefty had been 16–7 with a solid 2.82 ERA during the 1977 championship season, his first full season with the Yankees. The following year wasn't just proverbially on another level; it might have been about 10 levels higher. Ron Guidry won his first 13 games in 1978 and finished 25–3 with a league-best 1.74 ERA and 248 strikeouts in 273⅔ innings. He also pitched 16 complete games and tossed a league best nine shutouts, tying Babe Ruth (with the Boston Red Sox in 1916) for the most in one season by a lefty in baseball history. "For the team, every time that I'd take the mound, they would look at me knowing we were going to win," Guidry said in 2018. "They knew all they had to do was score one or two runs, and the game was over because that's how well I was pitching. I never thought about what I was actually doing in terms of me having a great year; it was about the impact I was having on my team. There were so many things going on during that season. In 1977 and 1978, there was a lot of turmoil in those years. I just felt like I needed to do a good job whenever I went out there because of the way the season progressed."

Guidry rightly was the unanimous winner of the American League Cy Young Award in 1978, but he should have won the MVP, too. He finished second to Boston slugger Jim Rice, who hit .315 with 46 home runs and 139 RBIs to garner 20 first-place votes to Guidry's eight.

"The most dominant performance I've ever seen from a pitcher in my time in baseball," teammate Willie Randolph said in 2019. "I know later on Doc Gooden was incredible, Pedro, you name it, but this guy was 165 pounds soaking wet, whipping the ball at the plate, that devastating slider. Gator, especially that year, was amazing, man. Obviously, Mariano just went into the Hall of Fame, and everyone knew he was coming with the cutter. It was the same with Guidry. Great hitters back in the day were being just mowed down by Guidry. He had a good fastball, too, but that slider was just hellacious. In those days, it was a *mano a mano* thing. We didn't pussyfoot around. It was: here it is; try to hit it. To watch him do that every pitch, every game for a full season, man, I'm telling you, I never saw anything like it. He was an unbelievable competitor, one of the most unbelievable feats I've ever seen."

Guidry, who started the 1977 season in the bullpen before Billy Martin moved him into the rotation, credited lefty reliever Sparky Lyle, the American League Cy Young winner that season, with teaching him his wipeout slider. "I always had a good fastball, but when you're starting, you have to have something else," Guidry said. "Sparky said, 'All I do with it is I just flip it. I think you could do it, too, because that's the way you throw.' Any way you help yourself to be a good as you can be, it's a tribute to how you hard you work."

The lithe lefty's most memorable performance in 1978 was a franchise-record 18–strikeout performance in a 4–0 win against the California Angels on June 17 at Yankee Stadium.

Twenty-two of his 35 starts that season followed a Yankees loss; they went 19–3 in those games, a prime reason the team was able to come back from a 14-game deficit in the AL East in mid-July.

Guidry's 25th win came in the Bucky "Freaking" Dent game against Boston, a one-game playoff on October 2 to decide the division title at Fenway Park. Guidry worked six-and-one-third innings of two-run ball before Goose Gossage recorded the final eight outs to advance the Yankees to the American League Championship Series. "To come back and win it on the last day of the season made my season complete," Guidry said. "If I would have lost it, I don't think that would have meant anything."

Teammate Roy White still marveled at Guidry's season 40 years later. "Without question, it was the best season I ever saw a pitcher have," White said. "I played left field and I didn't have to worry about too many hard-hit balls coming out there. He would just be putting guys away. We knew if we could get one or two runs we would win when he was on the mound. That's a great feeling to have. It was like an automatic win every time he went out there. Amazing how he got guys out. That slider was lethal." Mickey Rivers similarly joked,

Ron Guidry throws during one of the nine shutouts he recorded during his epic 1978 season.

according to the YES Network, "I don't know why I ever bring my glove out there" to center field on the days Guidry pitched.

The four-time All-Star and three-time 20-game winner served as co-captain of the Yankees with Randolph from 1986–88, just before Don Mattingly did, and as pitching coach under Joe Torre in 2006–07.

Guidry's uniform No. 49 was retired to Monument Park in 2003, a quarter-century after he'd posted one of the most memorable pitching seasons of my lifetime. His teammates agreed. "I never saw anybody have a season like that, not even close," Gossage said. "I saw guys have good seasons, 20-game winners. I'd never seen that before. It was almost like I got the frigging night off whenever this guy was pitching. It was incredible to watch. What came out of that little body—he was 170 pounds soaking freaking wet—what he got out of that body, pitching-wise, especially that season, was just amazing."

40

BERNIE WILLIAMS

When people raved about the Core Four, Bernie Williams too often was slighted or omitted altogether, so he's deservedly getting his own chapter to explain why. No. 51 was the first to arrive of the homegrown future All-Stars that fronted the Yankees to four championships in five years, beginning in 1996. He arrived at least four years ahead of Mariano Rivera, Derek Jeter, Andy Pettitte, and Jorge Posada. Why Williams is not grouped with them more often still isn't exactly clear. Ask anyone associated with those teams, however, and they will gush over Williams' popularity and importance to the franchise's most recent dynasty. "Bernie was the first one to get here and he doesn't take a back to seat to any of them in my opinion," former Yankees coach Willie Randolph said. "Out of all the players I've worked with and dealt with, Jeter all the way down the line, I would say Bernie is my favorite, just who he is, what he represents as a person. Talent-wise, we all knew, off the charts, what he could do. But he had such a beautiful soul and spirit, too. The Core Four gets a lot of credit, and deservedly so, but man, I really wish they would have come up with a different nickname or way of describing them."

Joe Torre also described Bernie as "probably my favorite" player from that era, which he insisted wasn't intended as a slight to the quartet of organizational lynchpins who lasted long enough to win a fifth ring together—after Williams and Torre had departed—in 2009. "I told him a long time ago, 'Bernie, you're a leader on this club,' which sort of shocked him. He said, 'I am?'" Torre said. "I think the game was a little harder for him to play. He wasn't blessed with the baseball instincts that someone like Derek had. If he had the instincts of some of these other guys like Jeter or Scott Brosius or Paulie, he would have stolen so many more bases. He had to work hard at being who he was, but he was a gamer and one of the best pressure players you'd ever want on your team. He was really something."

This is not to suggest Williams' career parallels those of Rivera and Jeter. The greatest closer ever and a 14-time All-Star shortstop with 3,465 career hits, they are slam-dunk Hall of Fame players. Williams' career is far more comparable with Pettitte's and Posada's. They both fell short of the Hall of Fame demarcation line, as did Williams, who dropped off the ballot after receiving 9.6 percent and then 3.3 percent of the vote in two years of consideration. "Bernie was as important as anyone in the team's success just because of his presence," said former teammate Joe Girardi while he was still the team's manager in 2015. "He was a switch-hitter breaking up the lefties in the middle of the lineup, and his ability to run and play defense made him special. He was as important as anyone, and the only reason it wasn't a 'Core Five' is because he was here a couple years earlier than the other guys."

Brian Cashman wishes the group would have been dubbed "The Fab Five," even though that nickname was taken by the five freshmen who led Michigan to the NCAA Final Four in 1992. He also referred to Williams as "one of the fabulous five that we have produced from our system that led to many of these 27 championships that we have."

For his part, the easygoing and widely adored Williams, who consistently receives one of the biggest ovations any time he returns to Yankee Stadium, typically and consistently has laughed off the notion that he feels slighted by his omission. "I always thought that there was some reason for the Core Four term, but I think the people that knew the team knew that obviously I was a big part of it as well," Williams said ahead of his jersey retirement in 2015. "Really, it was more fun for me to hear all the back and forth about 'He's part of it!' or 'No, he's not!' I thought it was more funny than anything, but whatever name you choose to call us, everyone knows we were all part of the great run, and I still take away the memories."

Williams' father, Bernabe Sr., was a merchant seaman and his mother, Rufina, was a high school principal and college professor. A scout discovered Bernie at the age of 16 playing in Puerto Rico, so the Yankees stashed him briefly at a baseball academy in Connecticut before they could sign him on his 17th birthday. He also considered pursuing a pre-med track in college but chose to concentrate on his baseball career, arriving full time in the Bronx at 22 in 1991.

Williams struggled on and off the field amid sporadic playing time over his first two seasons, batting just .256 with a .719 OPS (on-base percentage plus slugging percentage). Veteran outfielder Mel Hall also bullied and hazed him mercilessly, calling him "Mr. Zero" and "Bambi." Manager Buck Showalter said years later that the Yankees "put an end to it," and Hall was jettisoned. In 2009 he was sentenced to 45 years in prison for sexually assaulting a 12-year-old girl.

George Steinbrenner grew impatient with Williams' slow development, and the Yankees considered trading him and engaged in various trade discussions with several teams. Gene Michael and Showalter, his former minor league manager, believed in Williams' raw talent as a switch-hitter with power potential from both sides and impressive speed. They fended off The Boss, and Williams batted .307 with 18 homers and 82 RBIs during the Yankees' first playoff season in 14 years in 1995.

Within the next year, Williams blossomed into the middle-of-the-order bat the Yankees had envisioned, beginning a stretch of six straight seasons averaging .323, 25 homers, and 102 RBIs with an OPS of .946. Williams also won four Gold Glove awards in center field, and the Yankees won four World Series titles in that span. "Man, Bernie was a huge part," Pettitte said. "I mean, he was here before any of us, roaming center field, and he did it for so many years. What a great player. So for sure, we couldn't have won those championships without Bernie right in the thick of things."

During the Yankees' team-record 114-win regular season in 1998, Williams batted .339 and became the first player to win a batting title, a Gold Glove, and a World Series ring in the same year. He nearly signed with the Boston Red Sox as a free agent that offseason, and the Yankees came awfully close to replacing him with surly Cleveland Indians slugger Albert Belle. Williams made a last-minute appeal to Steinbrenner, telling The Boss he wanted to remain with the Yankees. He agreed to a seven-year deal worth $87.5 million—$2.5 million less than the Red Sox had offered.

The five-time All-Star remained in the Bronx for the remainder of his career, choosing not to go elsewhere after the Yankees offered him only a non-guaranteed contract for 2007. Williams finished with a career average of .297 and he ranks in the top seven in franchise history in hits (2,336), games played (2,076), runs scored (1,366), home runs (287), and RBIs (1,257) over 16 seasons. He also is the team's all-time postseason leader in home runs (22) and RBIs (80).

Though he would not appear in a major league game after 2006, in typical Bernie fashion, he did not officially retire until 2015. "After playing professional baseball with the Yankees, I decided to be a rock star," he joked.

Williams, a classically trained guitarist, earned a jazz performance degree at Manhattan School of Music during retirement. He has released two contemporary jazz albums and even was nominated for a Latin Grammy in 2009. He has played "The Star-Spangled Banner" and "Take Me Out to the Ballgame" at Yankee Stadium and even strummed both at Rivera's Hall of Fame induction in 2019. He once performed "Glory Days" with Bruce Springsteen at a charity dinner for Torre's Safe at Home Foundation and he's appeared on stage with The Allman Brothers at New York's Beacon Theatre.

He may never be Eric Clapton or Jimi Hendrix—just as he may not have been Joe DiMaggio or Mickey Mantle—but Williams certainly merits inclusion alongside his most accomplished teammates in the Fab Five. "Bernie was always so quiet and so unassuming. I would say to him, 'Bernie, you're the center fielder for the New York Yankees. Do you understand what that means?'" Randolph said. "Do you know who roamed this patch of outfield you're roaming? Joe D, Mickey Mantle, the greats of the greats. Over there in right field was Babe Ruth. I'm not saying he was those guys. No one was. He had kind of this deer-in-the-headlights thing sometimes. He was great, truly great, but he didn't ever think of himself as The Man. I'd say to him, 'You're The Man. You're playing center field, batting cleanup for a multi-championship Yankees team. Do you realize how great you are?' He gave me that look one day, and you could see it finally connected with him. I think he understands now that even with how talented he was he needed people to help him get there. Along with a lot of people who had a small part, I take great pride in that, and that's why I love him so much. It's why everyone loves him so much."

41

ALLIE REYNOLDS' TWO NO-HITTERS

Out of nearly 20,000 players to appear in a major league game, Allie Reynolds was one of only a half-dozen pitchers to throw two no-hitters in the same season. In addition to being one of the most renowned big-game performers in team lore—and a six-time World Series champion—Reynolds' personal accomplishments were highlighted by no-no's against the Cleveland Indians, his former team, on July 12, 1951, and then another against the Boston Red Sox in the opener of a doubleheader on September 28. "A no-hitter is not the best standard by which to judge a pitcher. That's just luck," Reynolds said, according to *The New York Times*. "I pitched four games better than the no-hitters and lost three of them."

Reynolds was born in Oklahoma, and the son of a Nazarene minister partly of Native American descent (Creek) earned the nickname "Super Chief." He was a three-sport collegiate athlete who initially accepted a track scholarship as a javelin thrower from Oklahoma A&M (now known as Oklahoma State). He also was a running back on the football team for three seasons, and after Henry Iba saw him tossing the javelin and discus, the legendary basketball and baseball coach also asked him try out for baseball. He eventually attracted the notice of the Indians, who offered him a $1,000 signing bonus in 1939.

By 1943 Reynolds held down a spot in Cleveland's rotation while ace Bob Feller was serving in the military during World War II. They then teamed together for two seasons. In October of 1946, the Yankees acquired Reynolds for 1942 American League MVP Joe Gordon, a second baseman who was elected to the Hall of Fame by the Veterans Committee in 2009.

When the Indians gave the Yankees their choice of Reynolds or right-hander Red Embree, team president Larry MacPhail requested input from Joe DiMaggio and Tommy Henrich. "He's their best outside of Feller," DiMaggio said. "Take Reynolds. I'm a fastball hitter, but he can buzz his hard one by me any time he has a mind to."

With Eddie Lopat and Vic Raschi, Reynolds was part of the Big Three atop another Yankees championship rotation. He started 209 games and relieved in 86 more over eight seasons in New York. Reynolds registered 131 of his 182 career wins for the Yankees, but he saved his best work for the postseason, going 7–2 with a 2.79 ERA in

TWO NO-HITTERS IN THE SAME SEASON

The following is an awesomely impressive shortlist and one of the most exclusive clubs in baseball history:

- Johnny Vander Meer, Cincinnati Reds, 1939
- Allie Reynolds, New York Yankees, 1951
- Virgil Trucks, Detroit Tigers, 1952
- Nolan Ryan, California Angels, 1973
- Roy Halladay, Philadelphia Phillies, 2010
- Max Scherzer, Washington Nationals, 2015

That's the list. Six guys.

Interestingly, the five other men alongside Allie Reynolds in the same-season club also did so with historical distinction. Vander Meer is the only pitcher to ever throw no-hitters in consecutive games. Trucks was the last pitcher to no-hit the Yankees in the Bronx, though there was a combined hitless game by six Houston Astros against them in 2003. Ryan, baseball's all-time strikeout king, also owns the record of seven no-hitters for his career.

Halladay pitched a perfect game during the 2010 regular season and then a no-hitter against the Cincinnati Reds in the National League playoffs, joining Don Larsen as the only pitchers to throw no-hitters in postseason history. (Halladay died in a crashed plane he was piloting in 2017, 38 years after Thurman Munson's tragic death in 1979.) Scherzer, a three-time Cy Young winner, no-hit the World-Series-bound New York Mets on the penultimate day of the 2015 regular season.

World Series play. "At the time the trade was controversial, but when Joe and Tommy went to bat for me, that was really all the Yankees needed to know to make it happen," Reynolds said in Phil Rizzuto's book, *The October Twelve*. "I made sure that Joe and Tommy knew I was grateful, but I slipped a needle in when I did: 'Guess you two guys didn't want to go to bat against me anymore, so you went to bat for me.' Playing in New York after playing in Cleveland was like going from the minors to the majors."

Reynolds also compared the move to "going from a church supper to the Stork Club," a prestigious nightclub on West 58th Street in Manhattan from 1929 to 1965.

In his first no-hitter, Reynolds outdueled Feller, who actually had thrown his second of three career no-hitters against the Detroit Tigers 11 days earlier, in a 1–0 game at Cleveland Stadium. Feller also hadn't been reached for any hits until Mickey Mantle's double in the sixth inning before Gene Woodling rocked a solo homer in the seventh for the game's only run. The final out was a strikeout of second baseman Bobby Avila.

For the final out of his second gem more than two months later, an 8–0 victory in the Bronx that clinched at least a tie for the American League pennant, Reynolds stared down Red Sox slugger Ted Williams with two runners on base via walks. Teddy Ballgame was granted a reprieve when Yogi Berra dropped his foul pop behind home plate. Clearly, this game would not be over 'til it was over. Williams proceeded to hit another pop foul, which was closer to the Yankees dugout, and Berra squeezed it to cement Reynolds' rarified place in history.

None of the 10 men to have thrown no-hitters for the Yankees— George Mogridge (1917), Sad Sam Jones (1923), Monte Pearson (1938), Reynolds (twice), Don Larsen (1956 World Series), Dave Righetti (1983), Jim Abbott (1993), Dwight Gooden (1996), David Wells (1998), or David Cone (1999)—are in the Hall of Fame.

Reynolds, who died at 79 in 1994 due to complications of lymphoma and diabetes, earned as much as 33.6 percent of the Baseball Writers' Association of America vote in 1968. He also fell one vote shy of election by the Veterans Committee in 2009, when Gordon was inducted.

With the Cy Young Award not presented until 1956, Reynolds placed third in AL MVP voting in 1951 (behind Berra and St. Louis Browns pitcher Ned Garver) and second the following year behind Philadelphia A's pitcher Bobby Shantz. Reynolds also was honored with a plaque in Monument Park in 1989, but it's not even the most exclusive club of which he's a member.

42

JOE McCARTHY

Joe McCarthy lived by the Ten Commandments—just not the biblical collection you probably are thinking about right now. McCarthy's religion was baseball, and he used these 10 credos—and the linking of two separate generations of Yankees legends—to become the most successful manager in baseball history both in career winning percentage (.615) and World Series championships (seven, tying him with Casey Stengel for the most all time).

Some of his words to live by were simplistic, some were profound, some were just common sense, and one or two bordered on Yogi-isms—even if McCarthy predated the incomparable Yogi Berra in New York by more than decade. According to the book, *The 10 Commandments of Baseball: An Affectionate Look at Joe McCarthy's Principles for Success in Baseball (and Life),* they are:

- Nobody ever became a ballplayer by walking after a ball.
- You will never become a .300 hitter unless you take the bat off your shoulder.
- An outfielder who throws in back of a runner is locking the barn after the horse is stolen.
- Keep your head up and you may not have to keep it down.
- When you start to slide, SLIDE. He who changes his mind may have to change a good leg for a bad one.
- Do not alibi on bad hops. Anyone can field the good ones.
- Always run them out. You never can tell.
- Do not quit.
- Try not to find too much fault with the umpires. You cannot expect them to be as perfect as you are.
- A pitcher who hasn't control hasn't anything.

"I loved him. One of the greatest men I ever knew," former Yankees outfielder Tommy Heinrich said, according to Donald Honig's book

Baseball Between the Lines: Baseball in the Forties and the Fifties as Told by the Men Who Played It. "I don't know where in the heck he learned all his psychology about ballplayers. He could handle almost anybody. And if he couldn't handle them, he'd trade them."

McCarthy never played in the major leagues, but after waiving Hall of Fame pitcher Grover Cleveland Alexander, he led the Chicago Cubs to the National League pennant in his fourth year as their manager before losing to the Philadelphia A's in five games in the 1929 World Series. He was let go before the end of the following season after a falling out with Cubs owner William Wrigley. In replacing him with the legendary Rogers Hornsby, Wrigley said, "I have always wanted a world's championship and I am not sure that Joe McCarthy is the man to give me that kind of team," according to *The New York Times*.

General manager Ed Barrow and the Yankees, however, turned to that stern man to replace Bob Shawkey, who'd provided a mediocre one-season bridge (86–68) in 1930 after Miller Huggins died suddenly the previous season.

Nicknamed "Marse Joe" (short for Master Joe), McCarthy no longer allowed hot dogs or peanuts in the dugout, but he otherwise avoided any personal clashes with Babe Ruth, who was disappointed he wasn't considered for the managerial position. He also instituted a stringent dress code, and players were ordered to shave before arriving at the ballpark.

By 1932, his second season in the Bronx, McCarthy became the first manager in baseball history to win the pennant in each league, fronting the Yankees to a four-game sweep of the Cubs, his former team, in the World Series. (There since have been six other managers to pull off the pennant-in-each-league feat: Alvin Dark, Berra, Dick Williams, Sparky Anderson, Tony La Russa, and Jim Leyland.)

In his first 14 seasons in New York, McCarthy's Yankees won eight pennants and seven titles, including becoming baseball's first four-peat champions beginning with Joe DiMaggio's rookie season in 1936. "I hated his guts, but there was never a better manager," former Yankees pitcher Joe Page said, according to *The Times*. "Never a day went by," DiMaggio said, "that you didn't learn something from McCarthy."

There was a notion that McCarthy was a product of his loaded roster, which also included Hall of Famers Lou Gehrig, Bill Dickey, Tony Lazzeri, Lefty Gomez, Red Ruffing, and others. In *New York Times, Story of the Yankees: Profiles and Essays from 1903 to Present*, McCarthy joked, "Sure, I spend every summer in Atlantic City and only come back to get ready for the World Series."

McCarthy left the Yankees amid reported drinking problems and gall bladder issues in May 1946 before finishing his career managing Ted Williams and the Boston Red Sox for three seasons from 1948 to 1950.

He remains the Yankees' all-time leader in wins (1,460) and baseball's all-time leader in winning percentage in both the regular season (.615) and the postseason (.698). He was elected to the Baseball Hall of Fame in 1957. "The McCarthy stamp was indelibly imprinted on his team, his Yankees," Arthur Daley wrote in *The Times* upon McCarthy's resignation. "This grim-visaged man was in a class by himself...You can't improve on perfection. Joseph Vincent McCarthy was exactly that."

43

RIGHETTI'S NO-HITTER

Outside of October, the Fourth of July might be the most significant and eventful singular date in franchise lore. It was the somber day in 1939, on which a dying Lou Gehrig referred to himself as "the luckiest man on the face of the Earth." Independence Day marks George Steinbrenner's birthday (as well as John Sterling's), the ultimate definition of a Yankee Doodle Dandy. And on July 4, 1983, Dave Righetti authored the sixth regular season no-hitter in Yankees history and the first since Allie Reynolds tossed two in the same season more than three decades earlier in 1951. (Don Larsen's World Series perfecto occurred in 1956.)

The Boss wasn't in attendance for Righetti's gem, but former president Richard M. Nixon spent the game in the owner's box with son-in-law David Eisenhower, the grandson of another former president, Dwight D. Eisenhower. "So much neat stuff came out of that day," Righetti recalled in 2019. "Nixon was there and he sent me a really nice letter. And I got cool messages from all over the world, a lot of servicemen and Yankees fans on vacation or listening down on the beaches on the Jersey Shore or Long Island. I just picked the perfect day, I guess. Red Sox-Yankees at the stadium, the anniversary of Gehrig's speech. George wasn't there, but he sent me a note thanking me for the birthday gift. Plus, it had been so many years since Larsen's perfect game. I think that's why that memory really endures."

Righetti had arrived just after the Yankees had appeared in three straight World Series and was acquired from the Texas Rangers for Sparky Lyle. The left-handed Righetti was named American League Rookie of the Year during the strike-shortened 1981 season, going 8–4 with a 2.05 ERA in 15 starts. He won three more games in the American League playoffs before the Yankees fell in the World Series to the Los Angeles Dodgers.

Righetti's gem in his final season as a starter before transitioning to the closer role the following year came on a sweltering Monday afternoon in the Bronx as temperatures soared well above 90 degrees. "You never think it's going to be a no-hitter. I was just trying to hold Boston down. They had been beating us up, and we needed a win," Righetti said. "It was so hot, so I wasn't going for strikeouts. I just happened to outlast them. I was 24 and strong and could throw 145 to 150 pitches. It's silly to think that now. But I was lucky I could handle the heat. I don't know why, maybe just growing up in California. It just fell my way that day."

The night before, Righetti, Don Mattingly, Goose Gossage, and several teammates had attended a festival-style concert at Giants Stadium featuring Willie Nelson, Waylon Jennings, Merle Haggard, The Stray Cats, and Linda Ronstadt, among others. Yankees manager Billy Martin also was there. "I ended up leaving pretty early because I had to pitch," Righetti said. "I remember Billy saying, 'What are you doing here?' And I said, 'I'm watching the concert, but I'm going home soon.' I just remember him saying, 'You better go home and you better pitch good tomorrow.' So that was the first thing I told Billy as we walked off the mound after the game: 'How was that?'"

A few key defensive plays also should not be overlooked. Shortstop Roy Smalley made an over-the-shoulder catch to take a potential hit away from Glenn Hoffman in the sixth inning. Right fielder Steve Kemp leapt into the stands to snare Dwight Evans' foul ball in the eighth.

And Dave Winfield, playing center field in place of regular starter Jerry Mumphrey, also ran down two Wade Boggs drives in the gap in right-center. "Mostly, I remember that the heat index was probably like 110 and those two rockets I hit to Winfield," Boggs said. "That stood out to me and then naturally being the last out, striking out, for the no-hitter. I don't think that we otherwise came close to sniffing a hit."

Boggs struck out only 36 times that season en route to his first of five career batting titles, but the future Hall of Famer fanned twice that day, including waving at a 2–2 slider with a runner on second for the final out of the game. Martin later said it was the first time he'd ever prayed during a game. "That picture of Rags spinning around after he finished that off against Boggsy, I'll never forget that," said Mattingly, a rookie that season.

Dave Righetti throws during the ninth inning of his July 4, 1983, no-hitter against the rival Boston Red Sox.

"The thing about Boggs is I had faced him a lot in the minors. I always pitched him well," Righetti said. "I was a tough at-bat for him. I kept him at bay, but that doesn't mean he's not gonna get a hit there. He was the best hitter in the league. To get him, what a feeling."

Amid the euphoria and a handful of on-field interviews, many of Righetti's teammates already had departed by the time he got back to the clubhouse because it was the Yankees' final game before the All-Star break. Winfield and Ron Guidry were headed to the Midsummer Classic, but others were scrambling to make flights. "I didn't get to see hardly anybody," Righetti said. "But George ended up giving every guy on the team—coaches, everybody—a watch commemorating the day. I thought that was cool. I didn't want anything extra."

That didn't stop Dick Young, the venerable New York sports columnist who had shifted from the *New York Daily News* to the *New York Post* in 1981, from taking shots at Steinbrenner for not giving Righetti a bonus for the gem. "I said to him, 'Dick, I know you like to go after George, but he's gonna kill me if you write that. I'll be in Columbus next week,'" Righetti said, referring to the team's Triple A affiliate.

Actually, Atlantic City was Righetti's next stop. Graig Nettles, who sat out the no-hitter with a case of pink eye, had been the lone teammate to speak with Righetti in the latter innings, checking on their plans to drive together for some southern New Jersey gambling that night. Nettles drove despite his limited vision, and the car he was driving got pulled over on the Garden State Parkway by a New Jersey state trooper. "We ended up getting a police escort to A.C.," Righetti said. "When we got down, the Beach Boys were playing on the boardwalk."

By the next season, Righetti was shifted to the bullpen, taking over as the team's closer after Gossage signed with the San Diego Padres as a free agent. It only was supposed to be a one-year stopgap arrangement because Steinbrenner eyed future Hall of Famer Bruce Sutter in free agency for 1985, but Righetti stayed in the job for seven seasons. He amassed 224 of his 252 career saves in that span, the most by a lefty in baseball history until John Franco surpassed him. All-time saves leader Mariano Rivera later shattered Righetti's club mark. "He blew everyone away—the hitters and all the records," Righetti joked. "I knew there were people next to George who were against me closing in the first place. I know Billy didn't want me doing it. He wanted me to start. People were torn about it and arguing about it really until the day I left. All I tried to do was take it as one of the greatest responsibilities a guy could have, the closer in New York for the Yankees, after Sparky and then Goose. I knew the pressure that comes with it. I thought I could handle it and I thought of it as a hell of a compliment. But I definitely was glad to have the no-hitter under my belt before making the change."

44

JIM ABBOTT'S NO-HITTER

Like kids all over America, Jim Abbott wanted to play Little League baseball with his friends, but this remarkable tale is not one of mere participation. In his first organized game, 11-year-old Jim Abbott of Flint, Michigan, tossed a no-hitter. That feat was made all the more incredible by the youngster being born without a right hand. "A true Little League no-no," Abbott said with a laugh in 2019. "Ten walks, all of that. It was just as wild as my major league no-hitter."

Indeed, it would not be Abbott's last pitching performance without allowing a single hit. He also did so for the Yankees during a 4–0 win against the Cleveland Indians on September 4, 1993 in the Bronx. More than a quarter-century later, Abbott continues to serve as an example of perseverance and possibility, a source of inspiration and motivation for the thousands of children and adults he speaks to regularly by recounting his story, almost always ending his speeches with memories of that Saturday afternoon at Yankee Stadium. "Even with all the World Series wins and the other great moments, it still stands out to me— both the feat itself and what he'd gone through. It was extraordinary to watch," longtime Yankees reporter and radio announcer Suzyn Waldman said. "You sat there with your mouth open that a human being could do this."

Abbott was born in 1967 to teenaged parents Mike and Kathy Abbott, who resolved from their son's earliest days to encourage Jim to not allow himself to be hindered or defined by his disability. Mike and Kathy initially believed soccer would be the ideal sport for Jim since he wouldn't need to rely solely on his hands. But he immediately gravitated toward baseball, a sport many of his school-aged friends played and enjoyed.

While he famously spent hours working to develop his hand-eye coordination by throwing a rubber ball against a brick wall, his father worked with him on learning to throw and catch with his left hand by resting his baseball glove on his right wrist before switching it to his left hand immediately after releasing the ball. By the time he got to Flint Central High School, Abbott also played football and basketball. Legendary Michigan coach Bo Schembechler even told him he could have played quarterback for the Wolverines had he concentrated on the gridiron. "He said that, but, honestly, I think he was being very kind," Abbott said. "He was a big baseball fan and loved watching us. He would come over from the football facilities and watch our games. He knew I had played some football in high school, but I think he may have been exaggerating my abilities a little bit."

Abbott's baseball abilities and exploits needed no embellishment. He was such a good athlete that Mariano Rivera recalled seeing Abbott hit "home run after home run" during one batting practice session in spring training of 1994. Playing mostly in the American League, Abbott managed two singles in 21 at-bats in the major leagues with the Milwaukee Brewers in 1999, though he did rip a triple against Rick Reuschel once in a Grapefruit League game. "If Mariano Rivera remembers a story about me, I'm never going to downplay it or deny it," Abbott joked. "But I certainly can admit that I wasn't in the majors because of my bat."

Before reaching the major leagues, Abbott was an All-Conference pitcher at Michigan, leading the school to two Big Ten championships. He was named the winner of the James E. Sullivan Award as the top amateur athlete in the United States in 1987. Abbott also pitched the unofficial gold medal-winning game (with baseball a demonstration sport) against Japan in the 1988 Olympics in Seoul after being drafted with the eighth overall pick earlier that summer by the California Angels. "Things were happening so quickly, but playing on the USA team was really a formative part of my baseball life," Abbott said. "That was kind of the point where I had started to have the feeling I could play in the major leagues."

Abbott never even appeared in a minor league game before making 29 starts and going 12–12 with a 3.92 ERA for the Angels in 1989, finishing fifth in the balloting for American League Rookie of the Year. Two years later he was among the best pitchers in baseball with a record of 18–11 and a 2.89 ERA for a third-place showing in Cy

Young voting behind Roger Clemens of the Boston Red Sox and Scott Erickson of the Minnesota Twins. "I felt a certain validation that I had maybe moved a little beyond the label of being a one-handed pitcher and a curiosity. Now there was some substance behind it," Abbott said. "Truthfully, that was always my real motivation. I wanted to be good. I wanted to be more than just the one-handed guy."

In December of 1992, Abbott was shipped to the Yankees, who were coming off four straight losing seasons for the first time since 1912–15, for a three-player package headlined by top first-base prospect J.T. Snow. His first season in pinstripes proved to be an uneven one, but on May 29 against the Chicago White Sox in the Bronx, Abbott carried a no-hit bid into the eighth inning until Bo Jackson broke it up with a bloop single with one out. "That was a really great preparation for the September no-hitter itself," Abbott said. "I had the excitement of a no-hitter, had that momentum, and then Bo kind of hit it off the end. He didn't hit it well. It was kind of a fluky hit, but it broke up the no-hitter, and then the next batter Ron Karkovice hit a home run. So I knew how fickle a no-hitter could be and how fleeting the excitement of it could go away. That really helped keep me dialed in when the next time rolled around."

The next time seemed just as improbable, as Abbott carried a 9–11 record and a 4.31 ERA into his September 4 start against a stacked Indians lineup that featured Kenny Lofton, Carlos Baerga, Albert Belle, Jim Thome, and a rookie named Manny Ramirez. The Tribe had knocked Abbott around for seven runs in three and two-thirds innings in his previous outing six days earlier. "I got beat up pretty bad. It was a real low point," Abbott said. "I didn't live up to the expectations the Yankees had for me and I didn't fulfill the role that they had hoped at the top of the starting rotation. I'm not trying to be overly dramatic, but the game before the no-hitter was a real down point."

In between those two series against Cleveland, the Yankees played a three-game set against the White Sox. Abbott sensed a change in his outlook after going to dinner one night with two close friends, former Team USA teammate Robin Ventura and former Angels teammate Kirk McCaskill. "I felt a little bit of a weight come off my shoulders," Abbott said. "It was good to see some old friends. I just felt sort of renewed a little bit, maybe from bouncing off the bottom. For whatever reason, the heaviness had dissipated. But not in a million years could I ever have imagined a no-hitter right up until the moment that it actually happened."

Abbott credits Yankees catcher Matt Nokes and pitching coach Tony Cloninger with altering his gameplan against Cleveland and mixing in more off-speed pitches and breaking balls. The plan worked. Harkening back to his initial Little League no-no, Abbott said he was "effectively wild," walking five and leaving the Indians with few meaty pitches to square up and hammer. In the seventh inning, third baseman Wade Boggs made a diving stab to his left and threw to Don Mattingly to barely nip Belle at first. "You could feel it in the stadium at that moment. Everything sort of kicked in," Abbott said. "I think you felt by the fans' excitement what was happening. From that moment on, everything had a different feel."

The buzz, the anticipation, and the delirium hit a crescendo when Baerga came to the plate with one out remaining in the ninth. Batting from the left side despite facing the lefty Abbott, the switch-hitting Baerga grounded out to shortstop Randy Velarde for the first of four no-hitters at the stadium in the '90s. "Absolutely electric," Abbott said. "I remember recalling the Olympics, standing out there in the gold-medal game in the ninth inning. I had the exact same feeling of really wanting this result, of really being excited and yet very much aware of the vagaries of the game and how things can go wrong, and you can throw a good pitch, and a bad thing can happen. I felt all of that swirling and was just trying to harness all of that and focus on Matt Nokes' mitt and throwing a quality pitch."

The fun continued that night, as Abbott and his wife met up with Mattingly in Manhattan at the popular restaurant Cronies. "So happy for Jimmy, such a competitor from the standpoint that he was really too hard on himself," Mattingly said. "That's what was most satisfying—to watch him get it. He'd been really struggling, and to see that, to share it all with him, was amazing."

By the time dinner was over that night, the paparazzi swarmed outside the restaurant waiting for them. The front-page headline of the *New York Daily News* already blared "DANDY!" "I don't know how they found out. They must have been tipped off, but cameras were everywhere," Abbott said. "We woke up the next morning, and there were cameras outside our apartment building. It was a Saturday night, and all of the early editions of the New York papers were on the newsstands. My picture was on the front page or the back page of all the papers. People were running up for autographs, cars were honking. To see Donnie that night, it was a pretty low-key celebration, to be honest, other than we drank a little too much champagne. But I really loved it. I just felt enveloped that night by the city itself, and it's a moment I'll never forget."

Of course, the moment, as such moments often are, would be fleeting. Abbott dropped three of his final four starts that season before pitching one more pedestrian season in pinstripes, finishing with a 9–8 record and a 4.55 ERA in 24 starts in the strike-abridged 1994 campaign.

That spring Abbott even felt the wrath of Yankees owner George Steinbrenner, who publicly accused him of focusing more on his charity work than his pitching in the offseason. "I was taken aback a little bit it," Abbott said. "Anybody who knew me knew how focused I was on pitching well. But it was fair at the same time. They traded for me, traded some good players for me, and I think they expected me to be a top of the rotation pitcher. I wasn't that unfortunately. I didn't think it was because of any lack of effort. I didn't think it was for any lack of focus. But it was really sort of the first time in my athletic career that I faced that sort of scrutiny and criticism. It was tough, and I had to face it, but it was true. As an owner, even if it was a little misplaced, I felt like I understood the sentiment."

Abbott's career never again reached the pinnacle of that September afternoon against the Indians. Back with the Angels in 1996, he dropped 18 of 20 decisions and was rocked for a 7.48 ERA. At age 29 he briefly retired before pitching two more nondescript seasons with the White Sox and the Brewers. Neither his career record of 87–108 nor his career ERA of 4.25 merited inclusion in the Baseball Hall of Fame, and he received just 2.5 percent of the polling in 2005, his lone year on the ballot. But his hat from the no-hitter represents him at the Hall of Fame, while the pitching rubber signed by his Yankees teammates and the umpiring crew hangs at his home in Southern California.

More importantly, the 10-year Major League Baseball veteran has inspired and personally encouraged thousands of children with various disabilities. One-handed goalie Joe Rogers played NCAA hockey at Notre Dame. One-handed linebacker Shaquem Griffin played college football at Central Florida and was drafted in the fifth round of the 2018 NFL Draft by the Seattle Seahawks. "It's been really the pride of my life outside of family," said Abbott, whose two daughters were students at Michigan as of 2019. "I still receive a lot of nice letters and emails and tweets. A lot of kids I met at Yankee Stadium, or Angels Stadium, or all over the country, are now growing up and doing fun, interesting things. It's a pretty amazing feeling.

"Almost every speech I finish up with the story of the no-hitter and sort of walking through that game. There's a really cool connection, and the feedback I've gotten about that moment and my story and the lessons that people take away from it, you never would have imagined waking up that September morning going to Yankee Stadium that it would have that kind of effect on my life and that people would be impacted by it in such a way."

45

THE 1999 YANKEES

Joe Torre said the emotions and heartache that underscored the 1999 season made it special. Everyone in the media wanted to dub the 1999 Yankees "The Team of the Century," even though they long ago had established that moniker. That was the wraparound front page of the *New York Daily News* after the final game of my third year on the beat, which ended with a four-game sweep of the Atlanta Braves in the World Series. But general manager Brian Cashman admits the circumstances surrounding that title made it "very different than the other years."

The Yankees reported to spring training in February determined to accomplish what they were unable to in 1997—defend the championship they had captured the previous year.

Pitchers and catchers barely had showed up to the training complex in Tampa, Florida, when Cashman pulled off a blockbuster trade, shipping David Wells—coming off an 18–4 year that featured a perfect game—along with lefty reliever Graeme Lloyd and popular utility infielder/pinch-runner deluxe Homer Bush to the Toronto Blue Jays for five-time Cy Young Award winner Roger Clemens. "I was excited because Clemens is Clemens. You hated him for a reason," Torre said. "He was a bulldog out on the mound. Not that Wellsy wasn't. But I didn't think twice about making the deal, even though Wells had a big year."

Cashman didn't either, explaining that he worked on various permutations with Toronto counterpart Gord Ash throughout that winter. "Our team had been 125–50. It was a historic team with a historic performance," Cashman said. "But that winter Roger Clemens, who was a multi-time Cy Young Award winner who had accomplished everything in his career but a World Series title, legendary work ethic, legendary competitor, all of that, was on the market. And that coincided with David Wells spending the winter celebrating and partying and traveling with [actor] Tom Arnold here and there on his private jet everywhere. There was a lot of internal thought about our particular team, and as we moved forward as a franchise, what would be the best interests to stay hungry and competitive? I felt like infusing Roger Clemens would be the pure benefit for that. It was a big risk, but a risk I was willing to take."

On a personal note, my son was six years old during that spring training and already a die-hard Yankees fan to surprisingly detailed levels for that age. When I returned to our Tampa, Florida, condo complex that night and informed him of the trade, his initial reaction wasn't about the Yankees acquiring Clemens or even trading Wells. "They traded Homer Bush?" He asked. "Who's gonna run for Chili?"

Chili Davis was an aging designated hitter who had missed much of the 1998 season with a foot injury. He would drive in 78 runs in 1999, the last season of a highly productive 19-year career. "Tell him I was thinking the exact same thing," Davis, who returned to New York as the Mets' batting coach in 2019, said with a laugh.

The next day, on Clemens' first day in pinstripes, Chuck Knoblauch and Derek Jeter emerged for live batting practice wearing full catcher's gear in an attempt to lighten the mood after years of being on the receiving end of brushback pitches from The Rocket. "It was such an important acquisition—even if it was a bit of a shock," Paul O'Neill said. "That's what I respected Mr. Steinbrenner so much for. It was like, whatever we needed in those years, we got."

That spring would feature another shock when Torre called O'Neill, David Cone, and Joe Girardi into his office on the morning of March 11—the same day Darryl Strawberry was slated to appear in his first spring training game in Fort Myers, Florida, against the Boston Red Sox, following his colon cancer treatment the previous season. Torre asked them to tell their teammates that he would be leaving for an undisclosed amount of time to receive treatment for a prostate cancer diagnosis. "Anytime you hear that word, especially with someone you respect like Joe Torre," O'Neill said, "that was a really hard thing to hear and have to do."

"Devastating," Torre said. "The worst was waiting for the results. You hear the word 'cancer' and you think the worst. I called my wife and my older daughter. It was scary, but the doctors sort of relaxed me a little bit, and I went in for the surgery the following week."

Although Torre wishes in hindsight he would have recommended pitching coach Mel Stottlemyre to fill in as the interim manager, Steinbrenner turned to the 68-year-old Zimmer to run the team in the manager's absence. "The Boss on his own tracked Zimmer down and met with him and said, 'You're up.' At that stage of his career, Zim really wasn't capable of manning the head chair," Cashman said. "We had a lot of disorganization. Zim stepped up to do the best he could, but at that stage of his life, there was only so much he was capable of providing."

Said Torre: "I've made a lot of mistakes, but the one big mistake I made was asking George if it was okay if Zim took over as the interim manager. That broke their friendship. You could see everything was wearing on Zim. In retrospect, I should have had Mel take over and just have Zim be the bench coach. He still could have essentially managed but without being out front and in the crosshairs so much."

Those crosshairs came into focus during the final game of spring training. With the Yankees slated to play an exhibition game the next night against the Dodgers in Los Angeles before starting their title defense in Oakland, Japanese pitcher Hideki Irabu failed to cover first base on a ground ball. I was standing next to a fuming Steinbrenner when he infamously emerged from the elevators and called Irabu "a fat puss-y toad." Reporters conferred with their offices to determine how to write "puss-y" (it rhymes with fussy), so it didn't appear that The Boss had called one of his players a "pussy." However you spell it, his insult led the team plane to be delayed for nearly two hours. "It was like a hostage-crisis situation, trying to talk Irabu into getting on the plane. It held up everything," Cashman said. "It truly was a circus for a while as we navigated the '99 season. It was very different than '98, where other than the little hiccup with the slow start, everything came easy. '99 was quite the opposite."

Irabu's rights had been acquired in a trade from the San Diego Padres in 1997. He initially stayed back in Tampa, Florida, but Steinbrenner told me and other reporters the next day by phone that his $12.8 million investment would rejoin the team and start later that week in Oakland. Zimmer flipped out when media members informed him of Steinbrenner's plan because he already had informed valuable rotation swingman Ramiro Mendoza he'd be taking Irabu's spot. Zim provided blaring headlines when he verbally laced into Steinbrenner cross-country from Dodger Stadium, hardly caring about the risk of getting fired. "Who called him a fat pig or plum?" Zimmer asked. "Who started it all? Nothing would have been said if he wasn't ranting and raving. But now it's history all over the world...I don't care. He says what he wants. I am a human being and I'm not in prison. I'm sure he isn't going to like it. I respect him, but I am going to say what I want to say, too. You can't be a little wimp. I have never been scared in my life and I am not scared now. I am saying things now that will get back to George, and he will read it. I can't run his life, but no one can run mine. That will go over good, too. He is The Boss and he has fired better people than me."

Irabu, who had gone 13–9 with a 4.06 ERA in 1998, was traded after the '99 season to the Montreal Expos. He started only 16 games with Montreal and the Texas Rangers over the next three seasons before returning to pitch in Japan. After multiple arrests for driving while intoxicated during his retirement, Irabu committed suicide in 2011, reportedly hanging himself at his Los Angeles home. An autopsy showed he had large amounts of alcohol and an anxiety medication in his system. Tragically, death and mourning would play a role during the 1999 season.

Torre returned to Boston on May 18, adding it "really meant a lot to me" that the fans at Fenway Park greeted him with a two-minute standing ovation when he brought out the lineup cards. The Yankees had been 21–15 under Zimmer and, despite winning only 11 of 20 upon Torre's return, they regained first place from the Red Sox on June 9 and remained there for the rest of the season, finishing with 98 wins. In addition to Cone's perfect game, Jeter batted .349 with a .438 on-base percentage (and more than 100 RBIs for the only time in his career). Bernie Williams was right behind him in both percentage categories at .342 and .435. Jim Leyritz even was reacquired at the trade deadline after opposing the Yankees in the 1998 World Series with San Diego. "I'd been hurt and was on a rehab assignment in July, and [Padres

Mariano Rivera jumps into the arms of catcher Jorge Posada after the Yankees defeated the Atlanta Braves 4–1 in Game 4 of the 1999 World Series.

GM] Kevin Towers told me he had a deal for me to go to the Red Sox," Leyritz said. "I was like, 'No, I can't do it, please no. Give me 24 hours.' So I called my agent and said, 'I don't want to be a Red Sox. See what you can find.' I personally called George's assistant in Tampa and told her to get a message to George that Boston was trading for me and I don't want to go there. Twenty-four hours later, I was in New York."

After sweeping Texas in the division series for a second straight year, the Yankees got back to the World Series with a five-game ousting of Boston in the first postseason series ever played between the longtime rivals (the one-game playoff in 1978 was considered an extension of the season). Williams nearly had signed with Boston the previous winter, but he ripped a 10th-inning homer to win Game 1 en route to a 2–0 series lead. Pedro Martinez dominated Game 3 at Fenway—while Clemens was hammered with chants of "Where is Roger?"—in a 13–1 Red Sox drubbing. "I remember Yogi walking in after that game," Davis said. "'What's this with you guys hanging your heads? Those guys haven't beat us for 80 years, and they're not gonna beat us now.' I'll never forget that."

Ricky Ledee belted a grand slam to seal Game 4. Jeter, Jorge Posada, and Williams went deep in Game 5 to set up another World Series matchup with the Atlanta Braves. "We're not going there to lose, I'll tell you that," Steinbrenner told reporters during the postgame celebration.

An editor at my newspaper, the *Daily News*, pulled that accurately reported quote out of my game story and changed it to "We're not going to lose" for a headline. Steinbrenner and Yankees media relations director Rick Cerrone were furious with the small but significant change, which made it seem as if he'd guaranteed victory.

The anger turned out to be unnecessary. The Yankees executed a second straight World Series sweep—the first team to do that since the 1938–39 Yankees—defeating tri-aces Greg Maddux, Tom Glavine, and John Smoltz for the second time in four Octobers.

Clemens, who had endured a shaky first season in New York with a 14–10 record and a career-worst 4.60 ERA while dealing with assorted leg ailments, even was on the mound for the clinching game. He allowed just one run in seven and two-thirds innings to outduel Smoltz before World Series MVP Mariano Rivera recorded his sixth save of an 11–1 postseason for the Yankees. Leyritz fittingly even went deep in the eighth inning of Game 4, the final home run of the century.

The enduring snapshot of that particular mound celebration, however, was O'Neill breaking down in tears in Torre's arms after the final out was recorded. Scott Brosius' father had died in September, and Luis Sojo's dad also had passed away in Venezuela earlier in the postseason. Each necessitated a brief absence. In the early morning prior to Game 4 of the World Series, O'Neill's father, Charles, died at Lenox Hill Hospital in New York of complications from heart disease. "We had the 3–0 lead going into Game 4, and I was on my way to the ballpark when I got a call from Nevele, Paulie's wife," Torre said. "She said, 'He has to play tonight. He has to. I know his dad just died, but he has to play.' And then I talked to Paul when I got there, and he just said, 'My dad would want me to play this game.' When we met at the mound after the game, it was like the emotion of that whole season took a toll on everyone. I know it wasn't '98, but that club was really special for different reasons."

Sojo wasn't surprised O'Neill suited up. "It was a heartbreaking year," Sojo said. "But that's what was so special about that team. Everybody was like, 'Your problem is my problem.' All the phone calls I got when I went back to Venezuela to bury my father, Joe Torre said, 'Your spot is here whenever you come back.' My mom said to me, 'Your dad wanted you to play baseball.' So I knew I'm going to be okay. I was able to come back and win the World Series with my teammates. All of our dads always wanted us to play baseball."

O'Neill now recalls the entire day as "a blur," but he insists he never really gave consideration to not playing. He did not take part in the champagne celebration in the clubhouse, however, instead spending it in quiet reflection in trainer Gene Monahan's office. "When I got to the ballpark that night, I figured out pretty quick that everyone knew. Even the Braves players were coming up to me and saying how sorry they were. It's a part of life, but a weird way to spend it on a baseball field," O'Neill said. "That's one World Series that I don't really remember like the others. I just remember when it was over. I didn't even feel like celebrating. It was more something I got through. It's a World Series, but you lose your father once in your life. It really took away all the memories. I was just numb. Looking back, I can't even remember a lot of plays from that World Series. I can remember every single play from every other year, but that one is just a total blur. But I'm also so proud of that World Series, especially, because we'd really been through so much as a team that year. They're all definitely special in their own way."

46

STICK MICHAEL

You know how so many of the Marvel Universe or DC Comics movies have an origin story? Well, call this the origin story for the superheroes known as the Yankees' 1990s dynasty.

The Yankees finally had bottomed out, following a series of free-agent failures—and zero World Series titles—through the entire decade of the '80s, finishing in last place in the American League East in 1990 with a 67–95 record. George Steinbrenner also was suspended by commissioner Fay Vincent for three years for paying a gambler and convicted felon named Howie Spira $40,000 to dig up dirt on Dave Winfield and his charitable foundation.

During The Boss' banishment, general manager Gene "Stick" Michael began a methodical transformation of the roster, notably acquiring fiery Paul O'Neill from the Cincinnati Reds for talented outfielder Roberto Kelly in 1993. Respected veterans such as Jimmy Key and Wade Boggs were signed as free agents, and Cy Young Award-winning pitchers Jack McDowell and David Cone were acquired to help change the culture. Bernie Williams became the first to arrive from a young core of homegrown talent that Michael made painfully sure to avoid trading unlike so many prospects over the preceding tumultuous decade. "No doubt, I think the quality of those guys that Stick brought in really is what started turning it," Don Mattingly said. "O'Neill, Jimmy Key, Boggsy came over. Jim Abbott was in there somewhere, and then Bernie came up. It was more like the character changed. We were getting more hard-nosed guys who played hard and went about it every day the right way. They were good fits for New York. They had the right intentions, and then when Buck came in and did a great job of putting it together and turning it around, suddenly, everyone all had the right attitude. Guys could feel it turning."

Buck Showalter was the 35 year old who improbably ascended quickly through the ranks of the organization to replace Stump Merrill as manager in 1992. "Mr. Steinbrenner and the front office just got tired of losing," Boggs said. "With Boston and Toronto winning the division every year and the Yankees finishing last, I just think going out and getting the players that Stick and Buck were going after were players of similar personalities. I think that was a sticking point. None of us were there for any BS reasons. I think that was a reason we all got along so well together."

Said O'Neill: "You could see that Stick had a lot of say in what they were going to do, getting rid of some people who, I guess, didn't really fit what they wanted to bring in [as far as] the right people in order to win. I thought that was interesting because the tradition of the Yankees always had been to win, but they hadn't done it in a long time. They obviously felt like something needed to change."

By 1994 Showalter and the Yankees owned the best record in the American League (70–43) when an August players' strike resulted in the cancellation of the rest of the season and the World Series. They returned to the playoffs the following year after a 14-year absence before squandering a two-game lead in a division-series loss to the Seattle Mariners. "In '94 you really started to see it was kind of the first step, and then '95 was another one," O'Neill said. "The change of Buck to Joe Torre for '96 was kind of the final thing with the Core Four showing up. It was kind of the perfect storm. But you saw what was happening, what Stick did those earlier years, and it was incredible to be considered a part of that turnaround."

Michael, who died of a heart attack in 2017, had been the prototypical sure-handed but light-hitting shortstop over a 10-year playing career, including seven seasons with the Yankees from 1968 to 1974. He was tabbed by Steinbrenner as general manager in 1980 but shifted to the dugout for the first of two half-season stints as manager in 1981 before being fired in September. After Bob Lemon returned to lead the Yankees to the World Series against the Los Angeles Dodgers, Michael replaced an axed Lemon in the second half of the next season. He later managed the Chicago Cubs for parts of two seasons before returning as the Yankees general manager upon Steinbrenner's ban in 1990. "I'm not looking for somebody to say yes to me," Steinbrenner said. "Gene is loyal. That's his greatest asset, but he'll tell me if he thinks I'm wrong."

Michael slid into roles as the head of scouting and senior advisor to Steinbrenner, following the 1995 season. When baseball scouting shifted to more analytics and statistic-driven decision making thereafter, Michael said in 2014, "Numbers are important only to the degree you can blend them with what a scout has seen with his own eyes." Through the draft, trades, and free-agent signings, Stick also was responsible for the acquisition—and more importantly the retention—of the majority of players who formed the nucleus of the team that won four World Series titles in five years, beginning in 1996.

Of course, personnel mistakes were made in those years, too. Free-agent acquisition Danny Tartabull's biggest contribution as a Yankees player might have been the two cameos he made on *Seinfeld*. The Yankees also wasted the No. 1 overall draft pick in 1991 on left-handed high school pitcher Brien Taylor, who suffered a career-ending shoulder injury two years later in a bar fight while still in the minors. The best player in that draft turned out to be New York City outfielder Manny Ramirez, who went to the Cleveland Indians at No. 13. The Yankees made up for that mistake the following year by grabbing a high-school shortstop from Michigan named Derek Jeter with the sixth overall selection.

Perhaps Michael's most important accomplishment was constantly fighting and convincing the ever-impatient Steinbrenner, who was reinstated to operating control of the team by 1993, to resist trading the likes of Jeter, Mariano Rivera, Andy Pettitte, and many others in that decade. "He would talk to us after these big blowups with The Boss and The Boss wanting to fire him," said Brian Cashman, who took over as GM in 1998. "He would just sit there and talk from his desk about it, more talking out loud than anything probably. It was: 'You can't sacrifice your integrity. You can't do something that sells your soul.' He'd say, 'George asked me to do things, and I just couldn't do it.' It certainly served me well, when all of a sudden, shockingly, I was offered the next step."

The Yankees eventually took the next step because of Michael's stewardship, one of the baseball's best origin stories ever told. "It all started in '93 when they brought Buck aboard after Stick was already there, and they started with that youth movement and then added all of those important guys from the outside," said homegrown 1996 World Series hero Jim Leyritz. "We'd been sitting around the minor leagues for a few years waiting for our opportunity, but I think most of us were praying to get traded. We knew if we got traded from the Yankees, we'd probably get to the big leagues faster with someone else. But Stick started building this thing the right way. By '93 when Buck took over, the team was starting to develop. The next year, it was ready to take off. And everyone knows what happened after that."

47

THE NEW BOSS

Meet the new boss. He isn't anything close to the same as The (old) Boss. Aside from the same insatiable desire to win championships, Hal Steinbrenner couldn't possess a more disparate personality or approach from his infamous father. "When I went into this, I was already close to 40 years old when I became the control person. I was not going to go into this, trying to be somebody that I wasn't," said Hal Steinbrenner, who took over as managing general partner of the Yankees in 2009. "That's just not my personality. I've got strengths and I've got weaknesses, and they're different strengths and weaknesses than my dad or any other person. I just try to do the best I can. It's a blessing to have this job, of course. And I know if my name wasn't Steinbrenner, I wouldn't be sitting here. I know that and appreciate it and try to treat the job with respect. But never did I try to be somebody that I wasn't. I'm not a very good actor. George was one of a kind. There's no doubt about it."

That much is abundantly clear, which only makes Hal Steinbrenner's handling of a monumental job he admittedly inherited by birthright so much more fascinating. Hal Steinbrenner is the youngest of George and Joan Zieg Steinbrenner's four children, a self-described "science geek" and impassioned pilot whose favorite childhood memory with his father was a trip the two of them took together to NASA's Kennedy Space Center near Orlando, Florida, when he was 11 years old. "I'm a left side of the brain guy. There's no doubt about it. I'm a pilot and was a psychology major with a lot of geology and astronomy in college. So yes, I've always been more of a math and science guy," Hal said. "George, he was an English major, so he was pushing me to be an English major, and I wanted nothing to do with that, so he wasn't too happy. But amazingly enough, since it's only about an hour away, I've only been to Kennedy Space Center one time, and it was actually with him—pre-shuttle years, probably like 1979 or '80. I still remember it well. I remember seeing the Saturn V rocket and thinking it was the biggest thing I'd ever seen in my life. It probably still is. It was a good experience, and my dad had never been there either. Clearly, he did it for me."

Like his father and siblings, Hal attended Culver Military Academy in Indiana. He also matriculated at his father's alma mater, Williams College, and earned an MBA from the University of Florida, while taking on executive roles with both the Yankees and the family's hotel business upon graduation in 1994. Initially, it was Steinbrenner sons-in-law Joe Molloy, who was married to daughter Jessica, and Steve Swindal, who was wed to Jennifer, who assumed the most prominent roles with the team in the 1990s. Both marriages ended in divorce, however, leaving them without jobs in the organization.

George's older son, Hank, also briefly became the face of the new regime in the late 2000s. His similarities to his father—both in temperament and outspokenness—were readily apparent. "Very intelligent, as George was, very cerebral. More intelligent than me, quite frankly, but yes, a lot more like George than I am," Hal said of his brother.

Hank, 12 years older than Hal, publicly referred to the notion of Red Sox Nation as "a bunch of bullshit." "Go anywhere in America and you won't see Red Sox hats and jackets," he said. "You'll see Yankee hats and jackets. This is a Yankee country." He took public potshots at Major League Baseball over the expanded playoff format and at teams such as the Tampa Bay Devil Rays (later known as the Rays) over how they spent revenue sharing dollars received from the Yankees and other large-market teams. Once, I got Hank on the phone during "The Joba Rules" era when they were determining whether pitcher Joba Chamberlain should be a starter or a reliever. Informed that Johnny Damon believed Joba should be in the bullpen, Hank replied, "I like Johnny, but let's face it, he isn't exactly Branch Rickey."

Hank remains a general partner and co-chairman on the pinstriped masthead, but he mostly remains in the background to concentrate on the family's hotel properties and horse breeding business. Hal has been front and center since 2009, when he authorized Brian Cashman to spend more than $420 million on free agents CC Sabathia, A.J. Burnett, and Mark Teixeira, leading to the lone World Series title since the 2000 championship against the New York Mets.

"I don't know if my excitement was because it was my first full year as managing general partner, as much as because we didn't make the playoffs the year before," Hal said. "To go from that, and then picking up a few key acquisitions, and them really paying off, and A-Rod contributing the way he did [after his PED admission], and the core guys who already had been on the team, it was a very rewarding year and clearly another memory that will be for the rest of my life."

Hal also has succinct memories of the Yankees from his childhood, noting his favorite players were Thurman Munson, Willie Randolph, and Lou Piniella, whose family also hailed from Tampa, Florida. "I'll never forget the first World Series, even though we lost, because it was the first for my dad, first for the family. That first American League pennant, when Chambliss hit the home run against Kansas City, I was there for that," he said. "It was beyond surreal and it ended up being chaotic in fact. And then the first world championship the next year, when Lee Lacy popped up to Mike Torrez for the last out, I was there and I remember that unbelievably, vividly, being down in the clubhouse afterward with Dad and Billy."

That is not to suggest that growing up as a Steinbrenner always was easy or pleasant.

"George was tough. His father was very tough on him, and he expected a lot out of us," Hal said. "There were no shenanigans allowed. He was a tough boss, too. I had him around the clock, so to speak. I started working here in '91, while I was doing a few other things. But my office has always been next to George's. As you can imagine, that was interesting, to say the least."

Whereas George Steinbrenner was infamously boisterous and blustery and prone to impulsive decisions, Hal is more reticent, reserved, and calculated in his decision making and everyday life. "The Boss was emotional and reactionary, and Hal is very methodical and pragmatic and wants all the info before he comes to a conclusion of what's the best decision," Cashman said. "He's the exact opposite of emotional and reactionary, completely opposite."

"We had different personalities. Let's just say that," Hal Steinbrenner said. "I like to take as much time as I can and get as much information as I can before I do anything. I just don't believe in rash decisions and getting rid of people without thinking it through and making sure that things actually are going wrong because of that individual. We're different in those ways definitely, but George was a very passionate man, and that's what people loved about him and appreciated about him, too. Sometimes it was good, and sometimes it definitely was not good."

Business definitely remains good for the Yankees. The franchise that George Steinbrenner originally purchased for $8.8 million—with a personal commitment of just $168,000—was estimated by *Forbes* to be worth $4.6 billion in 2019. Hal has insisted for years there are no immediate plans to sell. George Steinbrenner referred to handing down the family business to allowing the "young elephants in the tent."

Hal lists several of George's 14 grandchildren as having interest in one day taking over: Jennifer's son, Stephen Swindal Jr.; Jessica's son, Robert Molloy; Hank's daughter, Julia, and son, George Michael IV; as well as Hal's daughter, Katherine. "It's in the family. The grandkids are very involved, and that's a good sign because I'm not going to be here forever," Hal said. "That transition will happen easier under my watch. Believe me. There will come a point when I want to travel a bit and see the world and maybe build a hotel or two again. That day will come. Nothing in the near future, but I expect to have an easier time with that than George did. That's for sure."

48

YANKEE STADIUM

Five teams in baseball history have won the World Series in the first year playing in a shiny new home ballpark. It's only fitting that the Yankees were two of them. Bookended championships No. 1 and No. 27 came in 1923, the year the famed "House that Ruth Built" was so christened, and the year after The Cathedral in the Bronx was closed, respectively. The Yankees opened their new monolithic shrine to history and owner George Steinbrenner across 161st Street with their 27th World Series title in 2009. "It meant so much to win that first year in the new building," Hal Steinbrenner said. "We loved the old stadium. There was so much incredible history there, but there were a lot of maintenance issues, too. It was getting more and more difficult when 200-pound beams were falling and things like that. It's never easy to let go, but it was time. And we certainly opened it the right way."

The other three teams to accomplish that championship feat during a stadium debut season were the 1909 Pittsburgh Pirates at Forbes Field, the 1912 Boston Red Sox at Fenway Park, and the 2006 St. Louis Cardinals at the new Busch Stadium. The Yankees had shared the Polo Grounds in upper Manhattan for 10 seasons, surpassing the more established Giants in attendance three straight years upon Babe Ruth's heisted arrival in 1920. They topped a million each year, though they lost to their landlords in the World Series in both 1921 and 1922.

Yankee Stadium opened to great fanfare the next spring, across the Macombs Dam Bridge in the Bronx. The construction took barely 11 months and cost $2.4 million. John Philip Sousa's regiment band played "The Star-Spangled Banner" on Opening Day, and Ruth fittingly belted the first home run in a playing field with dimensions supposedly tailored toward his strengths. His three-run shot off Boston's Howard Ehmke carried into the right-field seats for a 4–1 Yankees win before what the team announced as a Major League Baseball-record crowd in excess of 74,000. "Some ballyard," The Babe exclaimed after the game, according to *Newsday*.

Fred Lieb of the *New York Evening Telegram* was more of a wordsmith and widely was credited with the first referral to "The House that Ruth Built." One year after enduring the worst World Series performance of his career (.118 with no homers), Ruth led the way with a .368 average and three longballs among six extra-base hits over six games against the Giants for the first of 26 championships and several historic moments to come over 85 years in the original Yankee Stadium.

In addition to the Yankees' unparalleled success, Yankee Stadium hosted various presidents, three popes, and rock concerts by stars such as Billy Joel, Pink Floyd, and U2 (which I attended). There also were numerous marquee events in other sports through the years, including the heavyweight title rematch in 1938 when Joe Louis regained his belt with a first-round knockout of Adolf Hitler-supported German champion Max Schmeling. Louis participated in seven other fights at the stadium, which also featured subsequent championship bouts involving Max Baer, Sugar Ray Robinson, and Muhammad Ali, who defeated Ken Norton in a unanimous decision in 1976. Additionally, nearly 40 college football games were played across the Yankee Stadium outfield, including 22 between Notre Dame and Army. The NFL's New York Giants played there from 1956 to 1973, including the 1958 NFL Championship Game, a 23–17 overtime loss to the Baltimore Colts widely referred to as "the greatest game ever played."

Yankee Stadium underwent various renovations over the decades, but none were more in-depth than a massive $100 million overhaul during the 1974–75 seasons, forcing the Yankees to play home games at Shea Stadium in Queens. "It just wasn't home," Roy White said. "It was no fun to have to share a stadium with the Mets. It was great to finally be back in our own stadium with our own fans in '76."

The Yankees returned to the World Series on Chris Chambliss' American League Championship Series-winning homer albeit, getting swept by the Cincinnati Reds before winning it all each of the next two years.

Cosmetically, the alterations were drastic. The expansive field dimensions were tightened considerably. Death Valley in left-center field was shortened by about 19 feet from 430 to 411, and the monuments for Ruth, Lou Gehrig, and Miller Huggins that used to be in deep center moved to a new museum-like area known as Monument Park beyond the moved-in wall in left-center. (Ten years later the outfield dimensions were further shortened.) There also was the removal of view-obstructing support columns throughout the stands, green seating was replaced by blue, a new press box and 16 luxury suites was constructed between the upper bowl and the field-level seating, and a chunk of bleacher seats were replaced by a blackened "batter's eye" in center, lowering seating capacity to less than 58,000.

George Steinbrenner spent the next two decades looking for another upgrade in the form of a new stadium, preferably in Manhattan. He also occasionally threatened to move the team to New Jersey, following the football Giants. On April 13, 1998, I was writing for the *New York Daily News* when a 500-pound beam from the upper deck crashed onto an empty seat a few hours before a scheduled game against the Anaheim Angels. The Yankees were forced back to Shea Stadium for the makeup game and shifted another scheduled home series against the Tigers to Detroit while engineers and inspectors tested the structural integrity of the 75-year-old stadium.

This only further emboldened Steinbrenner's desire for a replacement, though attendance continued rising as the Yankees won four championships in five seasons. They hit their first three million turnstile count in 1999, a figure they wouldn't dip below in their final decade in the original stadium. In fact, they surpassed four million in attendance for four straight seasons beginning in 2005, which culminated in a team record 4,298,655 in its final season in 2008.

In addition to the product on the field, the fans enjoyed and appreciated the sights and sounds unique to Yankee Stadium: the final years worked by legendary public-address announcer Bob Sheppard, Eddie Layton on the Hammond organ, fan Freddy "Freddy Sez" Schuman banging his frying pan throughout the stands, and the implementation of "Enter Sandman" as Mariano Rivera's entrance theme. Rowdy and creative-chanting fans in the right-field bleachers eventually would come to be known as "The Bleacher Creatures," dubbed so by *Daily News* columnist Filip Bondy, in the mid-1990s. They started their famed "roll call" around that time, in which each fielder's name (battery excluded) would be chanted until the player acknowledged them in some manner. The ground crew also started dancing to "YMCA" during the fifth-inning infield drag around this time. These traditions were carried over to the new Yankee Stadium in 2009.

The final game in its predecessor, a nationally televised Sunday night game against the Baltimore Orioles, was played September 21, 2008. According to the Yankees' website, more than eight decades earlier, Ruth had said, "I was glad to have hit the first home run in this park. God only knows who will hit the last." That player turned out to be backup catcher Jose Molina, who hit a two-run blast in the fourth inning.

The only silver lining of the playoff whiff (89–73) in Joe Girardi's first season as manager was that everyone knew for weeks when the final home game would be. Before the home finale, dozens of former stars or their widows or descendants took their respective positions alongside the current Yankees lineup. Yogi Berra went to home plate with Elston Howard's daughter, Cheryl, and Thurman Munson's son, Michael. Derek Jeter was joined by Cora Rizzuto. David Mantle, Kay Murcer, and Bernie Williams stood together in center. Randy Maris, Reggie Jackson, and Paul O'Neill were in right. Whitey Ford and perfect game hurlers Don Larsen, David Cone, and David Wells were among those on the mound. Ruth's daughter, 92-year-old Julia Ruth Stevens, even threw out the first pitch.

Afterward in the ultimate torch passing, Jeter grabbed a microphone and addressed the crowd and said: "We are relying on you to take the memories from this stadium, add them to the new memories that come at the new Yankee Stadium, and continue to pass them on from generation to generation."

That didn't stop the organization and memorabilia partner Steiner Sports form gouging those same fans for tangible mementos representing those memories in an everything-must-go liquidation sale. It sold seats ($1,500 per pair), pieces of the foul poles, even vials of infield dirt, and more. (Jeter took home the Joe DiMaggio sign, housing his quote thanking the "Good Lord for making me a Yankee.") Final demolition didn't take place until May 2010, and the old site transformed into a 10-acre park dubbed Heritage Field.

The new Yankee Stadium unmistakably was a $2.3 billion shrine to the Yankees and their vaunted past. The plaza outside was named for Ruth. The behemoth 500,000-square foot structure featured a replication of the infamous arched façade or frieze, rimming the top of the old stadium. Thurman Munson's preserved locker was moved in one piece for viewing in a new public museum. Concourses and sightlines also were vastly improved. Amenities and concessions were top drawer. There were 56 luxury suites and 30,000-square feet of clubhouse space for the players. On Opening Day, George Steinbrenner waved to the crowd, having lived to see the new stadium. (He died the following year.) My longtime *Daily News* teammate Anthony McCarron squeezed one more quote out of him: "It's beautiful," he said.

That level of beauty and extravagance came at a hefty cost, of course. Ticket prices ranged from $500 to $2,500 for premium seats behind and around home plate. TV shots regularly showed swaths of emptiness in that area. Hal Steinbrenner credited team president Randy Levine and chief operating officer Lonn Trost with much of the heavy lifting in getting the massive project done.

The new building hosted events, including an annual college football bowl game, the Pinstripe Bowl, and outdoor NHL games involving the three local teams, the Rangers, Islanders, and Devils. There also have been concerts by Jay-Z, Eminem, Paul McCartney, Madonna, and Metallica, who also showed up to play "Enter Sandman" on Mariano Rivera Day in 2013. Jorge Posada ripped the first home run that year, as Ruth had done at the original house he built 85 years before. "It was a big project, especially getting that done in New York City. But once it was opened, it was very rewarding," Hal Steinbrenner said. "Obviously, we opened it correctly by winning a world championship. It was a good year."

49

GEORGE COSTANZA

"Ruth. Gehrig. DiMaggio. Mantle...*Costanza*?" When the greatest sitcom of all time (go ahead, try to fight me on this) decided to have one of its main characters take up employment at Yankee Stadium and work alongside a hilariously dead-on caricature of George Steinbrenner, well, "Holy cow," as Phil Rizzuto would say.

The prominent inclusion of the pinstripes and several players, including Derek Jeter, Bernie Williams, and Paul O'Neill, and, especially of The Boss, in *Seinfeld* in the 1990s as a recurring storyline for Jerry Seinfeld's oft-unemployed friend, George Costanza, played by Jason Alexander was a stroke of comedic genius that even Steinbrenner and his family could not deny.

"First and foremost, we needed a job for George for the next season. He had been unemployed the year before. And we needed to give him a job," explained Larry David, the co-creator of the show. "I was thinking, *What's a cool job for George?* What job would I want to have? Well, I always wanted to work for the Yankees. So I said one day, 'Maybe he can work for the Yankees.' And that was it. You know, we didn't put as much thought into these things as people think. Everything was just a whim generally."

Of course, Jerry Seinfeld is likely the foremost celebrity New York Mets fan there is. He even featured 1986 team legend Keith Hernandez in an infamous two-episode arc in Season Three, making the retired first baseman a love interest of Julia Louis-Dreyfus' character, Elaine Benes. So why the Yankees and not their crosstown rivals from Queens? Clearly, the easiest answer was Steinbrenner. "The chaos, the turmoil, that personality, we just thought he fit perfectly," David said. "Frankly, the possibilities seemed endless."

David was a longtime friend of Seinfeld's, and the Costanza character was loosely based on him. David was born in 1947 and grew up in the Sheepshead Bay section of Brookly,n firmly in Dodgers territory. David's older brother, Ken, however, rooted for the Yankees, a rarity in their neighborhood. That was enough for Larry. "He was four years older than I was. So naturally whatever he did, I did," David said. "So I became a Yankee fan, the only one of my friends on the block. And they had Mantle. You couldn't help as a kid but idolize The Mick. The switch-hitting, all the tools, hitting it farther and being faster than everyone, he played hurt all the time, he was just a great story, a great guy to follow. I couldn't take my eyes off him when he was up."

David remained a die-hard fan through what he described as the "lean and horrible Horace Clarke years" in the late 1960s. When Steinbrenner purchased the team from CBS in 1973, he also remembered thinking, *Who is this guy?* Two more championships quickly followed on the heels of marquee acquisitions such as Catfish Hunter and Reggie Jackson, but the 1980s mostly were a constant source of frustration for fans such as David, as too many subsequent big-ticket additions didn't result in the same success. "I never liked personally how he always signed someone else's players, free agents, to these massive contracts," David said of Steinbrenner. "I was such a big fan that I would follow all the kids in the farm system. I actually would look them all up in *The Sporting News* to see how they were doing. I kept track of these guys, but after a while none of them ever got to the major leagues. They all got traded—Rijo, McGee, McGriff, Drabek, Buhner. It just kept happening. It was all very frustrating and infuriating. We all thought we could run the team better than he could."

That pain was worked into *Seinfeld* scripts easily and often. Quirky next-door neighbor Kramer, played by Michael Richards and based on David's former real-life neighbor Kenny Kramer, once bounded into Seinfeld's apartment and railed that Steinbrenner "is killing me" with his constant meddling, ticking off a similar list of prospects to the one David mentioned.

Kramer's recounting of a bench-clearing brouhaha he started involving a different laundry list of team legends—Joe Pepitone, Moose Skowron, Hank Bauer, and more—while pitching at a Yankees fantasy camp also remains a hilarious scene. "Joe Pepitone or not, I own the inside of that plate," Kramer said. "So I had to plunk him." In the ensuing melee, Kramer unintentionally slugged and decked his hero—David's, too—the great Mantle. "I looked down, and whoa man, it's Mickey," a distraught Kramer said. "I punched his lights out. So I got out of there."

No matter, Costanza soon replaced Kramer as the character interacting most frequently with the storied franchise. He even wanted to name his first-born child "Seven" to honor The Mick. In the finale of Season Five in 1994, Costanza decided to ignore every impulse he has to do the opposite, a practice that immediately helps him pick up an attractive female patron at Monk's Coffee Shop. The reversal soon also earned him an unlikely job interview with his favorite Bronx-based team. Costanza was introduced as a prospective applicant to Steinbrenner, who greeted him calmly enough by saying only, "Nice to meet you."

"Well, I wish I could say the same, but I must say, with all due respect, I find it very hard to see the logic behind some of the moves you have made with this fine organization," Costanza replied. "In the past 20 years, you have caused myself and the city of New York a good deal of distress, as we have watched you take our beloved Yankees and reduce them to a laughingstock all for the glorification of your massive ego."

Steinbrenner emphatically responded: "Hire this man!"

And so began Costanza's run as the Yankees' assistant to the traveling secretary, a storyline that lent itself to the *Seinfeld* writers exploring how outlandishly they could go with their over-the-top parody of Steinbrenner. Seinfeld and David received The Boss' approval to use his likeness and the Yankees' brand. "He thought we were making fun of him, thinking he was George Costanza. He didn't know much about the show before we approached him. He didn't realize that there already was this character named George for five years," David said. "There must've been at least one big *Seinfeld* fan in his immediate family who told him he should do it."

Indeed, Steinbrenner told Ira Berkow of *The New York Times* in 1996 that his grandchildren thought it was "cooler" that he was depicted in *Seinfeld* than "anything else I did in my life," including owning the Yankees. And while Hal Steinbrenner described to me his own television viewing habits as "more of a History Channel and Discovery Channel buff than a sitcom guy," George's youngest son allowed that he and the rest of the family thought *Seinfeld* and their patriarch's inclusion was "really very funny." "That's nice to hear," David told me. "I'm glad they liked it at least."

Even George Steinbrenner appreciated the humor after allowing his name and likeness to be used and lampooned throughout the series. "I was prepared not to like it, but I came away laughing my head off," Steinbrenner told *The Times*. "Hey, if you can't laugh at yourself, you're in bad shape. We need more laughs today. I go to too many funerals and not enough birthday parties."

Steinbrenner noted his favorite episode included the scene, in which he travels to Queens to the home of Costanza's parents to erroneously inform them their son had died. George's father, Frank Costanza, interrupted him and instead wanted to know: "What the hell did you trade Jay Buhner for? He had 30 home runs and over 100 RBIs last year. He's got a rocket for an arm. You don't know what the hell you're doing!"

The fictional Steinbrenner replied, "Well, Buhner was a good prospect, no question about it. But my baseball people loved Ken Phelps' bat. They kept saying 'Ken Phelps, Ken Phelps.'"

The kicker to the scene was Frank Costanza leaving a classic message on Seinfeld's answering machine: "Jerry, it's Frank Costanza, Mr. Steinbrenner's here, George is dead, call me back!" The real-life Steinbrenner loved every bit of it. "It was sick, but hilarious," Steinbrenner said.

"George Steinbrenner said that? I wasn't even aware of that. That makes me smile," David told me. "It's pretty obvious I did not like that Jay Buhner trade one bit—and still don't—I can tell you to this day."

The 23-year-old Buhner was traded to the Seattle Mariners in 1988 for Phelps, a 34-year-old designated hitter who totaled only 292 at-bats over parts of two seasons with the Yankees before he was dealt again to the Oakland A's, where he earned a World Series ring in 1989 alongside Mark McGwire, Jose Canseco, and Tony La Russa. Buhner went on to belt 307 home runs in 14 seasons with the Mariners. "It's great to be remembered for something, I guess," Phelps joked about his *Seinfeld* mention when he and Buhner were reunited at Mariners spring training in 2015.

David didn't initially intend to provide the voice for the Steinbrenner character, but it should be no surprise that it took two people to portray The Boss. An actor named Lee Bear played the physical version of Steinbrenner. Bear only was shown from behind, often flailing his arms maniacally, while David sat nearby off-camera and rambled about the Yankees and topics as diverse as calzones, cupcakes, and Cuban cigars. He once even butchered the lyrics to Pat Benatar's "Heartbreaker." "I turned him into a bit of a nut," David says. "It was just my sense of what he sounded like. That's what he sounded like to me—that abrupt, staccato style he had. You know he would talk very quickly and very emphatically about things, just going on and on about different topics in different directions, kind of all over the place. I did my version of it for what we should be looking for, and Jerry said to me, 'You know, you should just do it. It's perfect.'"

The first pinstriped player to appear in the series was Danny Tartabull, who signed a five-year, $27 million contract with the Yankees as a free agent in 1992. He was traded to Oakland to conclude a largely disappointing Bronx tenure in 1995. Tartabull had cameos in two episodes in Season Six with then-manager Buck Showalter joining him in one appearance. George Costanza convinced Showalter that the Yankees should switch their uniforms from polyester, which was "not a natural fiber" to a more breathable cotton. "They're more comfortable, they're happier, they're gonna play better," Costanza told the nodding manager. Later in the episode, the plan blows up in Costanza's face when the cotton uniforms shrunk and tightened on the players, prompting an announcer to exclaim: "Oh my God, Mattingly just split his pants!"

After David left the show following Season Seven, Williams and a young Jeter also took part in the episode shortly after the Yankees' 1996 World Series title. Costanza extolled the two emerging stars on the art of hitting in the episode known as "The Abstinence," in which he claims to be thinking clearer than ever because he's abstaining from sex. "Guys, hitting is not about muscle. It's simple physics," Costanza explains as he cracks a few batting-practice pitches over the center-field wall at Yankee Stadium. "Calculate the velocity—V—in relation to the trajectory—T—in which—G—gravity, of course, remains a constant. It's not complicated." That leads to this memorable exchange:

> **Jeter:** "Now, who are you again?"
> **George:** "George Costanza, assistant to the traveling secretary."
> **Williams:** "Are you the guy who put us in that Ramada in Milwaukee?"
> **George:** "Do you wanna talk about hotels, or do you wanna win some ballgames?"
> **Jeter:** "We won the World Series."
> **George, dismissively:** "Yeah. In six games."

The real Steinbrenner actually filmed one scene in front of the camera with Louis-Dreyfus for the Season Seven finale titled "The Invitations," in which he volunteers to accompany her to Costanza's wedding. David and Seinfeld ultimately decided not to use the scene, but someone had to tell The Boss. "It was much funnier just to see him from the back with my voice than to see him act, but I had to be the one to tell him that," David said. "He said in that famous voice of his, 'You can tell me. I can take it like a man.' So I said, 'Look, I'm sorry, Mr. Steinbrenner. We have to cut you from the show. I just wanted to let you know.' He didn't seem that disappointed about it. It just didn't work."

As for O'Neill's Season Eight turn, Kramer promised a sick child in the hospital that the longtime right fielder would hit two home runs for him that night. Kramer was attempting to recoup a birthday card for Steinbrenner signed by the entire Yankees organization that he mistakenly sold to his friend, who dealt in sports memorabilia. "It's terrible," O'Neill said in the show. "You don't hit home runs like that. It's hard to hit home runs. And where the heck did you get two from?"

O'Neill scoffed when Kramer told him, "Babe Ruth did it." Kramer then asked if he's calling the Yankees legend a liar. O'Neill retorted: "I'm not calling him a liar, but he wasn't stupid enough to promise two."

Those cameos earned O'Neill some additional fame. "Honestly, I didn't even know anything about the show. The first time I was asked, I said no. But these things only happen when you're part of the New York Yankees," O'Neill said. "They picked me up from Anaheim. They drove me over to the studio. We did the shots, and I remember I had a horrible game against Chuck Finley [of the Angels] that night. When it aired you don't know how it's going to come out. But even now you meet people, and some will tell you about a play or a game they remember. But just as many will tell me, 'I remember you from *Seinfeld.*' So that's really cool."

Eventually, even Costanza had enough of Steinbrenner. He tried to get himself fired late in Season Eight so he could take a better-paying scouting job with the Mets. He wore Babe Ruth's uniform, rubbed strawberry juice on it, wore a nude-colored bodysuit, and streaked across the Yankee Stadium field. He even dragged the World Series trophy around the parking lot behind his car. But Costanza failed in getting fired. In the next episode, Costanza was traded to Tyler Chicken in exchange for a conversion of all stadium concessions to chicken-based products, including a beer substitute made of fermented alcoholic chicken.

50

THE BABY BOMBERS

"All Rise" instantly became a felicitous and fitting catchphrase in 2017, as Aaron Judge blasted his way into the national consciousness as the latest homegrown Yankees player to emerge as the face of the franchise. Judge and the rest of the impressive passel of next-wave talent acquired by Brian Cashman over the second half of that decade clearly have reinvigorated the Yankees, following a decade without any World Series appearances. Now it is time for them to rise up and deliver the organization's first championship in more than a decade following three straight playoff appearances. "Any year you're not the last man standing, the season is a fail," Judge said in 2019. "You can win every single game in the regular season, but if you lose in the postseason, it doesn't matter."

Every successful era in franchise lore had to start somewhere, but it usually begins with the same pointed mantra. From the time players stand at the lowest rungs of the minor league ladder, Yankees are taught the organizational priorities as defined by late owner George Steinbrenner. "Winning is the most important thing in my life—after breathing," Steinbrenner often said. "Breathing first, winning second."

As Judge already has learned, sometimes it can feel at times as if that order is reversed. Such is life in a franchise that has made 40 World Series appearances and won 27, the most by far in both categories. The Yankees fell one game short of reaching the Fall Classic during Judge's unprecedented rookie season in 2017, losing to the eventual champion Houston Astros in Game 7 of the American League Championship Series. It resulted in Joe Girardi's removal as manager. The next year with Aaron Boone at the helm, they advanced past the Oakland A's in the wild-card game only to fall again to the pending champs, the rival Boston Red Sox.

The roster building, though, began at home, and by the middle of the 2010s, Cashman famously pushed back on the public narrative that the Yankees' depleted farm system was failing after producing Bernie Williams and The Core Four in the 1990s and little thereafter aside from All-Star second baseman Robinson Cano. "That's where I'd get upset. I don't mind if somebody writes something that's accurate and I deserve it, and they have an opinion that I deserve to get whacked around, but this was different. This was personal in many cases," Cashman said. "I was like, okay, if you want to fight this way, I have to fight for myself. And I did. The bottom line was the process that we'd played out was always healthy and strong, but it always needed to be improved, too. The bottom line is we want a positive outcome, we want to produce great players both internationally and domestically through the draft. I think we've done that."

The arrivals of Judge, Gary Sanchez, and Luis Severino by 2016 was a strong starting point. With the Yankees slipping to 84–78 and missing the playoffs, that season also marked the lone year of Cashman's first 21 years as general manager in which they sold off pending free agents at the July trade deadline. And he swung a series of significant deals that further restocked the team's prospect coffers. Cashman leveraged highly ranked infield prospect Gleyber Torres from the desperate Chicago Cubs for closer Aroldis Chapman, the final piece as Chicago finally ended its 108-year World Series drought for its first title since 1908. He then re-signed Chapman that winter, and Torres emerged as a potential superstar in 2018 and 2019. At just 22 he made the All-Star team both years and slugged a team-best 38 home runs with 90 RBIs in his sophomore year. "He's smart and he's confident, and that's a really good combination when you're talented," Boone said.

"To do what he's doing when he's still just 21 or 22 years old?" Judge said. "I was still in Class A Charleston when I was his age, still trying to figure out how to play the game at that level. And here he is doing it in the playoffs on the biggest stage in the game. It's incredible when you think about it."

Cashman also acquired outfielder Clint Frazier and pitching prospect Justus Sheffield from the Cleveland Indians in a deal for reliever Andrew Miller and pitching prospect Dillon Tate for veteran outfielder Carlos Beltran. Tate was flipped to the Baltimore Orioles for reliever Zach Britton, and Sheffield was traded to the Seattle Mariners for lefty starter James Paxton ahead of 2019, a move that helped the Yankees win 103 games and their first American League East title since 2012.

Cashman also took on the contract of 2017 National League MVP Giancarlo Stanton, who hit 59 home runs that season, in a lopsided salary-dump trade with Derek Jeter's rebuilding Miami Marlins. Another underrated signing ahead of 2019 was former NL batting champion DJ LeMahieu, who emerged as an MVP candidate with a .327 average and a team-high 102 RBIs in a season, in which the Yankees had a whopping 31 players land on the injured list.

The lynchpin to all of it remains Judge, the 6'7", 280-pound behemoth from California who garnered football interest from major college programs such as Stanford, UCLA, and Notre Dame as a high school wide receiver. Judge instead chose to attend Fresno State, and the Yankees drafted him with the 32nd overall pick in the first round of the 2013 draft. He blasted a home run in his first major league plate appearance in August 2016, but Judge didn't exactly have everyone rising with a hardly inspiring 42 strikeouts and a .179 batting average during that six-week audition.

One year later, however, Judge was the story of baseball. He won the Home Run Derby in July with a prodigious display to wow his fellow All-Stars and crushed 15 home runs in September to overtake Mark McGwire's record for rookies, finishing three better at 52. (Pete Alonso of the New York Mets eclipsed Judge's mark in 2019.)

The Yankees erected the popular Judge's Chambers seating section in right field, where fans donned white wigs and long black robes. "He's good for Major League Baseball. He's bad for the teams you're playing against," Indians manager Terry Francona said. "He's really good. From all accounts he's a really special young man. If you throw in the wrong place, he's going to hit it a long way."

Judge's first postseason started poorly. He went 1-for-20 with 16 strikeouts against Cleveland in the 2017 American League Division Series, but he rebounded with three homers in seven games against Houston in the ALCS. Despite stints on the injured list each of the

Aaron Judge hits a two-run home run in the fourth inning of Game 2 of the 2019 ALCS.

next two seasons, Judge has done his share to deliver in October, also batting .375 with a pair of home runs against the Red Sox in 2018.

The Yankees led the majors with a .294 batting average with runners in scoring position during the 2019 regular season, but they batted just .171 (6-for-35) in such situations in their six-game loss to Houston in the ALCS. "It's a failure," Judge said. "Each year it left a bad taste in my mouth...That keeps us hungry."

[Acknowledgments]

This project could not have come at a better time for me, about halfway through a 15-month layoff between full-time jobs, and I dug into it with everything I had over the summer and fall of 2019 for an early 2020 release.

My most daunting challenge was how do you narrow down the most prolific franchise— a team boasting an unprecedented 27 championships and nearly 50 Hall of Famers when you tally up all of the players and managers that wore the fabled pinstripes—in the history of sports to 50 men or moments that shaped its existence over more than a century? The short answer is you don't, you can't, but you lump together a few of the related title seasons into one chapter, you combine all of Babe Ruth's or Derek Jeter's historic moments into others, and you attempt to be mindful that you aren't going to please everyone, but you hope those decisions spur the kind of animated debates that always have made fandom fun. I have read other books in *The Big 50* family, and with all due respect to some of those franchises, there were players and moments from those teams who received their own chapters who wouldn't rank in the top 500 with the Yankees.

I have to start with a massive thank you to Bill Ames at Triumph Books for giving me the opportunity to tell these stories, and especially to editor Jeff Fedotin, whose patience and guidance helped me reach the finish line. A very special thank you to everyone associated with the Yankees who took time to speak with me or provided quotes for the project: Jim Abbott, Dale Berra, Aaron Boone, Wade Boggs, Homer Bush, Robinson Cano, Brian Cashman, Chris Chambliss, David Cone, Bob Costas, Matt Dahlgren, Johnny Damon, Chili Davis, Bucky Dent, Terry Francona, Brett Gardner, Jason Giambi, Goose Gossage, LaTroy Hawkins, Michael Kay, Jim Leyritz, Bill Madden, Lee Mazzilli,

Don Mattingly, Kay Murcer, Paul O'Neill, Willie Randolph, Dave Righetti, Mariano Rivera, CC Sabathia, Luis Sojo, Hal Steinbrenner, John Sterling, Joe Torre, Suzyn Waldman, Roy White, and Ralph Wimbish.

Additional thanks to Jason Zillo and Michael Margolis of the Yankees' media relations department with their help reaching a few of them and to Yankees advisor and former batboy Ray Negron for hooking me up with the great Chazz Palminteri, who unquestionably is among the team's foremost and legitimately impassioned celebrity fans. Speaking with Chazz about his nearly 60 years of loyalty was remarkable, and that certainly comes through in his wonderful and appreciated foreword. Thank you to Bernie Williams and his longtime manager, Steve Fortunato, for helping with an in-depth and amazing foreword.

Also, anyone who knows me or follows me on Twitter knows what it meant to me to speak with Larry David, the genius behind *Seinfeld* and *Curb Your Enthusiasm*, for his insight and help with the George Costanza chapter, my personal favorite. Larry made my year when he called me back and told me he remembered me from my years doing the *New York Daily News*' fifth inning on the radio with John and Michael and Suzyn—and that he unsubscribed from the paper when I and several colleagues were let go in 2018 due to budget cuts!

To that end I have worked with and competed against dozens and dozens of esteemed New York baseball writers. There are far too many to list, but especially to those I covered baseball with regularly before practically all of us left the *News*—Billy, Harp, Mac, Sandy, Cred (and Lil' Red), Kristie, Rog, Andy, Brennan, Mazz, Lisa, Mike, Fil, Raiss, and so many others—I thank you for your friendship and solidarity through the years. Yes, Isola, too, a hometown friend from Long Island, who never forgets to remind me he helped get me my first job out of college at the *New York Post* and my next one at the *News*, as well.

To current bosses Chris Shaw and Mark Hale at the *Post* for bringing me back in October 2019 to the terrific sports section I started my career with from 1990–97 under former sports editors Bob Decker and Greg Gallo, who gave me first chances in the business. To all of my former sports editors at the *Daily News*, too, especially Barry Werner,

Leon Carter, Teri Thompson, and Bill Price, who meant so much to my career professionally and personally.

Last, but anything but least, my family.

My dad (Big Pete) died in 2018, but his imprints are all over this book from his reverence of DiMaggio despite growing up a Dodgers fan in Brooklyn to a love of the game that he passed on to me as far back as I can remember, a love that lasted throughout his 82 years. My mom, Lucy, forever has been my No. 1 fan; she's probably read and clipped more newspaper accounts of the Yankees, Mets, Islanders, Knicks, you name it, over my nearly 30 years covering New York sports than she ever thought possible. Her love and unwavering support always has been the lifeblood of our family.

To my younger brother, Mike, who died of lymphoma at just 40 years old in 2011, no one loved to share a beer and a dog at the ballpark more. I miss talking to you about sports, music, family, everything. To my sister, Danielle, who put up with my baseball obsession for years, to my sister-in-law Jenn and my nieces and nephews, I love you all. To Tammy, the most loving mom to our kids I ever could envision, thank you.

To my aunts and uncles and cousins, especially Chrissy and Marty Neff, who always will know me better than the friends and folks I see more regularly, I hope they know what they mean to me. To my former father-in-law, Jimmy "Vinny Boom Bots" Ciccarelli, among the biggest die-hard Yankees fans that I know, I always will consider you family. To my various circles of friends, from NB High, to BU, to the soccer and baseball fields, to the work crowd, to later in life, I hope you've had as much fun as I have.

And, finally, to my amazing children, Tyler and Hayley, now incredibly 27 and 25 at the start of 2020, just know that *everything* I do, I do for you. I could not be prouder of the compassionate, well-rounded adults you have become as you chase down your respective dreams. I never have to think twice when I consider the best moments of my life. You get all the chapters.

[Bibliography]

Books

Abbott, Jim, and Brown, Tim. *Imperfect: An Improbable Life.* Ballantine Books (2012).

Anderson, Dave (Editor). *New York Times, Story of the Yankees: Profiles and Essays from 1903 to Present.* Black Dog (2012).

Appel, Marty. *Casey Stengel: Baseball's Greatest Character.* Doubleday (2017).

Appel, Marty. *Pinstripe Empire: The New York Yankees from Before The Babe to After The Boss.* Bloomsbury USA (2012).

Berra, Dale. *My Dad, Yogi: A Memoir of Family and Baseball.* Hachette Books (2019).

Berra, Yogi. *The Yogi Book: I Really Didn't Say Everything I Said.* Workman Publishing Company (2010).

Bouton, Jim. *Ball Four.* World Publishing (1972).

Castro, Tony. *Gehrig and the Babe: The Friendship and the Feud.* Triumph Books (2018).

Clavin, Tom, and Peary, Danny. *Roger Maris: Baseball's Reluctant Hero.* Atria Books (2010).

Cone, David, and Curry, Jack. *Full Count: The Education of a Pitcher.* Grand Central Publishing (2019).

Cramer, Richard Ben. *Joe DiMaggio: A Hero's Life.* Simon & Schuster (2001).

Dahlgren, Matt. *Rumor in Town: A Grandson's Promise to Right a Wrong.* Woodlyn Lane (2007).

Eig, Jonathan. *Luckiest Man: The Life and Death of Lou Gehrig.* Simon & Schuster (2006).

Feinsand, Mark, and Hoch, Bryan. *Mission 27: A New Boss, A New Ballpark, and One Last Ring for the Yankees' Core Four.* Triumph Books (2019).

Ford, Whitey, and Pepe, Phil. *Slick: My Life in and Around Baseball.* William Morrow and Co. (1987).

Ford, Whitey, and Mantle, Mickey, and Durso, Joe. *Whitey and Mickey: A Joint Autobiography of the Yankee Years.* Viking (1977).

Frommer, Harvey. *Remembering Yankee Stadium.* The Globe Pequot Press (2016).

Frommer, Harvey. *The Ultimate Yankee Book: From the Beginning to Today.* Page Street Publishing (2017).

Hemingway, Ernest. *The Old Man and the Sea.* Charles Scribner Sons (1952).

Honig, Donald. *Baseball Between the Lines: Baseball in the Forties and the Fifties as Told by the Men Who Played It.* Nebraska Press (1993).

Howard, Arlene, and Wimbish, Ralph. *Elston: The Story of the First African-American Yankee.* University of Missouri (2001).

Jackson, Reggie, and Baker, Kevin. *Becoming Mr. October.* Doubleday (2013).

Kahn, Roger. *The Boys of Summer.* Harper and Row (1972).

Larsen, Don, and Shaw, Mark. *The Perfect Yankee: The Incredible Story of The Greatest Miracle in Baseball History.* Sagamore Publishing (1996).

Leavy, Jane. *The Last Boy: Mickey Mantle and the End of America's Childhood.* Harper Perennial (2010).

Levitt, Daniel. *Ed Barrow: The Bulldog Who Built the First Yankees Dynasty.* Nebraska Press (2008).

Madden, Bill. *Steinbrenner: The Last Lion of Baseball.* Harper Collins Publishing (2010).

Madden, Bill. *Pride of October: What it Was to Be Young and a Yankee.* Warner Books (2003).

Meany, Tom. *Babe Ruth: The Big Moments of the Big Fellow.* Bantam Books (1947).

Montville, Leigh. *The Big Bam: The Life and Times of Babe Ruth.* Doubleday (2006).

Neyer, Rob, and Epstein, Eddie. *Baseball Dynasties: The Greatest Teams of All-Time.* WW Norton and Co. (2000).

Olney, Buster. *The Last Night of the Yankees Dynasty.* Harper Perennial (2005).

Rizzuto, Phil, and Horton, Tom. *The October Twelve: Five Years of New York Yankee Glory, 1949–53.* Tom Doherty Associates (1994).

Roberts, Selena. *A-Rod: The Many Lives of Alex Rodriguez.* Harper (2009).

Steinberg, Steve, and Spatz, Lyle. *The Colonel and Hug: The Partnership that Transformed the New York Yankees.* Nebraska Press (2015).

Stewart, Wayne. *The Gigantic Book of Baseball Quotations.* Skyhorse Publishing (2007).

Torre, Joe, and Verducci, Tom. *The Yankee Years.* Anchor Books (2009).

Thorne, J.D. *The 10 Commandments of Baseball: An Affectionate Look at Joe McCarty's Principles for Success in Baseball (and Life).* Sporting Chance Press (2009)

Vaccaro, Mike. *Emperors and Idiots: The Hundred Years Rivalry Between the Yankees and the Red Sox.* Broadway Books (2005).

Wells, David. *Perfect, I'm Not: Boomer on Beer, Brawls, Backaches, And Baseball.* William Morrow (2003).

Wilner, Barry. *Pinstripes and Pennants: The Ultimate New York Yankees Fan Guide.* North Star (2019).

Periodicals

New York Post
New York Daily News
The New York Times
Newsday
Boston Herald
The Bergen Record
The Boston Globe
Sport
Sports Illustrated

Websites

baseballhall.org
baseball-reference.com
baseball-almanac.com
espn.com
mlb.com
sabr.org
sny.tv
yankees.com
yesnetwork.com
youtube.com